Reading Eating Disorders

NEUE STUDIEN ZUR
ANGLISTIK
UND
AMERIKANISTIK

Herausgegeben von Willi Erzgräber † und Paul Goetsch

Band 87

PETER LANG
Frankfurt am Main · Berlin · Bern · Bruxelles · New York · Oxford · Wien

Greta Olson

Reading Eating Disorders

Writings on Bulimia and Anorexia as Confessions of American Culture

PETER LANG
Europäischer Verlag der Wissenschaften

Bibliographic Information published by Die Deutsche Bibliothek
Die Deutsche Bibliothek lists this publication in the Deutsche Nationalbibliografie; detailed bibliographic data is available in the internet at <http://dnb.ddb.de>.

Zugl.: Freiburg (Breisgau), Univ., Diss., 2000

ISSN 0170-8848
ISBN 3-631-50619-8
US-ISBN 0-8204-6406-6

Printed in Germany 1 2 3 4 5 7

www.peterlang.de

For Kirsten

Gratitude

I would like to thank my *Doktorvater* Prof. Dr. Paul Goetsch, whom I—child of the late twentieth century—would prefer to call my *Doktor-Hebamme*, for his help with this project. Like a good midwife Prof. Goetsch allowed me to labor alone when I wished to and lent assistance whenever required. He gave me my head with regard to the unconventional subject matter of this study and offered continuous support in the form of recommendations for further reading and rapidly-completed and attentive corrections of early drafts. Prof. Goetsch's erudition and professionalism set standards I will continue to aspire to.

I wish to express my gratitude to my very dear friends Petra Deistler and Susanne Strobel for their help with this manuscript. Passionate readers and lovely and loving companions, they proofread carefully, challenged me to structure better, pointed out contradictions, and lent me their great support and affection during *anni horribili.* I would also like to thank my step-parents and parents Nancy and Jon Olson, and Tom Bryan and Jean Olson for their generous material help with the publication of this book.

Finally, I would like to thank my dear sister Kirsten Ann Olson Lanier for more than just her help with completing this study. Kirsten curbed my tendencies to get Bill Buckleyish about American culture, interrogated my distaste for confession, and reminded me often to push on towards the finish line. More importantly, she has given abundantly of her humor, insight, and care. To her I wish to dedicate this book with thanks and great love.

Grateful acknowledgement is made to Eavan Boland for permission to reprint "Anorexic" from *Collected Poems* (Carcenet Press Limited, 1995) and to Frank Bidart for permission to reprint parts of "Ellen West" (1977) from *In the Western Night: Collected Poems 1965-90* (Farrar Straus Giroux, 1990).

Contents

Howl

I.
I saw the best bodies of my generation destroyed by self-control, starving,
determined well-healed,
jogging through suburban streets at noon looking for a set of scales,
slimhipped sweethearts burning for the ancient physical connection to the lean
discipline of the empty dawn,
who affluence and goals and perfect and nude nibbled celery before full-lengths
floating through remembered recipes contemplating eggs,
who bent like nun nurses over pure white porcelain to count pieces of carrot in a
gastric sea,
who passed through universities with mute clouded eyes hallucinating
hamburgers and makeovers among the arbiters of success
who picked kernels off rice cakes, doled out curds of cottage cheese, chewed 50
times a side,
who spent lunch money on cigarettes and clothes to shrink into,
who deathgripped dance barres, whispering the mantra "I'm so fat I can't do this
I'm so fat I can't do this I'm so fat I can't do this" until their thin blood
swished to the beat,
who stepped like shy antelope on swollen toes before Misha's framed inscrutable
stare,
who clenched and released their buttocks while riding the bus or purgatoried their
torsos night after night
with movies, with candy, with popcorn, fingers and throats and endless
abdomens,
calorie clouds of refrigerators, kitchen white knives hospital dawns, Metamucil
and raw fruit bursting over the sink, drugstore families and aspririnhead
denial inches pounds cholesterol counts and RDAs for pigs in the soap
opera afternoons, poolside calculations and harsh daughter's control of
mind,
who sized up every woman they saw, x-ray eyes blazing through the subterfuges
of bold prints and vertical lines,
who mixed powders in shotglasses of blue milk, popped pills and gloried in the
banquet,

who leapt from bed to toilet to scales dropping their nightgowns snipping nails
    and shaving legs to make the wand wave lower,
who meditated on glasses of stylish sexy water and eight times a day drank the
    cleansing draught,
who weaned themselves on the wizard's tit of sugarfree lifesavers,
who rocked 'til they dropped at the dance-a-thon in ecstatic communion with
    dissolving thighs,
who tweezered pubic hair, toothpicked vomit from braces and walked the beach
    once a year in throat-to-ankle raincoats,
who treadmilled their minds into lockstep obsession pared themselves like
    potatoes and apologized for every inch of earth they occupied,
who struggled with snaps in department store dressing rooms as the discreet and
    polished toes of size 2 salesladies clicked up and down the numbered
    aisles,
who served seven-course meals on fine china while violins oozed butter in their
    ears and fat-fingered CEOs reached for non-existent asses,
who broke down crying in white gymnasiums naked and trembling before the
    machinery of other skeletons,
who scribbled "my body, my choice" on the stretcher sheets in their own blood
    the stink of rotting cells and stomach lining leaking from their lips,
who hid huge weights in rectum and vagina to show the smocked irrational judges
    how much they'd gained,
who yanked IVs and bubbling nostril tubes with chopstick arms in the fluorescent
    stroke of midnight,
who corseted their skulls with celluloid and silicon,
who dried up like apricots, asexual Alices singing happy good-byes to their
    monthlies

ah, Mandy, Bella, Rosalie, while you are not safe I am not safe

You chose from the few roles available
That of the most perfect subject for poetry (a beautiful woman dying)
Played it to perfection so the audience gasped.

Were we right? Is heaven clouds of whipped cream?
Are you angels lighter than air?

- Heather Stephenson[1]

I begin this introduction with an explosive, attention-grabbing poem. With it I want to show that eating disorders command our attention and that a growing number of literary treatments of them exist to do so. "Howl" represents a call to arms, a demand that the hell of eating disorders and the violence to the body they entail be recognized and addressed. Amongst the horrors the speaker testifies to in this poem are how women painfully squeeze themselves into clothes too small for them, compulsively exercise, diet on water and sugar free candies out of a hatred of their body fat, and how school girls consume cigarettes instead of lunch in pursuit of thinness. The preoccupation with having a thin body may involve the waste of university education and take a toll on the health of average women.

In the poem's list of varieties of disordered eating and body abuse images of average dieters are among the least frightening ones. More alarming is the dense imagery concerning bulimics—while vomiting, they resemble nurses or nuns lowering themselves before the altar of the toilet to let laxatives and fruit explode out of their mouths—and severe anorectics, those women who "hid weights in rectum and vagina to show the smocked irrational judges / how much they'd gained, / who yanked IVs and bubbling nostril tubes with chopstick arms in the fluorescent stroke of midnight [...]."

Inspired by Allen Ginsberg's "Howl" (1955-1956)—a lament for the lost souls of Ginsberg's generation—Stephenson's poem mourns the current squandering of women's lives and energy that eating disorders and diet obsessions bring with them. With its literary allusions to Ginsberg's poem, *Alice in Wonderland*, and Edgar Allan Poe's explanation of his poetic fascination with dead beauties,[2] "Howl" also demonstrates that literary accounts of eating

---

[1] Heather Stephenson, "Howl," *Eating Our Hearts Out: Personal Accounts of Women's Relationship to Food,* ed. Lesléa Newman (Freedom, Ca: Crossing Press, 1993) 32-33.

[2] "From what I have already explained at some length the answer here also is obvious—'When it most closely allies itself to *Beauty*: the death then of a beautiful woman is unquestionably the most poetical topic in the world, and equally is it beyond doubt that the

disorders now have a position within English-language poetry and prose. Numerous recent début novels about eating disorders and spontaneous outpourings of poetry on food and food-related abuse on the Internet express the frequency of women's problems with food in American culture. These novels and poems describe such unaesthetic experiences as forcing oneself to vomit, consuming ground-up glass, defecating without end, and the minutiae of obsessions with weight, food, calories, and thinness. Poems and novels about eating disorders also reflect on the reasons why women become bulimic and anorexic. In so doing these texts demonstrate how literature is a focal point for the expression of cultural tensions.

This study examines literary accounts of eating disorders as a method of reading American culture. I want to show what novels, poems, and literary autobiographies tell us about women's disordered relations to food and their bodies that medical, psychological, and sociological texts about eating disorders cannot. Eating disorders present grave health problems in other industrial and post-industrial countries as well as in those developing countries in which American eating patterns are being mimicked. Yet the combination of increasing rates of obesity in the United States with an unrealistically thin ideal of feminine beauty and a moralistic attitude toward overweight individuals render disordered eating coupled with weight obsession a peculiarly salient American problem.[3] Hence the texts studied here stem almost exclusively from American writers or are set in America, and the locus of the culture I refer to is the United States.[4]

---

lips best suited for such topic are those of a bereaved lover.'" Edgar Allan Poe, "The Philosophy of Composition," *The Centenary Poe: Tales Poems, Criticism, Marginalia and Eureka* (London: The Bodley Head, 1949) 495.

[3] Almost a third of all adult Americans are obese or super-obese, and the rate of obesity continues to increase. Eric Schlosser, *Fast Food Nation: the dark side of the all-American meal* (2001; New York: Harper Collins, 2002) 239-240, Notes 342.

[4] Autobiographical accounts of anorexia and bulimia as well as novelistic portrayals of eating disorders are arguably as wide spread in Canada, Europe, Japan, Australia, New Zealand and South Africa as they are in the States. Like their American counterparts, these texts portray

The speaker of the poem "Howl" describes her starving subjects as "well-healed" women from "suburban streets" who embody "affluence and goals and perfect," who sit by pools while they make caloric "calculations" and who have the leisure to "treadmill[] their minds into lockstep" and are expected to "serve[] seven-course meals on fine china while violins oozed butter in their ears / and fat-fingered CEOs reached for non-existent asses." Clearly, these individuals come from affluent backgrounds. Having bulimia or anorexia remains an ironic prerogative of the well-to-do, as members of the middle class react more strongly to the media-propagated condemnation of overweight. The other side of the coin is that obesity is encouraged among America's poor due to the targeting of fast food to the economically disadvantaged. I will argue that eating disorders represent a class and even a racial issue in the United States, to the degree that class is coupled with race. Having a thin body is associated with wealth and status in American society. Hence immigrant women and members of minority groups who aspire to adopt the values of the American middle class are increasingly afflicted by eating disorders. That the vast majority of individuals who suffer from disordered eating are women demonstrates that this phenomenon is a gender issue.

Eating afflictions represent more than just anorexia, which has historically affected only a small group of strong-willed individuals. More and more, eating disorders come in a variety of forms. Each edition of the

---

the profound sense of discomfort with food, weight, and body that many Western women have. However, such texts also address preoccupations specific to the cultural fields out of which they arise. To demonstrate this I will name just two examples within the field of English-language literature. Elleke Boehmer's *Screens Against the Sky* (1990) portrays an anorexic South-African woman's struggles with weight, individuation, and independence from her overly-protective mother; yet the novel also depicts the protagonist Annemarie's growing awareness of the economic and political injustices of Apartheid as well as her own untenable position as a privileged white within this system. While the sixteen-year-old Lisa of Esther Freud's *Peerless Flats* (1993) displays some symptoms of anorexia, her disassociation from food and her body has as much to do with her lack of a sense of self in the downtrodden London world of the Council flats where she lives as with the prevailing

American Psychiatric Association's *Diagnostic and Statistical Manual of Mental Disorders*—the diagnostic bible of mental health providers—contains new and newer subdivisions of already documented eating disorders.[5] Binge eating is now recognized alongside anorexia and bulimia as an eating disorder in its own right. Activity anorexia (the addiction to exercise coupled with weight concerns) may follow in being acknowledged as a discrete eating disorder as may the night-eating syndrome (the compulsive consumption of food between midnight and 6 am).

Written accounts of gorging and starving oneself and of forcing oneself to vomit or exercise to the point of exhaustion mirror the wide spectrum of eating disorders. This study looks specifically at literary accounts of disordered eating. By "literary" I do not necessarily mean fictional versus non-fictional texts. Indeed, this study devotes a chapter to Marya Hornbacher's *Wasted: A Memoir of Anorexia and Bulimia* (1998),[6] an example of "life-writing" that blurs the distinction between the categories of fiction and non-fiction. Rather, the texts included in this study are in some sense exemplary. Either they tell something new about the experience of being a woman with a profoundly troubled relation to food, or they use language and employ imagery in a rich and unusual way, or they test the paradigms of conventional thinking about eating

---

beauty ideal. Concentrating on American texts in this study will avoid, I hope, needless over-generalizations.

[5] American Psychiatric Association, *Diagnostic and Statistical Manual of Mental Disorders*, 4th ed. (Washington DC: American Psychiatric Association, 1994). Hereafter abbreviated as DSM-IV.

[6] Marya Hornbacher, *Wasted: A Memoir of Anorexia and Bulimia* (New York: HarperFlamingo, 1998) 154. Hereafter abbreviated as *W*.

disorders.[7] Research remains to be done on the vast number of autobiographical texts on anorexia, bulimia, and binge eating not included in this study.[8]

The majority of literary writings on eating disorders concern anorexia. Anorexia nervosa is the most well-known of the eating disorders in popular culture and the one that has most frequently been made the object of scientific, historic, and cultural discourse. The literary interest in anorexia reflects Western culture's infatuation with self-control and the historical fascination with thin

---

[7] To describe what is literary I have leaned heavily on ideas in an essay from David E Bell, "A Moratorium on Suspicion," *PMLA* 117.3 (May 2002): 487-490; for a critical reflection on the problematic nature of traditional definitions of literature, see Terry Eagleton, "Introduction: What is Literature?" *Literary Theory: An Introduction,* 2nd ed.(Oxford: Blackwell, 1996) 1-14.

[8] Prominent among autobiographies of anorexia are Sheila Macleod's *The Art of Starvation: A Story of Anorexia and Survival* (1982) which is written from a British perspective. With its strong Christian orientation, Cherry Boone O'Neill's *Starving for Attention* (1982) tells the story of an anorexic television personality and singer's illness and recovery. The autobiography includes letters from Cherry's parents to their daughter as well as accounts of Cherry's anorexia by her husband and doctor. The "narrative" *Solitaire* (1979) by Aimee Liu describes how Aimee was raped at age seven by two twelve-year-old boys, her subsequent anorexia, modeling career, early marriage, and gradual recovery. The current bestseller by Lori Gottlieb, *Stick Figure: A Diary of My Former Self* (2000) is the published diary of an anorexic eleven-year old who decided on her half-birthday in 1978 to become the thinnest girl in the school if not in the world. Camie Ford and Sunny Hale's *Deadly Diet* (1983; 1995) presents two recovered anorectics' accounts of disease and recovery through Christian faith. Regarding bulimia, Caroline Adams Miller's *My Name is Caroline* (1988; 1991) is probably the best-known account; Miller embraces Overeaters Anonymous twelve-step approach to overcome the bulimic practices she learnt from a friend in high school. This account is significant because it demonstrates that an outwardly attractive and successful athlete and Harvard graduate may suffer from bulimia for years without anyone knowing about it. The autobiography is complimented by a diagnostic test for bulimia and a list of eating disorder organizations. Marianne Apostolides's *Inner Hunger: A Young Woman's Struggle through Anorexia and Bulimia* (1998) also recounts an outwardly successful (Ivy League) young woman's 10-year long struggle first with anorexia and then with bulimia. The autobiography begins with a factual account of the causes of eating disorders and ends with a chapter of advice to communities and individuals about how to combat or avoid eating disorders. Perhaps the best-known account of the binge-eating disorder is Margaret Bullitt-Jonas's *Holy Hunger: A Memoir of Desire* (1998) which describes the again outwardly over-achieving author's long-term addiction to food and bingeing. I would argue that this text is less about food addiction than family dysfunction and the search for meaning in spiritual pursuits. It is striking how many of the titles described here have a very strong religious and specifically Christian orientation. Complete information on this by no means exhaustive list can be found in the bibliography.

"spiritualized" women. Anorectics[9] provide a particularly salient symbol of cultural contradictions. These women and girls figuratively starve in a supermarket brimming over with food. Autobiographical novels such as Jenefer Shute's *Life-Size* (1992)[10] and Stephanie Grant's *The Passion of Alice* (1995)[11] provide extended insiders' views of the lives and hospitalizations of severe anorectics. *Life-Size* in particular illuminates the attractions of anorexia. The narrator's initial account of Josie's spartan and ritualized life is so aesthetic that readers may find the protagonist's anorexic mindset invading their everyday lives.[12] Josie's infatuation with death and her romance with illness recall the late poetry of Sylvia Plath. This novel and others resembling it describe the anorectic's obsession with limits: the limits of the body, the limits of control, and the limits of the individual's ability to perfect or actualize herself. Numerous poetic accounts of suffering from anorexia nervosa complement these novels.

By contrast, Hornbacher's *Wasted* describes bulimia and how this less well-known eating disorder is related to anorexia. I include Hornbacher's memoir in this study, because this hybrid text presents a powerful articulation of the bulimic experience and illustrates differences between bulimic and anorexic preoccupations. During the course of my research I found no full-length novel about bulimia in English that was not intended primarily for young adults.[13]

---

[9] The spelling of the noun that denotes individuals who suffer from anorexia nervosa is variable, as will be seen in the variety of textbooks on eating disorders quoted from below. In this study "anorectic" will denote a woman who has anorexia, and "anorexic" will be used as the adjective to describe things or behaviors pertaining to anorexia.

[10] Jenefer Shute, *Life-Size* (1992; London: Minerva, 1995). Hereafter abbreviated as *L-S.*

[11] Stephanie Grant, *The Passion of Alice* (1995; London: Hodder and Stoughton, 1996). Hereafter abbreviated as *PoA*.

[12] One woman with whom I read the novel described mentally cataloging the caloric values of all the foods she saw in the store windows of the main street in town after reading the description of Josie's tortured and ritualized meal.

[13] A popular example is Liza F. Hall's *Perk!: The Story of a Teenager with Bulimia* (Carlsbad, CA: Gürze Books, 1997) which tells how a troubled and insecure teenager nearly loses her baby sister to death by drowning while she is purging. This incident leads to her hospitalization, treatment, and recovery.

Fewer published poems about bulimia exist, while poetry about bulimia appears with about the same frequency on web sites as that about anorexia. This study asks why literary writing on bulimia nervosa is less available than that on anorexia, although the experience of having bulimia is at least twice as common. Why is it easier to translate starving oneself into writing than gorging and purging?

I want to venture a few preliminary explanations. Bulimia has only recently become a widespread phenomenon and is sometimes referred to as the disease of the 80s. Hence literary and non-literary accounts of this disorder have emerged much more recently and there are still fewer of them.[14] The absence of a literary tradition from which to draw from represents another obvious reason for the lack of extended literary treatments of bulimia. Literary history offers many intriguing narratives about self-starvation. This history lends current literary treatments of anorexia an associative richness lacking in those of bulimia. Samuel Richardson's Clarissa Harlowe (1747-8) starved herself at long-suffering length and wrote many eloquent letters to tell about it. Franz Kafka's short-story "A Hunger Artist" (1922) provides a portrait of the real phenomenon of the *Hungerkunstler*, those so-called artists who earned their daily bread by starving themselves in public. As late as in 1926 six men publicly fasted for money in Berlin.[15] And Kafka's story highlights the public aspect of self-starvation: When the audience stops bothering to check whether or not the hunger artist is still fasting, he dies of starvation.

Furthermore, the vanishing bodies of those who suffer from it make anorexia obvious. Anorexia represents a public statement, although anorectics may conceal their emaciation under many layers of clothes. Conversely, one

[14] Similarly, one may assume that extended accounts of cutting or self-mutilation, which is closely associated with eating disorders, will emerge in the next few years, whereas today this phenomenon is written about extensively in poetry web sites and discussion groups.

[15] Tilmann Habermas, *Zur Geschichte der Magersucht: Eine medizinpsychologische Rekonstruktion* (Frankfurt: Fischer Taschenbuch Verlag, 1994) 89.

cannot see that a woman is bulimic. Of normal weight or a bit overweight, most bulimics keep their bingeing and purging behaviors carefully hidden. The character of the "typical" bulimic is also less easy to classify than the anorectic's. Whereas psychologists and psychiatrists characterize anorectics as having perfectionist and compulsive personalities, they most often diagnose bulimics with having borderline personalities—a classification that implies a contradiction between the outer appearance and the inner life. The character Maeve from *The Passion of Alice* is an extraordinarily visible but psychologically opaque bulimic. Tall, voluptuous, verbally aggressive, and sexually active, Maeve overshadows all the other patients in the eating disorder clinic that the novel depicts. Yet the novel's first-person narrator—and hence the reader—never discovers the reasons for Maeve's severe bulimia: She offers several different conflicting biographies of herself, which are never resolved.

Even if anorectics and bulimics react to the same desire to comply with current standards of extreme feminine slenderness, they elicit different reactions in those who view them. Whereas the anorectic awakens memories of holy martyrs and may even invite us to envy her self-control and seeming autonomy from urges to eat, the bulimic baffles and disgusts us with her behavior. The emaciated anorectic much resembles a feted hundred and ten-pound, 5' 10" supermodel, while the bulimic of 150 pounds looks like an average American woman. I suspect that the distaste for bulimia reflects a discomfort with average dietary habits. Most American women are on, or are in between, diets. Americans vacillate between eating too much, regretting excess, and dieting and exercising out of a sense of remorse. As Marya Hornbacher writes:

> And yet this is a culture where we seesaw madly, hair flying and eyes alight, between crazed and constant consumption, where the insatiable hunger is near universal, as is the fanatical belief in the moral superiority of self-denial and self-control. Culturally, we would be diagnosed as bulimic, not anorexic, daily veering back and forth between two extreme points, bingeing and purging. The frenzied adoration of the anorexic body,

> and the violent hatred of fat, on ourselves, and on others, reveals not that anorexia is beautiful, nor that fat is particularly despicable, but that we ourselves are intolerably torn, and we have to choose sides. (*W* 154)

In accord with the above I contend that bulimia is associated in American culture with the uncontrollable urge to eat and, hence, with fat, both of which are alternately condemned or feared. As long as anorectics are admired for their self-discipline and bulimics and overweight individuals elicit feelings of disgust for their lack of self-control, it will be difficult for writers to put bulimic experience into textual form.

The same holds true for binge eaters, who, if addressed at all, are generally treated with humor in fictional contexts. The novels *Lady Oracle* (1976) by Margaret Atwood and *Final Payments* (1978) by Mary Gordon offered comic treatments of binge eaters before we knew what properly to call them. Joan Foster, the protagonist of *Lady Oracle*, accurately surmises that the discrimination and cruelty she witnesses as a fat girl will be judged ludicrous by others. One feels sorry for beautiful thin heroines, one laughs at the pitfalls of fat ones: "If Desdemona was fat who would care whether or not Othello strangled her?" Joan asks herself.[16] Wally Lamb's *She's Come Undone* (1992) describes the relationship between sexual abuse and binge eating in fictional terms. In literary descriptions of binge eating the narrator's humorous derision of the protagonist's fat plays a central role. Even while readers are made to understand the binge eater's psychological pain and her good reasons for abusing food, we are also confirmed in our dislike of her overeating.[17] Whereas the anorectic inspires admiration, if not emulation, the fat woman stuffing food into her mouth makes us laugh with *schadenfreude* or simply appears grotesque. Yet the obese binge eater and the emaciated anorectic both respond to societal

---

[16] Margaret Atwood, *Lady Oracle*, (1968; London: Virago, 1982) 52. Hereafter abbreviated as *LO*.

pressures on women and resort to destructive food and body abuse.[18] The anorectic's and the binge eater's abuse of food represent the outer limits of a spectrum of disordered eating found in American culture.

Another kind of literary prose depicts the experience of living with and loving women whose relationship to food is tortured. While describing her own difficulties with weight and occasional use of purging techniques, the narrator of Jillian Medoff's *Hunger Point* (1997) focuses chiefly on her sister's severe anorexia and resultant death. Cathi Hanauer's *My Sister's Bones* (1996) also gives a 15 year-old's view of her much-admired older sister's struggle with anorexia. Jonathan Rosen's *Eve's Apple* (1997) depicts a college graduate's inability to comprehend his lover's obsessions with food and her body and his own obsession with her illness. Margaret Atwood's short story "Spring Song of the Frogs" from *Bluebeard's Egg* (1983) describes a man's befuddled perception of the seeming withdrawal of the women around him due to their perpetual dieting, anorexic, and bulimic behaviors. Will's confusion reflects the state of consternation men may feel in the face of many women's charged relationship to eating. In the words of one binge eater's boyfriend, "'I don't understand. What is it about women and food? To me, it's just fuel.'"[19]

Still another type of fiction interrogates the culture of dieting. Researchers report the existence of an enormous group of sub-clinical individuals, who, while not having enough of the symptoms to classify them as bulimic, anorexic or binge eaters, suffer from the mood alteration and behavioral changes of the chronically food-deprived. Since most authorities

---

[17] By contrast, Andre Dubus's "The Fat Girl" from *Adultery and Other Choices* (1975) tells of an obese girl's painful yearlong diet, her conventional triumphs as a thin woman, and her joyful return to fleshiness during and after her pregnancy.

[18] "I wish to offer here the hypothesis that obesity and anorexia nervosa are related to faulty hunger awareness, that 'hunger' is not innate knowledge; learning is necessary for its organization into recognizable patterns." Hilde Bruch, *Eating Disorders: Obesity, Anorexia Nervosa and the Person Within* (New York: Basic Books, 1973) 4.

[19] Patricia J. Washbum, "Losing It," *Eating Our Hearts Out: Personal Accounts of Women' s Relationship to Food*, ed. Lesléa Newman (Freedom, CA: The Crossing Press, 1993) 56.

agree that dieting is the first step towards the development of seriously disordered eating, narratives about dieting are included in this study. Like bulimics and binge eaters, chronic dieters think obsessively about food and tend either to overeat or to be extremely restrictive of food intake. Enjoyment of food and eating on a regular basis become unknown experiences. Two stories by Ellen Gilchrist detail the nearly fatal, and fatal, effects of severe dieting. "The Gauzy Edge of Paradise" from *Victory Over Japan* (1984) describes how a speed-induced "Major Diet" ends when the dieters are held up at gun point and drown their sorrows in stale ice cream sundaes afterwards. "The Last Diet" in *Drunk With Love* (1986) tells how a desperate dieter, hallucinating due to a lack of food, runs over her overweight professor while on her way to the diet center to be weighed. These stories illustrate the normative madness of America's dieting culture, a culture that encourages bizarre food behaviors and eating disorders.[20] This study argues that restricted eating and eating disorders represent a continuum of behaviors. All of these practices demonstrate American women's profound concern about how they should look, what they should eat, and how much they should weigh and consume.

Many researchers understand eating disorders as "ethnic disorders," as syndromes that express cultural conflicts and tensions through the psychosomatic exaggeration of socially condoned behaviors.[21] Often hysteria is compared to anorexia and bulimia. Like eating disorders, hysteria occurred almost exclusively in women and appeared to spread as though by contagion. Arising during the second half of the nineteenth century, hysteria was a way in

---

[20] In a British context Helen Fielding's comic *Bridget Jones's Diary* (1996) documents how a young professional woman's sense of self worth is largely determined by her weight, which she records daily, and the amount she has eaten and drunk the day before.

[21] Richard A. Gordon, *Anorexia and Bulimia: Anatomy of a Social Epidemic* (Oxford: Blackwell, 1990) 10-11, 84; Habermas, *Zur Geschichte der Magersucht* 166 -175; Brian Turner, *The Body and Society: Explorations in Social Theory* (Oxford: Blackwell, 1984): Turner does not use the term "ethnic disorder"—borrowed from the psychoanalyst George Devereux—to describe eating disorders, but he means much the same thing when he states:

which middle- and upper-class women could rebel against the circumscription of their lives—the repression of their sexuality, the limited forum for their voices. This protest, however, took the form of an exaggeration of the so-called feminine characteristics of unreasonableness, affect, and moodiness and was cited as a reason for banning women from the responsibilities of work and the public world. Hysteria then was created by the culture in which it arose and served both to enforce the dictates of that society and to protest against them. In the same manner contemporary eating disorders represent grotesque versions of conventional feminine behavior in the late twentieth and early twenty-first centuries. The concern with outward appearance, the preoccupation with body image, weight, and dieting are ubiquitous features of contemporary middle-class life in the U.S.

While anorectics and obese binge eaters may seem to embody protest against the slim ideal of femininity, they also enforce stereotypes about women's unreasonableness and superficial obsessions with appearance. Becoming obese or dangerously thin renders individuals weak and incapacitates them from participating in public working life. Obese women suffer from discrimination, and when anorectics reach a certain level of emaciation they become incapable of doing anything other than starving themselves. How the bulimic and the chronic dieter express and support cultural mores is less obvious. Their vacillations between restricting caloric intake and then overeating are grotesque versions of most of American women's dietary habits. Two thirds of American women are unhappy with their weight, and a half of these women would trade several years of their lives to have a thin figure.[22] Hence the bulimic and chronic dieter's experience symbolizes many women's struggles with appetite, consumption, and control.

"In particular the disorders of women—hysteria, anorexia, and agoraphobia—are considered as disorders of society" (2).

[22] For documentation, see chapter I, section 1.1) below.

Just as psychologists and sociologists interpret eating disorders as expressions of societal malaise, literary theorists read texts as sites for voicing of cultural conflict and struggles. The interface of literature and culture becomes the center of interest: What do literary texts tell us about the circumstances in which they arise, and how do these circumstances affect literary expression and production?

Literary treatments of eating disorders serve several functions. The literary qualities of these texts render unaesthetic experiences, such as gorging, abusing laxatives, or watching one's body die due to self-induced fasting, compelling and ultimately more readable than many autobiographical accounts of eating disorders. In this manner prose and poetic accounts of eating disorders heighten public awareness of the plight of many young women. By depicting the cultural conditioning that has contributed to their protagonists' becoming eating disordered, literary treatments of anorexia and bulimia also indict American culture for fostering destructive food behaviors in women. More than in non-literary texts, literary treatments of anorexia and bulimia explore the symbolic meaning of disordered eating. These texts show how identity is sought in illness and emaciation as well as how fat and eating are demonized as the other.

Conversely, literary treatments of eating disorders spread the lore on bizarre food behaviors and may function as vehicles for the proliferation of disordered eating. Bulimics, in particular, report that they have learnt how to purge by reading books, watching talk shows, or visiting Internet sites on eating disorders.[23] *Wasted*'s detailed rendering of the narrator's techniques to make her

---

[23] Pro-ana (pro-anorexia), pro-mia (pro-bulimia), and pro-E.D (pro-eating disorder) web sites provide meeting places and sense of solidarity and community to those young women who regard eating disorders as "a lifestyle choice" (20) and not an illness. The positive sense of identity these sites provide bespeaks an unwillingness to give up their eating disorders that many individuals feel. Mim Udovitch, "A Secret Society of the Starving," *New York Times Magazine* 9 August 2002: 18–67. On the very similar situation in Germany, see Astrid Geisler, "Skinnygirl. 1,74 Meter, 47 Kilo," *die tageszeitung* 27 November 2002: 6.

body thin has been cause for the book to be banned in some eating disorder clinics.[24]

Finally, eating disorder narratives work on the premise that telling the story of one's illness effects a cure. Putting negative feelings into story form has become a popular form of treatment for the eating disordered as is reflected in the title of a recent book *Eating in the Light of the Moon: How Women Can Let Go of Compulsive Eating Through Metaphor and Storytelling* (1996). This type of therapy reflects a tendency to confess and forgive aberration that has become a recognizable pattern of behavior in American public life. The popularity of memoirs and fictional accounts of unusual sexual practices, psychological problems, and substance abuse exemplifies our culture of confession. I show that literary treatments of eating disorders belong to the "confessional genre" first described by the literary critic and poet M. L. Rosenthal. They reflect American culture's interest and vicarious pleasure in narratives about secret illnesses and deviant bodily experiences. I will argue that this overemphasis on somatic experience bespeaks an uncertainty about where identity is to be located, on the one hand. On the other hand, the one-sided focus particularly on women's bodily experience in confessional writings about eating disorders fosters traditional essentialist and reductive conceptions of women.

With their conflicting messages and intentions literary treatments of eating disorders illustrate current cultural tensions regarding femininity. Women remain the primary meal makers and food buyers in America. Yet the pressure to be thin is enormous. Hence women's magazines feature diet and fitness articles alongside recipes for high caloric foods. The terror of food that speakers of poems and novels on bulimia, binge eating, and chronic dieting express reflects these contradictions. American women feel insecure about how much food they may "legitimately" consume; they judge themselves and are judged by others accordingly.

---

[24] See chapter II, section 2.3) below.

This study is composed of two parts. The first part describes types of eating disorders, their etiology, and how I look at them though the twin lenses of cultural and literary studies. Chapter one examines anorexia, bulimia, binge eating, and chronic dieting and uses poems to illustrate them. These poems provide initial impressions of the motifs and forms of eating disorder literature. Common themes include speakers' obsessive interest in mirrors, their demonization of fat, flesh, and the urge to eat as well as their fear of food, and their idealization of thinness and anorexia. Speakers identify themselves as diminutive innocents who are entrapped and imprisoned by their eating disorders, which they picture as aggressive demons or witches. Nine out of the sixteen poems printed in this chapter were posted on the Internet; voices are exclusively female, raw, and self-revelatory. They offer unmitigated impressions of American women's current struggles with food.

To place eating disorders within their cultural context, a history of anorexia and the fashion for thinness are described in chapter one. Recognition is also given to growing rates of obesity in America. Moreover, an analysis of the cultural significance of weight as a moral issue in America is provided. The chapter concludes with a discussion of medical, psychological, and sociological explanations for the current proliferation of eating disorders.

The second chapter describes the cultural studies method I use to read and interpret literary accounts of eating disorders. I understand American culture to be a dynamic process which is motivated by economic as well as social forces: The consolidation of firms that create diet products and produce snack foods and the burgeoning beauty industry clearly relate to the literary texts discussed here. I see culture as a way of life that includes television, advertising, and comics rather than as discrete literary texts, artistic objects, and musical performances. Furthermore, I understand myself to be a socialized product of American culture, if a critical one. My job is to point out and name the cultural pressure points and conflicts that are exposed by an analysis of writings on eating disorders. By viewing eating disorders as representations of, and comments on, American culture, I may legitimately draw information to elucidate texts about them from a variety of sources including Internet sites, film, television, and the popular press.

The section on previous research describes limitations of two previous cultural analyses of literature on eating disorders and details how this study differs from them. Chapter two also outlines the confessional genre of literature to which most of the writings analyzed here belong. In this genre the testimony of illness aims to be a form of metaphorical healing.

The second part of this study examines longer literary narratives on eating disorders in detail. I analyze two novels on anorexia and one memoir on anorexia and bulimia to show how these texts employ confessional motifs and criticize the cultural milieu that made their protagonists eating disordered.[25] Chapter three looks at *Life-Size*. This novelistic account of hospitalization illustrates the cultural conditioning that encouraged its protagonist Josie to become anorexic and paints a picture of an anorectic's idealization of her emaciation and corresponding profound fear of fat. Chapter four examines *The Passion of Alice*. This second novelistic portrayal of a woman's hospitalization for anorexia scrutinizes and ironically criticizes the clinic for its atmosphere of coerced confession. Chapter five provides an explication of *Wasted*—a hybrid literary memoir—as the apotheosis of confessional writing. Using a method from literary studies, novels such as Margaret Atwood's *Lady Oracle* (1976), Ken Keysey's *One Flew Over the Cuckoo's Nest* (1962), and John Fowles's *The French Lieutenant's Woman* (1969) are brought into the textual analysis on a comparative basis.

Reading eating disorders and their literary treatments works like those triptych mirrors in fancy dressing rooms. These texts provide readers with

[25] Missing in this analysis are treatments of extended literary texts on binge eating and chronic dieting. This work remains to be completed by others.

startling images of our backsides. Americans exist in an atmosphere of constant temptation to overeat and to eat unhealthily, while fashion dictates an extraordinary level of dietary asceticism. Women who do not control their appetite for food are punished with social ostracism, moral condemnation, and economic loss. Literary accounts of eating disorders reveal how many women battle with fork, food, and fat every day. They also document how the culture of confession has come to be a dominant form in public and literary discourse.

Part I

I Eating Disorders and their Causes

What do we mean when we talk about eating disorders? Despite a great deal of sensationalistic media coverage of anorexia and bulimia, misconceptions about eating disorders abound. Dr. Ruth Striegel-Moore summarized the most common of these during a congressional briefing on eating disorders in July 1997. She mentioned seven myths regarding eating disorders: 1) anorexia is the only eating disorder; 2) an eating disorder is a transient problem; 3) only white women have eating disorders; 4) only rich and famous people have eating disorders; 5) eating disorders have just one cause; 6) eating disorders can be treated easily and effectively; 7) eating disorders are impossible to prevent.[1]

In part this chapter aims to address such misconceptions. By delineating what kind of eating disorders there are, who has them, and for how long, the scope of the literature dealing with these problems can be determined. Each one of the eating disorders mentioned here will be illustrated with poems. Much more suggestively than textbooks, these poems describe the experience of having anorexia, bulimia, or being a compulsive eater or dieter. Furthermore, a variety of explanations will be offered for why people, predominantly young women, get eating disorders and what the historical roots of these illnesses are. Again, these sketches of the common explanatory models for the etiology of eating disorders will be filled out with poetry.

The poems quoted here, some from well-known poets, most posted anonymously on the Internet, provide a preliminary view of the themes treated more extensively in novels and literary memoirs about eating disorders. Being obsessed by thoughts of food, hating one's own body, despising feminine flesh in general, and feeling powerlessness over one's eating obsessions number

[1] Ruth Streigel-Moore, "Statement of Ruth Striegel-Moore, PhD at the APA CoSponsored Congressional Briefing," *American Psychological Association* 2002, 4 November 2002 <http:// www.apa.org/ppo/issues/pruth.html>.

among them. Speakers employ pseudo-religious images to describe the purported purity of emaciation and the fall from grace that consuming food represents to them. Mirrors find frequent mention. Confrontations with "full-lengths" (in "Howl" above) or "silver picture[s]" (from "The Angel That Feeds Me" below) work as catalysts for eating-disordered behavior: the speaker feels so much self-loathing when she perceives the image of her ugly flesh that she goes on a binge ("The Bulimic Experience; Today Will Be The Last" and "The Angel That Feeds Me"). Mirrors also reveal the eating-disordered woman's divided sense of self, the discrepancy she senses between her public functioning self and her private eating-disordered one. The divided selves reflected in these mirrors are reminiscent of the explorations of horrific hidden selves in *The Strange Case of Dr. Jekyll and Mr. Hyde* (1886) and *The Picture of Dorian Gray* (1891). Furthermore, food is alternately regarded as an all-powerful temptation or as the incarnation of evil. Moreover, the desire to eat is experienced as so hateful that speakers of poems on eating disorders project their appetites outwards and personify them as demons or witches. The "good" woman is abstinent, the "bad" woman exercises no self-control, binges, and may be cursed with fat. These poems also reflect on how and why American culture encourages women to become eating disordered.

As new types of eating disorders are discovered and clinicians alter their understandings of the existing ones, the diagnosis and classification of eating disorders will change. At present three types of eating disorders are enumerated in the standard handbook for diagnosing psychological conditions and disorders in America, the *Diagnostic and Statistical Manual of Mental Disorders-IV* (1994): these are anorexia nervosa, bulimia nervosa, and the binge-eating disorder.

1.1) The History of Anorexia Nervosa and the Cult of Thinness

Following the guidelines of the DSM-IV anorectics are described as dangerously underweight girls, women, and very occasionally men who are intensely concerned with their body shapes and weight. They refuse to maintain "normal" weight for their height and age, or their weight loss has led them to weighing less than 85% of their minimum expected weight. Despite being severely underweight, anorectics fear gaining weight and growing fat intensely. For this reason the psychologist Richard Gordon has suggested that the German term *Pubertätsmagersucht* (the addiction to thinness during puberty) more accurately describes the symptoms of anorexia than the English term, which means a nervous loss of appetite.[2] Anorectics have a disturbed perception of their bodies and size. Although they are emaciated, they believe that they are "fat" or that a body part is "too fat." Anorectics who have gone through puberty suffer from an absence of menstrual cycles, called amenorrhea. Some anorectics restrict their food intake to lose weight. Others, called bulimic anorectics, or bulimarexics, induce vomiting or abuse laxatives.[3] The fatality rate for anorexia lies between 5% and 20%, making it the most "life-threatening" of all psychiatric disorders. Most often, anorectics die from starvation or heart failure.[4] Anorectics suffer from osteoporosis—which leads to bone fractures—and stunted growth. Other problems involve electrolyte imbalance, anemia, skin discoloration, hair loss on the head coupled with the growth of fine body hair

---

[2] Richard Gordon, *Anorexia and Bulimia* 66.
[3] DSM-IV, 544-545.
[4] On fatality rates for anorexia nervosa, see Hans-Christoph Steinhausen, "The Course and Outcome of Anorexia Nervosa," *Eating Disorders and Obesity: A Comprehensive Handbook* 235; For the long term effects of anorexia, see Steinhausen 234-237 and Kathryn Zerbe, *The Body Betrayed: A Deeper Understanding of Women, Eating Disorders, and Treatment*, (Washington, DC: American Psychiatric Press, 1993; Carlsbad, CA: Gürze Books, 1995) 250.

(lanugo)—probably for warmth.[5] On a more subjective level anorectics report an inability to sleep, hyperactivity, constipation, and an extreme sensitivity to cold.[6] Generally, the onset of anorexic behaviors occurs during adolescence. Conservative estimates suggest that one percent of American girls between the ages of 13 and 20 suffer from anorexia, though the incidence may be much higher.[7] Less than 10% of anorectics are males.[8]

In a classic work on the subject *The Golden Cage: The Enigma of Anorexia Nervosa* (1978), the psychiatrist Hilde Bruch, who worked with eating-disordered patients for forty years, provides a psychological portrait of the anorexic girl. Typically, she is the pampered daughter of a well-to-do family in which the parents are controlling and overly involved in their children's lives. The best-behaved child in the family, the girl gave her parents the pleasing sense that they were doing a good job of parenting. Frequently, she made her father's interests in sports or science her own, fulfilling the role of the heir apparent in families notable for their "paucity of sons."[9]

Good at school, compliant, and physically attractive, the pre-anorexic girl embodies all the characteristics of conventionally successful youthful femininity. Her anorexia begins with a diet, which as often as not was initiated by her father's remark about her developing a fat bottom or thighs.[10] Weight-conscious parents initially react to their daughter's weight loss with great praise.

---

[5] David S. Goldbloom and Sidney H. Kennedy, "Medical Complications of Anorexia Nervosa," *Eating Disorders and Obesity: A Comprehensive Handbook* 266-270.

[6] Zerbe, *The Body Betrayed* 255-259.

[7] ANRED (Anorexia Nervosa and Related Eating Disorders, Inc.) cites the 1% figure, 4 November 2002 <http://anred.com>. Hans W. Hoek suggests a far lower prevalence among young females, of 0.2.8% in "The Distribution of Eating Disorders," *Eating Disorders and Obesity: A Comprehensive Handbook* 208; Zerbe suggests the higher figure of 1-5%, *The Body Betrayed* 15.

[8] Hans W. Hoek, *The Distribution of Eating Disorders*, 207. See also *DSM-IV*: "More than 90% of cases of Anorexia Nervosa occur in females" (543).

[9] Hilde Bruch, *The Golden Cage: The Enigma of Anorexia Nervosa* (1978; New York: Vintage Books, 1979) 25.

Peers envy the dieting girl's resolve: "How does she do it, how does she exert such self-control?"

The diet escalates, and the anorectic's life becomes one of conceit: She lies about how much she has eaten, hides uneaten food, and exercises compulsively. She becomes intractable about continuing to lose weight. At this point the formerly compliant child turns willful: she insists on her autonomy, on her right to diet, and on the fact that she is still too fat and not at all hungry. Conflict escalates, and all the family's energies are now directed at the young woman and the necessity of her eating. Once the anorectic has grown sufficiently emaciated, she becomes unable to reason: She fervidly maintains the rightness of her dietary habits and has a kind of magical thinking about her body's ability to exist only on air. Patients recurrently use religious imagery to explain their behavior: they want to perfect themselves and transcend their bodies to become pure spirit. Only later, when the anorectic has gained weight, can she admit that she was obsessed by thoughts of food during her period of deprivation.

Risking starvation or cardiac arrest, the young woman is hospitalized, often against her will, to restore minimal functional weight. Only then is individual and family therapy possible. Even after regaining normal body weight, anorectics remain preoccupied by their body and food and suffer from depression. Their personalities are described as perfectionist, and obsessive-compulsive. Said to be difficult to treat, they have trouble engaging in social relationships: As adolescents they have delayed sexual development, as adults they tend to be asexual.

The following poem illustrates the themes of control over the body, the paradoxical powerless dependence on the family, and the testing and

---

[10] Bruch, *The Golden Cage* 29; On the weight-consciousness of parents of the eating disordered, see also Sharlene Hesse-Biber, *Am I Thin Enough Yet?: The Cult of Thinness and the Commercialization of Identity* (Oxford: Oxford UP, 1996) 84-89.

transcendence of bodily limits, which are all characteristic of the anorexic mindset. This untitled poem was posted anonymously on an eating disorder web site under the rubric "From Kate":

I'm in control
In control of mind body and soul
I am clean and pure
As they friv[ol]ously look for a cure

Hungry, starving is what I am
But I don't give a damn
So in control am I
To their faces I can lie

I will urge my problems away
I don't have to deal with them on this day
I will starve until I no longer feel the pain
No, I will not die in vain

They know it's helpless
This whole big mess
They know I'm lost
To try and save me they have paid every cost

There is no chance
Maybe in starvation I will always prance
Sailing my problems out to sea
I would die if the tide came back to me[11]

The speaker reveals the hostility anorectics feel towards those who would make them eat, those who "have paid every cost," and those who vainly "look for a cure." These lines also reveal the anorectic's economic dependency: the speaker cannot pay for her own treatment, either because she is too young, or—in the less likely event that she is an adult anorectic—because she is too sick to work. These words also reveal her family's relative affluence: They have the resources to invest extensively in their daughter's betterment. That she doesn't "give a damn" betokens her adolescent struggle to gain independence. The speaker's use of the third-person plural has a disdainful note. This is no direct address to family and health care servers, but a report on their idiocy. The anorexic "I" stands at the center of the poem; "they" do not deserve to be addressed directly with the use of "you."

The line "To their faces I will lie" expresses the perceived necessity of deception. In the last stanza the speaker explores her need to retain and protect her anorexic identity. Mixing metaphors, she insists that she will "prance" like a horse above her problems and send them out to sea by maintaining her starvation diet. Were her problems to return to her with the tide she also "would die." Whether she eats again or not, the speaker has worked herself into a highly dramatic position in which she feels bound to be destroyed whatever she does. Anorexia appears to be a life or death issue.

Bruch points out that the anorectic strives for independence by, paradoxically, making herself weak through self-starvation. This struggle between activity—the anorectic's fierce defense of her right not to eat—and passivity—weakness in starvation—is characteristic. The following poem from an English web site by an author who calls herself Beryl explores this conflict:

Beginnings

I never seem to get it right!
They say they care for me
Yet all I hear are rigid rules
Of how I "ought" to be.
They issue lists of "right" and "wrong"-
what's "good" and what is "bad"
Yet they want me to stay cheerful
"Can't bear" to see me sad.

---

[11] "From Kate," 4 November 2002 <http://www.mindspring.com/~cwildes/kate2.htm>. I have preserved original punctuation and changed spelling only where necessary in poems posted on the Internet.

I'm not allowed to put my views.
"Don't contradict; it's rude!"
"You're far too young to understand!"
"Be quiet, and eat your food."
They tell me how I "ought" to dress
So as to match their dream
And how to think, look, act and speak.
No wonder I could scream!!
But screaming's not acceptable.
I'm not supposed to feel.
It seems they'd rather have a doll
Cute, passive and unreal.
A puppet to manipulate
Compliant, mute and sweet.
A doll who will not "rock the boat".
    But dolls don't have to eat ...[12]

The speaker summarizes psychological work concerning the anorectic's inability to feel and express her own emotions in words (a phenomenon known as alexithymia). Bruch describes the difficulty of conducting family therapy with parents and siblings of anorectics: Because family members are so busy taking care of and interpreting each other's feelings, they fail to speak for themselves. For example, they say "we think" rather than "I feel."[13] "Beginnings" describes a family in which parental authority dominates and is signified by an excess of "ought(s)."

If a young woman's first words of rebellion are metaphorically gagged by her parents' injunction to be quiet and eat, it seems natural that she should react by throwing down her fork and closing her lips to food. According to the psychiatrist and eating disorder specialist Kathryn Zerbe, the anorectic keeps food out of her body as a way of symbolically circumventing her family's desire to invade her feelings, privacy, and autonomous self.[14] For her parents the

---

[12] Beryl, "Beginnings," 4 November 2002 <http://www.geocities.com/Hollywood/Set/ 1607/ poem.html>.
[13] Bruch, *The Golden Cage* 36.
[14] Zerbe, *The Body Betrayed* 62-64.

speaker is a "puppet to manipulate," "A doll," or the personified projection of their "dream." She defies them by making their would-be doll disappear.

Both "From Kate" and "Beginnings" tell their readers about the nature of contemporary middle-class girlhood. The youthful speakers employ their bodies as a form of signification; they identify themselves exclusively with their weights. In doing so they react to a reality of American culture: Female bodies—particularly lean youthful-looking ones—are valued more highly than women's accomplishments in American public media. Take the potential role model Hillary Rodham Clinton as an example. The senator and former First Lady's achievements—her health-care policy, her *It Takes a Village* (1996)—were never regarded as reason enough for her to appear on the cover of the women's magazine *Vogue*. Rather her decorum regarding the publicizing of yet another extramarital affair of her husband's and, more importantly, her having *lost weight* were cause for her to be chosen as the cover model of the December 1998 issue of *Vogue*. As *Vogue*'s editor stated in an interview, "I think the way she's behaved this past year has been *amazing*. And when I saw how *amazing* she was looking, we asked her to do the cover."[15] Were the lean female form not such a valuable commodity in the States, fewer girls would diet and become anorexic.[16] Were achievements of women valued more and their appearances de-emphasized, fewer girls would copy their mothers' dieting as a method of improving themselves.

When Bruch published *The Golden Cage* twenty-five years ago, typical anorectics were "young, rich, and beautiful [...] the daughters of well-to-do, educated, and successful families, not only in the United States but in many

[15] Rick Marin, "She's Still in Vogue," *Newsweek* 7 December 1998: 56. The decision to feature the First Lady was subsequently revoked after the House of Representatives voted to impeach President Clinton.

[16] See Joan Jacob Brumberg's exploration of the importance of having a "good body" to an American girl's positive sense of herself: *The Body Project: An Intimate History of American Girls* (New York: Random House, 1997) 97-137.

other affluent countries."[17] Probably, the anorectics she described came from families as conventional and overly concerned with appearances as the one described in "Beginnings." It goes without saying that the anorectics whom Bruch portrayed were overwhelmingly white. Increasingly, anorexia affects women of all ethnic groups, particularly immigrants to industrialized Western nations. For immigrant women, fitting in means adopting local standards of beauty.[18] Similarly, the extent to which anorexia besets African American and Latino women depends on how much they have adopted the values of the white American middle class. Part of this culture involves women's extreme dissatisfaction with their bodies.[19]

Anorexia remains most prevalent in Western industrialized societies in which there is an overabundance of food.[20] The middle class reacts to this excess by maintaining a disciplined-looking body has that belies the excess of food.[21] Commenting on the class-aspect of anorexia is the poem by the New Zealander Lauris Edmond that follows:

---

[17] Bruch, *The Golden Cage* vii

[18] Linguists note that women are more apt to adopt the accents and speech styles of dominant classes. It is interesting that this phenomenon is mirrored in the language and style of the body. John Lyons, "Language and Society" in *Language and Linguistics: An Introduction* (Cambridge: Cambridge UP, 1981) 273-274.

[19] Significantly, the "epidemic" of eating disorders remains confined to the white female population according to Bridget Dolan, "Cross-Cultural Aspects of Anorexia and Bulimia: A Review," *International Journal of Eating Disorders* 10, No. 1 (January 1991): 67-78; On white girls' dislike of their bodies as compared to black girls' pride in theirs, see Michele Ingrassia "The Body of the Beholder," *Newsweek*, 24 April 1995, 49-51; Steve B. Chandler et al. "Pathogenic Eating Attitudes and Behaviors and Body Dissatisfaction Differences Among Black and White College Students," *Eating Disorders The Journal of Treatment and Prevention* 2, No. 4 (Winter 1994): 319-328.

[20] Confirming the connection between anorexia and abundance is a comment made in conversation by a psychologist who treats women with "eating issues" (a new euphemism) at Yale University. Dr. Lisa Cross said that students, who had come from countries where eating disorders are virtually unheard of, such as China, seek treatment from her. Within a year of coming to the States, these students start to develop the abnormal eating behaviors that their American contemporaries demonstrate.

[21] In her article "Anorexia Nervosa: A Syndrome of the Affluent Society" from *Transcontinental Psychiatric Reseach Review* 22, No. 3 (1985) the Italian psychiatrist Mara Selvini Palazzoli notes, for instance, that during the war years when food was scarce no hospitalizations for anorexia occurred in Italy. This changed immediately when food became abundant again after the war (199); On the class issues involved in anorexia, obesity, and the modern fear of fat, see Stephen Menell, "On the Civilizing of Appetite," *The Body: Social*

Anorexic Girl

If she could only fly, the sick girl,
let her light limbs take her away and away, so
the pestering solicitude of parents and nurses
can no longer hang like a hot dress in summer
over her flimsy body, thin-angled shoulders—

can they not hear her disgust at their talk
of giant eating, slurp of eggs, bread,
overripe fruit, thick cake . . . she turns
from them painfully, devoured by
the great hungers nobody will acknowledge—

and remembers the Indian girl in the store
at the corner, how her tired eyes shine
in their purple shadows as she speaks
of parcels sent to the brother she hardly knows
in Calcutta . . . how she can never stay,

being carried away by the tide of work
the urgent, the necessary work. *These patients*
had a golden childhood from which they cannot escape
notes the doctor: but the Indian girl
moved straight into the cold clinic of hardship

—there like rough linen close to the skin
ride the purposed denials, the exhaustion,
the celebration at news of the families—ah
the thing needful, the strong hand enclosing
the soul; its ancient, forgotten food.[22]

The repetition of "away" in the descriptions of the hospitalized anorectic and her hard-working Indian counterpart links the girls' experiences together linguistically. The cloth and clothing metaphors used to portray their situations illustrate the material differences between the two girls' lives: The first girl experiences the concern of her caregivers and family like a light, "hot dress in

Process and Cultural Theory, ed. Mike Featherstone, Mike Hepworth, and Bryan S. Turner (London: Sage Publications, 1991) 126-153.

[22] Lauris Edmond, "Anorexic Girl," *Selected Poems* (Auckland: Oxford UP, 1988) 176.

summer," whereas the Indian girl's harsh existence is likened to "rough linen close to the skin." The spiritual poverty of the anorectic is revealed in her desire to be taken "away and away" from her caregivers and their talk of material food. She longs instead for spiritual nurture, but this longing is ignored: "the great hungers nobody will acknowledge." The Indian girl by contrast does not long to be taken away. Instead, she is forcefully "carried away" from the present—the store—by material demands upon her to work and support her family in India. She too suffers from a spiritual hunger for "the thing needful, the strong hand enclosing / the soul; its ancient, forgotten food." Yet though both girls suffer from "great[er] hungers," the lot of the Indian girl is obviously the harder one. Without a "golden childhood," she was born into the prison of poverty—"the cold clinic of hardship."[23]

As Western dictates of feminine beauty and eating habits are disseminated through advertising and the media, eating disorders spread with them. Hence Mervat Nassar reports on a "globalization of eating disorders" already affecting women in non-Western societies. The spread of the fast-food culture combined with the estimation of slender female bodies brings anorexia, bulimia, binge eating, and chronic dieting in its wake.[24] One might envision the Indian girl of the preceding poem becoming anorexic as an unconscious strategy for becoming more like the affluent, white girl who thinks about her.

The history of anorexia has been far better researched and speculated about than the history of bulimia or binge eating. Since many more women suffer from bulimia and binge eating than anorexia, this imbalance is striking. American culture's fashion for and persistent fascination with emaciated women is reflected in historical discourse. The historical development of anorexia

[23] In this poem the horror of food that typifies so many eating-disordered women's writing is also apparent in the lines: " [...] her disgust at their talk / of giant eating, slurp of eggs, bread, / overripe fruit, thick cake."

[24] "Eating Disorders: Between Cultural Specificity and Globalization," *Eating Disorders Review* 9, No. 5, (1998): 3.

receives intensive attention here because it is identical with the history of the idealization of thinness. This idealization, in turn, is the primary cause of the latter-day eating disorders of bulimia and the binge eating.

A regular pattern of feminine fasting occured as early as in medieval times. The historian Rudolph Bell establishes a connection between what we now know as anorexia nervosa and the *anorexia mirabilis* (miraculous anorexia) of the period between 1200 and 1500 exercised by Italian holy women. Bell asserts that more than half of the 261 holy women whose lives are documented in some detail were anorectics. Striving for autonomy, holy anorectics chose to renounce material comforts and embrace a spiritual quest by entering convents rather than marrying. This choice was often met with resistance; male relatives tried to preserve girls' potential economic value in marriage and used force to make them comply with family wishes. Modified fasting before Christmas and during lent was common to Catholic practice of the time and was modeled after Christ's forty-day fast in the wilderness. Yet persistent fasting was a practice at odds with the Benedictine-style moderation in food or drink, popular at the time. Francis of Assisi actually ordered the first famous holy anorectic, Clare of Assisi, founder of the poor Clares, to eat.[25] Clare's behavior was revered and copied, and holy anorexia became a model of pious behavior for medieval Italian women in convents and at home. In contrast to other forms of religious fasting, *anorexia mirabilis* had no stated ending point. In its extreme form this holy fasting ended in death by starvation as in Catherine of Siena's case. Bell argues that anorexia was a viable response to the patriarchy of medieval Catholicism. Fasting saints were so highly regarded for their spiritual lives that they were no longer subordinate to men.[26]

The distinction between holy anorexia and anorexia nervosa may then be one of modifiers, because cultural context determines whether a woman's

---

[25] Rudolph M. Bell, *Holy Anorexia* (Chicago: Chicago UP, 1985) 124.
[26] Bell 116

refusal to eat is a form of holiness or a nervous disorder. Medieval religiosity accompanied by holy fasting represented an "ideal state" for women. The extreme of slenderness embodied by modern anorectics is likewise an exaggerated ideal of feminine beauty.[27] Bell attributes the gradual decline of holy fasting in the sixteenth-century saints to women's having been newly credited with the ability to do good works. Exemplariness in women was no longer restricted to their leading self-abnegating, ascetic lives. Were women to be more greatly valued apart from the ideal of slender beauty, Bell suggests, then the current high incidence of anorexia nervosa might also decline.

Bell has been criticized for equating the symptoms of anorexia in medieval holy women with the actual eating disorder.[28] Yet his thesis that anorexia's meaning is in the eye of the beholder—a holy act or a form of sickness—is compelling. Bell also draws attention to the fact that restricted eating has been a powerful behavioral model for women in various cultural settings: holy fasting was unusual for medieval Italian men, and modern anorectics are almost exclusively female.

In the eighteenth and nineteenth centuries numbers of girls became famous for existing, as it were, only on air. These young women were celebrated by Spiritualists who interpreted their fasting as *anorexia mirabilis* or denigrated by skeptical doctors, who saw them as charlatans. The lives and occasional deaths of these "fasting girls"[29]—often when they were monitored too closely—received extensive media coverage. The ensuing debate about whether the human body could or could not be sustained by spiritual means alone mirrored contemporary tensions between religious and scientific

---

[27] William N. Davis, epilogue to *Holy Anorexia* by Rudolph M. Bell (Chicago: Chicago UP, 1985) 181.
[28] Joan Jacobs Brumberg, *Fasting Girls: The History of Anorexia Nervosa* (1988; New York: Plume, 1989) 42-43.
[29] Brumberg, *Fasting Girls* 61-62.

viewpoints. "Fasting girls" did not display any of the horror of fat or overweight of contemporary anorectics.

A great deal of debate centers on when anorexia nervosa was first diagnosed.[30] The English physician Richard Morton is commonly credited with having discovered anorexia in 1694, when he described a young patient who was so thin that she looked "like a Skeleton only clad with Skin."[31] In this case anorexia is understood as extreme emaciation in a young woman not due to food scarcity or another medical cause. The German psychologist Tilmann Habermas, by contrast, credits the Italian doctor Giovanni Brugnoli with having first diagnosed anorexia in case studies published in 1875. Brugnoli's studies describe two young women who died due to self-induced fasting: Neither evidenced any physical problem that interfered with eating. The patients denied being ill and were extremely physically active despite their severe weight loss. They had both matured physically quite early. These facts led Brugneli to speculate that one of the women's desire to drink vast quantities rather than to eat may have been motivated by her wish to become thinner.[32] Later commentators such as Gull and Lasègue assumed that anorectics suffered from a physical lack of appetite, which led to their weight loss, not from a desire not to eat.

Female self-induced fasting came to be regarded as medical condition rather than a spiritual state in the English-speaking world when Sir William Gull, physician to Queen Victoria and the Royal family, gave the phenomenon a

---

[30] This debate is caused by differing conceptions of anorexia and the frequency with which the modern anorectic's obsession with thinness is projected onto emaciated women in the past. Brumberg *Fasting*, 43.

[31] Richard Morton, *Phthisiologia or, A Treatise of Consumptions,* 2nd ed. (London, 1720) 8-9, quoted in Rudolph Bell 4.

[32] "Bei beiden hebt Brugnoli die frühreife körperliche Entwicklung in der Pubertät und ihren beträchtlichen Körperumfang hervor, womit er anzudeuten scheint, daß sie gezielt zu fasten begannen, um abzunehmen. Guendalinas Vorliebe für Suppen und später für große Mengen Flüssigkeit mag dafür sprechen, daß sie versuchte, sich ein Völlegefühl zu verschaffen, ohne dabei Nahrhaftes zu sich zu nehmen, eine Praxis, die auch heute von vielen Magersüchtigen betreiben wird" (Habermas 111).

medical name in 1873 in a brief paper. A few months before the French doctor Charles Lasègue had described the same ailment as *l'anorexie hystérique.*[33] Gull's term "anorexia nervosa" (a nervous loss of appetite) relates the disorder to a failure in the nervous system and implies that the disorder may also occur in men. "*L' anorexie hystérique,*" by contrast, relates the condition to a variety of ailments occurring only in women: "hysteria" stems from the Greek word for uterus. Both physicians noted that the condition occurred almost exclusively in females. The patients they described in their case studies ranged between 15 and 23 years of age. All were from bourgeois families and did not work. This does not necessarily imply that only the affluent suffered from anorexia; rather, well-to-do families had the resources to consult specialists like Gull and Lasègue about their daughters' medical problems. All the anorectics described by Gull and Lasègue lived at home. Although Gull's psychological description of his anorexic patients is minimal, he, like Lasègue, recognized that the condition was related to family enmeshment. Both physicians recommended that anorectic girls be treated outside of her family. Lasègue acknowledged the difficulties in treating them, their enjoyment of the status their starvation brought them, and their tendency to deceive others about their food intake. Both Gull and Lasègue understood anorexia to be a psychic disorder, closely related to the hysteria.[34]

On the basis of these early descriptions of anorectics the medical historian Joan Jacob Brumberg draws an analogy between the family settings of Gull and Lasègue's patients and those of anorectics today. She aims to demonstrate that the emotional problems of adolescent Victorians mirror those of middle-class girls today. Brumberg paints the Victorian family as being as closely-knit as those of the anorectics whom Bruch describes: A decrease of birth rates, children's marrying late, and the centering of family life on the

---

[33] Brumberg, *Fasting Girls*, 119.
[34] *Fasting Girls*, 118-136.

notion of love rather than authority—this characterized comfortable Victorian family life. Although food was abundant, denying it to children was the preferred mode of discipline. Victorian children were taught not to express food preferences and were encouraged to behave cheerfully. Girls were subject to particularly close scrutiny, as their good behavior was instrumental to their making good marriages and their family's prestige. Refusing food because of some vague malady was one of the few ways in which a Victorian girl could assert herself.[35] She behaved decorously while demonstrating her will. And because Victorian girls notoriously suffered from poor appetite, some due to real maladies such as iron deficiency and tuberculosis, food refusal was ambiguous.

Furthermore, a fashion for thinness began at about the time that anorexia was diagnosed. Physical debility was associated with grace and class and the wasting tubercular girl was both the object of pity and admiration in Victorian society.[36] Victorian women were in a quandary regarding food. Reticence in regard to eating was both a sign of gentility and good moral character.

---

[35] Brumberg draws on evidence assembled by J.A. Banks, *Prosperity and Parenthood: A Study of Family Planning among the Victorian Middle Classes* (London, 1954) etc.; For changing values of children she cites Viviana Zellizer, *Pricing the Priceless Child: The Changing Value of Children* (New York, 1985) among other sources; For information on Victorian dietary habits, she refers to Priscilla Robertson's "Home as Nest: Middle-Class Childhood in Ninteenth-Century Europe," in De Mause ed., *History of Childhood* (New York, 1975) etc., cited in *Fasting Girls* 126-140, 316-321.

[36] *Fasting Girls* 183-185; Miriam Bailin, *The Sickroom in Victorian Fiction: The Art of Being Ill* (Cambridge: Cambridge UP, 1994): "The erotic possibilities of the female invalid were more overtly promoted in the latter years of the century by George Du Maurier's hugely successful *Trilby*, for instance, or by Eliza Linton's suggestion in *The Girl of the Period* that the ill-health and 'fragility' and 'the long, loose folds of falling drapery' can revive marital passion: 'Many a drifting husband has been brought back to his first enthusiasm by the illness of a wife who knew how to turn evil things into good, and to extract a charme even out of suffering'"(23); Barbara Korte traces the evolution of the topos of the *femme fragile* in literature and art and shows that the height of the fascination with the sickly, elegant woman occurred in Victorian times, when sex was thought of as evil, tuberculosis was romanticized, and female frailty came to represent the economic prosperity of men who did not need their wives to work. "The 'Femme Fragile': Decline and Fall of a Literary Topos," *Anglia 105*, (1987): 366-389.

Helena Mitchie has shown that while the dinner table is central to Victorian literature, images of eating women are largely absent. Hence she detects an "anorexia at the center of many Victorian texts."[37] Images of women eating fruit were particularly resonant for the Victorian imagination. Citing Elizabeth Gaskell's *Cranford* (1853), in which the ladies of Cranford retire from company to perform the vulgar operation of eating oranges, and Thomas Hardy's *Tess of the D'Urbervilles* (1891), where Alex forces Tess to eat strawberries before having sex with her, Mitchie shows that a disciplined appetite and abstemious body were signs of female spiritual purity for Victorians.

Curiously, Mitchie does not address the likening of appetite for fruit with sexual desire represented by Christina Rossetti's long narrative poem "Goblin Market" (1862). The barkers of goblin market tempt two maidens with luscious looking fruits, offering one of them a taste of the forbidden fruit for the price of a lock of hair—a symbol of virginity. Laura, who tastes the fruit, is "ruined," grows gray hair and nearly dies. Her virtuous sister Lizzie saves her by going to buy fruit from the goblin men with money and refusing their attempts to get her to eat it. I quote from the second stanza of the poem:

> Evening by evening
> Among the brookside rushes,
> Laura bowed her head to hear,
> Lizzie veiled her blushes:
> Crouching close together
> In the cooling weather,
> With clasping arms and cautioning lips,
> With tingling cheeks and finger tips.
> "Lie close," Laura said,
> Pricking up her golden head:
> "We must not look at goblin men,
> We must not buy their fruits:

[37] Helena Mitchie, *The Flesh Made Word: Female Figures and Women's Bodies* (Oxford: Oxford UP, 1987) 28.

Who knows upon what soil they fed
Their hungry thirsty roots?"
"Come buy," call the goblins
Hobbling down the glen.
"Oh," cried Lizzie, "Laura, Laura,
You should not peep at goblin men."
Lizzie covered up her eyes,
Covered close lest they should look;
Laura reared her glossy head,
And whispered like the restless brook:
"Look, Lizzie, look, Lizzie,
Down the glen tramp little men.
One hauls a basket,
One bears a plate,
One lugs a golden dish
Of many pounds weight.
How fair the vine must grow
Whose grapes are so luscious;
How warm the wind must blow
Thro' those fruit bushes."
"No," said Lizzie: "No, no, no;
Their offers should not charm us,
Their evil gifts would harm us."[38]

The two sisters' divergent views of the goblin men's fruits represent two conflicting views of sexuality and consumption. Laura extols the sensual pleasures to be enjoyed by tasting the fruits. She can well imagine how "warm the wind must blow" and how "luscious" the grapes must taste for those who consume them. By consuming the fruit, she at first comes to know the "fruit globes fair or red: / Sweeter than honey from the rock."[39] In so doing she becomes—if only temporarily—a fallen woman, doomed like the character Jeanie to die a shameful death. Jeanie, whose life represents a cautionary tale in the poem, once tasted many of the goblin men's fruits and now lies in a grave upon which no flowers will grow.

[38] Christina Rossetti, "Goblin Market," *The Complete Poems of Christina Rossetti*, ed R.W. Cramp (Composed 27 April 1859; edition 1862; Baton Rouge: Louisiana State UP, 1979) 12.
[39] Rossetti, Lines 130-131, 14

In contrast to Laura, Lizzie embodies the Victorian ideal of maidenly virtue and circumspection. Unlike her sister, she does not look at the goblin men and later successfully resists their efforts to make her eat their wares. Whereas Laura imagines the sweetness of the proffered fruits, Lizzie envisions only the dangers that eating them would bring: "Their evil gifts would harm us." The implicit condemnation of women for buying and enjoying fruit in Rossetti's poem suggests that an ambivalence about how much women should consume of anything—fruit, sex, consumer goods—has deep historical roots in Western culture.

Brumberg points out that it was less fruit—symbolic of the Fall—that caused Victorian women anxiety about eating than meat, which was considered dangerously conducive to promoting sexual appetite. She cites Eliot's *Daniel Deronda* (1876), in which a group of gentry associate women's desire for venison with a sure sense of moral corruption. They are most particularly disgusted by one woman's desire to eat animal fat.[40] In part due to prohibitions regarding meat consumption many Victorian girls were anemic, and their paleness contributed to the aesthetic ideal of feminine fragility.

In his history of anorexia Habermas goes farther than Brumberg or Mitchie in associating Victorian anorexia with the punishment of burgeoning flesh. He posits a different cause for the desire to control appetite and weight amongst turn-of-the-century women than contemporary ones.[41] Asceticism motivated fin-de-siècle anorectics. Controlling physical appetite was a means to control sensory appetite, particularly sexual desire. Quoting several early patient testimonies—notably lacking in Gull and Lasègue's case studies—Habermas

---

[40] George Eliot, *Daniel Deronda* (1876; London: Penguin Books, 1995) 116. It is noteworthy that both the Jewish and the Gentile heroine of the novel are pale and extremely thin.

[41] This differentiation is quite important, since there is a danger of projecting our current understanding of anorexia onto a period in which the obsession with thinness did not yet exist. Physical fragility was considered attractive in Victorian contexts because it bespoke gentility and sexual innocence, as Mitchie and Brumberg show. Thinness as a mark of sexual desirability is a new concept, which appears to have arisen during the 1920s at the earliest.

gives us a portrait of an anorectic who was psychically far closer to the medieval holy woman than today's fashion-conscious middle-class anorectic.

The patient "Renata" was admitted to the Berne clinic in 1907, suffering from depression, underweight, hyperactivity, and a compulsion to vomit up whatever food she ate.[42] Renata reported to her psychiatrist that the experience of puberty was unbearable for her. In her own words:

> I was ashamed to be a woman, to have the bodily form of a woman. I asked myself what a man could possibly think about a woman that was good. I felt degraded by being a woman and ashamed when I noticed that someone was looking at me. Being fat seemed particularly humiliating to me, because then the form of the body was even more noticeable. I wished that one would not be able to discover the least bit of a feminine body under my clothes.[43]

Despising the roundness of the mature female body, the turn-of-the-century anorectic regarded her flesh as the embodiment of sin. This attitude is reflected in contemporary case studies of anorectics including one of the existential analyst Ludwig Binswanger's patients. Binswanger writes that his patient "Irma" punished all of her appetites and her other failings with self-flagellation and by biting herself, explaining, "I thought this was how witches were tortured, and when I lie I am a witch!"[44]

In a poem from a 1995 collection the Irish poet Eavan Boland explores the hatred of the female body as a sexual entity that Renata and Irma express:

---

[42] Habermas 70.

[43] "Ich schämte mich, eine Frau zu sein, die Körperformen einer Frau zu haben. Ich fragte mich, was ein Mann wohl Gutes über eine Frau denken könne. Ich fühlte mich erniedrigt, Frau zu sein, und schämte mich, wenn ich bemerkte, daß man mich betrachtete. Fett zu sein schien mir besonders erniedrigend, weil so die Form des Körpers noch mehr ins Auge fällt. Ich wünsche mir, man möge nicht das geringste eines weiblichen Körpers unter der Kleidung entdecken können." [Trans. mine] Schnyder, Louis, "Le cas de Renata: Contribution à l'étude de l'hystérie," *Archives de psychologie* (1912), quoted in Habermas 72.

[44] "Ich dachte, so wurden die Hexen gefoltert, und wenn ich lüge bin ich eine Hexe!" [Trans. mine] Ludwig Binswanger, "Versuch einer Hysterieanalyse," *Jahrbuch für psychoanalytische und psychopathologische Forschung, I* (1909), quoted in Habermas, 98.

Anorexic

Flesh is heretic.
My body is a witch.
I am burning it.

Yes I am torching
her curves and paps and wiles.
They scorch in my self denials.

How she meshed my head
in the half-truths
of her fevers till I renounced
milk and honey
and the taste of lunch.

I vomited
her hungers.
Now the bitch is burning.

I am starved and curveless.
I am skin and bone.
She has learned her lesson.

Thin as a rib
I turn to sleep.
My dreams probe

a claustrophobia
a sensuous enclosure.
How warm it was and wide.

once by a warm drum,
once by the song of his breath
and in his sleeping side.

Only a little more,
only a few more days
sinless, foodless.

I will slip
back into him again

as if I have never been away.
Caged so
I will grow
angular and holy

past pain
keeping his heat
such company

as will make me forget
in a small space
the fall

Into forked dark,
Into python needs
heaving to hips and breasts
and lips and heat
and sweat and fat and greed.[45]

This poem is extraordinary because its controlled use of language may be seen as a metaphor for the anorectic's control of her body. Nothing is superfluous. Language is elegant and lean. The images the speaker uses to describe her detested body are reminiscent of *Malleus Maleficarum* (1478)—the manual for witch hunters. According to this manual, the female is by nature prone to witchcraft because of her "carnal lust, which is in women *insatiable*," and her desire to fill the "*mouth*" of her womb.[46] Female "[f]lesh is heretic." Her needs are "python." These needs recall the snake that tempted Eve into committing the original sin.

The speaker seeks to forget her fall from grace into the sinfulness of carnal knowledge, the recognition of the naked sexual self. The need to disown her own body is so great that the speaker avoids owning it linguistically. She burns "it" and not herself. The disowned body is henceforward portrayed as a witch. This witch once had the power to "mesh[]" the speaker's "head," to

[45] Eavan Boland, *Collected Poems*, (Manchester: Carcanet, 1995) 58-59.

seduce her with "the half-truths of her fevers" and her hunger for "milk and honey." Stripped of female flesh, ridden of the witch/bitch, the spiritualized "I" may slip into Adam's rib again, as a diminished and small accompaniment to his heartbeat.

Despite the speaker's desire to flee into the forgetful amnesia of the rib, the last stanza reveals a compelling image of selfhood with all its messy wants. "[P]ython needs" are overwhelming and dangerous and attractive. The repetition of clusters of sibilant and plosive and sibilant and dental sounds in the last stanza force the reader to lick her lips in a mimicry of eating and by implication having sex: "heaving to hips and breasts / and lips and heat." The repetition of "ands" reminds us of another Irish writer's telling of female sexuality—Molly Bloom's "and then he asked me would I yes to say yes my mountain flower and first I put my arms around him yes and drew him down to me so he could feel my breasts all perfume yes and his heart was going like mad and yes I said yes I will yes."[47] The backhanded affirmation of female sexuality in the last stanza reveals that the poem was written retrospectively, at a time when calling women's secondary sexual characteristics "evil" has become at the very least politically incorrect.

"Anorexic" introduces imagery common to many literary accounts of eating disorders. The association of the hungry self with a witch or a demon in this poem is a frequent motif; we shall discover it again in the poems "The Bulimic Experience; Today Will Be The Last" and "The Angel that Feeds Me" discussed below. The heaping up of religious and biblical images done so masterfully in "Anorexic" is common to many poems on eating disorders. In the first poem mentioned in this chapter, the anorexic speaker spoke of her emaciated self as being "clean and pure," thus likening her lack of a need for

---

[46] Susan Bordo, *Unbearable Weight: Feminism, Western Culture and the Body* (Berkeley and Los Angeles: California UP, 1993) 161, quoting from *Maleus Maleficarum*.
[47] James Joyce, *Ulysses* (New York: Vintage Books, 1961) 783.

food to a spiritually exalted state. By contrast poems about the bulimic experience treat religious imagery satirically. In both "Howl," which opened this study, and "The Bulimic Experience," which will be discussed below, the toilet into which bulimics vomit is referred to as an altar. Since the speakers of these poems regard bingeing and vomiting as shameful activities, the toilet represents an anti-altar to them.

Perhaps the most famous anorectic before Karen Carpenter was "Ellen West," the pseudonym Binswanger gave another eating disordered patient. Highly articulate, Ellen inspired Binswanger to write a lengthy case study about her, in which he quotes from her poems and lengthy sections of her diary.[48] Binswanger describes Ellen as bright, passionate, and ambivalent about her sex. She refused to drink milk at the age of two, wore boy's clothes until she was sixteen, waited impatiently for social revolution to occur, and felt frustrated by her inability to fulfill herself intellectually. Ellen turned her extraordinary will and creativity into the business of becoming thin. She has become a kind of feminist martyr whose life and death provides a parable for what happens to creative women when they are not allowed to express themselves.[49]

Her life and suicide also inspired two major poets to write about her anorexia, Adrienne Rich and Frank Bidart. In the following poem from 1971 Rich composes an elegy for the wasted life and talents and flesh of Ellen West:

For Ellen West, Mental Patient and Suicide

Lethal poison: revenge
on a world of definitions

---

[48] Ludwig Binswanger, "The Case of Ellen West" (1944), trans. Werner M. Mendel and Joseph Lyons, *Existence: A New Dimension in Psychiatry and Psychology*, ed Rolla May, Ernest Angel, Henri F. Ellenberger (New York: Basic Books, 1958) 237-364.

[49] Kim Chernin makes Ellen West's sad life and obsession with thinness the centerpiece of her book *The Obsession: Reflections on the Tyranny of Slenderness* (1981; New York: HarperPerennial, 1994). See also L. Studer, "Ellen West," in *WahnsinnsFrauen*, ed. S. Duda and L.F. Pusch (Frankfurt: Suhrkamp, 1992) 226-254.

coiled in the bird's nest
swimming in the milk
you refused getting yourself a name
for stubborness
You weaning yourself
striding in boy's clothes
dreaming of freedom
in the skirted parlor
of pre-war Europe
you child and poet
delivered at birth
into enemy hands

I am not of your woman!
the poet in you
could only choke
on hunger
shame and self-loathing
Every ounce of your female flesh
revolted you
they took you to clinics
for willed starvation
for dread of swollen breasts
and swollen belly
They analyzed you twice
committed you to Kreuzlingen
in Switzerland
Your husband
understood you so perfectly
he came with you everywhere

Ellen West, a non-Swiss—
your title in Binswanger's history—
Ellen, not ski-ing the planes of the mountain
not-carving the frozen air
with your eager, longing breath
not-living for thirty years
the definitions
they had prepared for you
not-giving-in
though hunger haunted you
in a false and fatal form
O Ellen

I sift your life up out of their negatives
I read of you
in anger   you surrounded
by understanding, understood
to the brink of your throttled life
by parents, husband, the greatest doctors
in Kreuzlingen, in Switzerland
in the nineteen-twenties

you surrounded
by snow-peaks   by glaciers
by chocolate creams
and Easter eggs   the poems
of Goethe and Rilke   you
hungry for a forbidden life
guilty   starving   condemned

by a world of definitions

taking lethal poison
with a tranquil face
— Adrienne Rich[50]

The second stanza introduces a theme that is nearly universal in literary accounts of eating disorders: the profound disgust for female flesh. This disgust is palpable in "Anorexic," when the speaker refers to her breasts and thighs and hips as "curves and paps and wiles." The reference to breasts as "paps," defined as "soft or semi-liquid food[s] suitable for babies or invalids,"[51] displays the speaker's derisive attitude towards their potentially life-giving function. This loathing for the reproductive potential that fat represents in women is amplified on in Rich's description: "Every ounce of your female flesh / revolted you / they took you to clinics / for willed starvation / for dread of swollen breast / and swollen belly." Swollen breasts and belly accompany pregnancy and, to a lesser degree, lactation, and Ellen loathes these characteristics of maternity.

[50] Adrienne Rich, "For Ellen West, Mental Patient and Suicide" (1971) in Kim Chernin, *The Obsession* 178-179.

The poem's blanks refer both to Ellen's anonymity, her namelessness, as well as the gaps in her life, all that might have been had she been allowed to create her own "definitions" of herself. The negation of Ellen's possibilities is reiterated when the narrator plays with Binswanger's description of "Ellen" as a "non-Swiss": "not-ski-ing," "not-carving," "not-living," "not-giving-in." The cumulative effect of these negations is that Ellen was not allowed to determine her own identity. She was named by others, "understood" by others, and defined by others to the extent that her own creative powers were destroyed. Her inability to nourish herself in a world of "chocolate creams" and Rilke's poetry fills the speaker "with anger." The anger expressed here at the wreckage that eating disorders create in women's lives was palpable in the poem "Howl"; we shall come across it again in the poem "Conform," the novel *Life-Size,* and the memoirs *Wasted.*

Because Bidart's poem is thirteen-pages long, I include only one complete section from its twelve parts here. Interspersed with three actual quotations from Binswanger's case study, Bidart's poem presents Ellen's thought processes concerning her ideal of thinness, her dislike of being a female, her desire to transcend nature, time, and her material self. The final section renders a letter Ellen might have actually written to a fellow patient on the day she poisoned herself. In this letter she expresses her regret at having disappointed her husband and the letter's addressee due to her inability to give up her ideal of bodilessness. Like Rich's representation of her unhappy life, Bidart's poem emphasizes West's dismay at being a woman:

> Why am I a girl?
>
> I ask my doctors, and they tell me they
> don't know, that it is just "given."

---

[51] *Oxford Advanced Learner's Dictionary of Current English*, 4th ed., ed. A.P. Hornby (Oxford: Oxford UP, 1989) 894.

But it has such
implications—;

                                        and sometimes,
I even feel like a girl.[52]

Being a girl with all its "implications" of circumscribed movement and narrow career options also entails that one's physical image is of paramount importance. In the first section of the poem Ellen muses that she adores ice cream and sweets but that these pleasures cannot be enjoyed because their indulgence would lead to weight gain. A fatter body would be anathema to Ellen's image of her essential self:

But my true self
 is thin, all profile
and effortless gestures, the sort of blond
elegant girl whose
                                        body is the image of her soul.[53]

This blond, elegant, surely, very thin and very beautiful girl represents Ellen's ideal. Her "body" represents her "soul." In other words, if her body is "fat and ugly" her soul will be defective as well. Tragically, Ellen is never able to embody this stereotypical image of idealized femininity and hates herself for once having weighed 165 pounds. Nor is she able to abandon the pursuit of this ideal for any more sustaining activities such as writing. The seventh section of the poem represents how Ellen compares her own experience to that of her favorite opera singer Maria Callas. Callas lost an enormous amount of weight very rapidly after she had already become famous; Ellen assumes that the singer had to become thinner in order to achieve the full measure of her expressive powers:

---

[52] Frank Bidart, "Ellen West" (1977), *In the Western Night: Collected Poems 1965-90* (New York: Farrar Straus Giroux, 1990) 109-110.
[53] Bidart 109 -110

But soon she felt that she must lose weight,—
that all she was trying to express

was obliterated by her body,
buried in flesh—[54]

Yet in attempting "to express" all she had to say by becoming thin, in attempting to embody the ideal of the beautiful heroine, Callas also lost her powerful voice, first the volume and then her high notes.

With the comparison of Ellen's and Callas's lives, the poem suggests that a common conundrum for creative women is the need to embody the ideal of the beautiful artist. Artistry itself appears insufficient. In working to achieve the beauty ideal, women like West and Callas lose their ability to write, sing, or articulate themselves.

Popular wisdom attributes the roots of modern anorexia nervosa to the appearance of the model Twiggy in 1965. This wisdom is confirmed by various accounts of women who date the beginning of their food obsessions to the dawn of Twiggy's popularity.[55] Five feet seven inches tall and weighing 98 pounds, Twiggy embodied a new ideal. The craze for slenderness in the 1960s recalled the flapper era in the 1920s—when woman bound their breasts to appear slimmer and dresses were shortened to reveal calves for the first time. In both periods the fashion for slimmer bodies was associated with women's new independence.[56]

---

[54] Bidart 114.

[55] See the following testimonies of two bulimics: " [...] very very soon all those parts of me which had so recklessly been fleshing out without consent over the last few years would flesh in, shrink in, deflate, and I would be as petite and happy as Twiggy." Michelle Blair, "The Key to Happiness—A monologue—," *Eating Our Hearts Out: Personal Accounts of Women's Relationship to Food*, ed. Lesléa Newman (Freedom, CA: The Crossing Press, 1993) 122; "It was then the mid-sixties, the time of toothpick-thin Twiggy, and other icons of a culture suddenly insisting that a woman could never be too thin." Hendle Rumbaut, "An Image of Myself," *Eating Our Hearts Out* 123.

[56] Brumberg, *Fasting Girls* 245.

One may interpret this phenomenon variously. On the one hand the fashion for slim-hipped, small-breasted women in the twenties and sixties may have signified women's emancipation from the traditional wife-and-mother role. Women could symbolically stride out into the world without nursing infants in tow, when they looked more like androgynous boys. That this taste for androgyny would turn into a form of rigid social control was an unfortunate side-effect.

On the other hand the thin female body may be associated with pre-pubescence and sexual immaturity. The thinned, overtly girlish body of the flapper and the 60s hipster may have visually offset the threat of women's sexual autonomy.[57] Twiggy's first appearance in *Vogue Magazine* occurred roughly simultaneously with the mass introduction of the pill on the American market. Her extreme thinness may have suggested an asexuality that counterbalanced women's sexual and reproductive freedom: Twiggy appeared more in need of a good meal than on the prowl for sexual adventure. *Vogue* wrote about her at the time: "Her legs look as though she has not had enough milk as a baby and her face has that expression one feels Londoners wore in the blitz."[58]

Whatever the cause of Twiggy's immense popularity, Americans had become a nation of dieters before she appeared. Insurance agencies introduced weight tables in America at the beginning of the century, leading to the standardization of so-called normal body weight. The production of ready-to-wear clothes meant that larger-than-normal women were prevented from acquiring new fashions. As early as in the 1920s diet advice and diet manuals

---

[57] Both of these theories are speculative. One can find counter-evidence to the theory that thin women are equated with sexual innocence in the person of Marilyn Monroe. The voluptuous Monroe was also praised for her innocent quality just as thin beauties before and after her have been.

[58] Naomi Woolf, *The Beauty Myth: How Images of Beauty Are Used Against Women* (1981; New York: Anchor Books, Doubleday, 1982) 184-5, quoting Nicholas Drake, ed., *The Sixties: A Decade in Vogue* (New Work: Prentice Hall, 1988).

became popular. They exhibited a moralistic attitude towards personal responsibility for one's weight and looks. *Vogue* stated in 1918: "There is one crime against the modern ethics of beauty which is unpardonable; far better it is to commit any number of petty crimes than to be guilty of the sin of growing fat."[59] Personal appearance is treated as a question of morality here. The disgust with "growing fat" evident in the 1918 article from *Vogue* persists in America today and informs discriminatory treatment of the obese.

As a general cultural practice dieting has been giving Americans what we need for over a hundred years. As religious values have declined in importance moral values associated with controlling the body's appearance have grown. At the end of the nineteenth century work took on a more sedentary nature, and it became necessary to control consumption in order to maintain previous weights. At the same time the middle class discovered new ways to exercise their economic prosperity in consumerist indulgence. Dieting then has become a sort of persistent religious rite. It provides Americans with something to discipline—bodies and weights—while other forms of consumption, for instance sexual or monetary, are indulged. Guilt about monetary excesses can be expiated in diet and exercise plans. Standards of slenderness also provide seemingly objective criteria by which to judge how self-controlled or self-indulgent others are. This negative brand of American individualism informs the disgust for the obese, who are blamed individually for their lack of moral fiber.[60] It also explains the residing popularity of weight loss advertisements that feature one lucky soul who has conquered her weight problem alone by just using this or that product. Americans do not wish to see fat as a universal problem of a consumer culture but as a measure of individual character and worth.

[59] Brumberg, *Fasting Girls* 243.
[60] See the discussion of obesity below.

The views I have summarized are taken from the book *Fat History: Bodies and Beauty in the Modern West* (1997).[61] Peter Stearns, the author, compares a century of dieting in the States and in France to explore the question of what dieting means for Americans and why Americans have grown steadily more overweight. The French take a less moralistic stance on dieting: they regard overweight as unaesthetic, not as an indication of moral failure. Significantly, the French have been more successful in effectively controlling their weights than Americans have been. Stearns concludes that efforts to improve the treatment of the obese—anti-sizism—or even new medical findings supporting the hypothesis that being moderate overweight may be healthier than being underweight are unlikely to alter America's dieting culture. He suggests that we need the moral code that dieting provides. Even if we were to stop using weight and size as a measure of personal worth we would have to find some other standard by which to judge the characters of the individuals whom we meet.

Yet the culture of dieting is not simply an outgrowth of American moralistic individualism. It is also a reaction to increasing levels of overweight and obesity. Not coincidentally, the desire to be thin has grown proportionally with the widening of the American waistline. We Americans are among the fattest peoples of the world. More than half of the population is clinically obese, and obesity is on the rise.[62] America has become a site for promiscuous eating: "on the run," Americans eat food items that are easy to transport and consume and which are marketed to please the taste for fats and sugar.[63] An increasingly sedentary life-style and the alteration of dietary habits from ritualized family meals to an informal pattern of snacking, grazing, and constant oral

---

[61] Peter N. Stearns, *Fat History: Bodies and Beauty in the Modern West* (New York and London: New York UP, 1997).

[62] W. Wayt Gibbs, "Gaining on Fat," *Scientific American* August 1996, 4 November 2002 <http://www.sciam.com.html>.

consumption have all contributed to the fattening of America.[64] Moreover, the food industry contributes to increasing rates of obesity. Whereas 3,800 calories of processed food are produced per individual per day, the average adult should only eat between 2,200 and 2,500 calories. Investing enormous budgets in the marketing of fast foods even to children in schools, the food industry has contributed to the normalization of oversize portions. And with 12% of children and 14 % of adolescents now ranking as obese, the next generation of Americans threatens to be even fatter than the last.[65]

Hence there is very powerful economic incentive exists for keeping people obsessively worried about losing weight. In 1990 Americans spent $33 billion on weight-loss aids,[66] making the weight-loss industry a powerful economic engine. Since there is no cure for obesity and 95% of dieters gain back what they have lost and more, the amount of diet products and programs that may be developed is limitless. One obesity specialist estimates that for every dollar spent on preventing obesity in America, a hundred more dollars are spent by the food industry on creating and marketing new fast foods.[67] Advertising encourages Americans to snack on highly processed foods and to drink carbonated sodas rather than water. Simultaneously, new "lite" diet foods and sodas are marketed under the premise that they will undo the harm caused by snacking on unhealthy foods. Many of the conglomerates that produce so-called diet products also market cookies, sugar-laden breakfast cereals, candy bars, and other snack foods. This fact leads the sociologist Sharlene Hesse-

---

[63] Eric Schlosser makes a powerful case for how Americans are taught at an early age by the fast-food industry to crave saturated animal fats. *Fast Food Nation* 120, 241.
[64] Pasi Falk, *The Consuming Body* (London: Sage Publications, 1994) 29-35.
[65] Duenwald, Mary, "A Conversation with Marion Nestle: An 'Eat More' Message for a Fattened America," *New York Times* 19 February 2002: F6. On the connection between the growth of the American fast food industry and the fattening of America and those countries affected by American globalization. See also Schlosser.
[66] Gibbs.
[67] Sharlene Hesse-Biber, *Am I Thin Enough Yet?* 35.

Biber to describe the marketing strategy of American food and diet product producers as "fatten them up" to "slim them down."[68]

While Americans have grown steadily heavier, the standard of feminine beauty has grown steadily thinner. Numerous studies document that the weights of fashion models, *Playboy* centerfolds, and beauty pageant winners have all decreased in the post-war era, while their heights have increased.[69] On an anecdotal level, that formal icon of female desirability, Marilyn Monroe, is referred to by a current woman student as "a cow."[70]

In her history of American girlhood Brumberg comes to the depressing conclusion that the importance of girls' bodies has steadily increased during the last century.[71] Despite Victorian images of frail, gentile ladies, in 1880 or 1890 collegiate women might write home to proudly report that they had gained weight. By the 1920s "slimming" to achieve the flat-chested, long legged flapper silhouette had become common. By the end of the 1990s dieting and insecurities about one's body were ubiquitous elements in American girls' lives. High school yearbooks now feature photos of senior girls in fashion model postures. These girls chose images of their bodies to represent themselves, not of their faces as in yearbooks of the 1950s. One seventeen-year old based her decision on where to go to college on the basis of bad food; she went to the school with the poorest food in order not to gain weight.[72]

One reason for the century-long intensification of focus on women's bodies has been a change from the localization of feminine beauty and

---

[68] Hesse-Biber 34-38.

[69] Roberta P. Seid, *Never Too Thin: Why Women Are at War with Their Bodies* (New York: Prentice –Hall Press, 1989) Chapter 10; and Roberta P. Seid, "Too 'Close to the Bone': The Historical Context for Women's Obsession with Slenderness," *Feminist Perspectives on Eating Disorders* (New York: The Guilford Press, 1994) 3-16.

[70] Susan Bordo, "Anorexia Nervosa: Psychopathology as the Crystallization of Culture," *Feminism and Foucault: Reflections of Resistance,* ed. Irene Diamond and Lee Quinby (Boston: Northeastern UP, 1988) 89; and Susan Bardo, *Unbearable Weight* 141.

[71] Joan Jacob Brumberg, *Body Project.*

[72] Brumberg, *Body Project* 120.

desirability from the face to the body. Brumberg cites the importance of the swimmer and silent-movie star Annette Kellerman. Kellerman's frequent appearance in various states of undress in films led to the development of a new icon—the beauty queen in a bathing suit. From the 1920s onwards beauty pageants made the bathing-suit competition the highlight of their programs.[73]

The preference for slim female bodies has grown during the twentieth century, despite a respite during which time hour-glass shaped women were favored. The popularity of voluptuous vamps like Mae West in the 1930s and 1940s and "full-figured" Hollywood goddesses such as Marilyn Monroe, Jayne Mansfield,[74] and Jane Russell in the 1950s attests to mid-century's breast fetishism. During this era having full uplifted breasts seems to have been a prerequisite to happiness and success. Breast obsession became institutionalized in Sweater Girl contests and with the introduction of "training bras" for pubescent girls in the fifties.[75] The name of these undergarments implies that breasts need training presumably in order to reach their "full" potential.

However, in the post-war years readers were informed by magazines like *Seventeen* that "Nobody loves a Fat Girl," and advertisers promised girls and their parents smooth sailing through troubled adolescent waters if only this or that product were bought.[76] As advertising made the connection between female desirability and slenderness, the diet industry grew and directed its efforts towards women. Most commercials for weight loss products address women.

---

[73] Brumberg, *Fasting Girls* 245-248.
[74] *Playboy* centerfold model from 1955 and actress.
[75] Sweater Girl contests featured young women in tight sweaters versus bathing suits. These contests, in which the focus was clearly on the contestants' large breasts, find their contemporary equivalent in wet tee-shirt contests. In these contests, which are often held in bars, beer is poured over t0he contestants' tee shirt-clad breasts or contestants' breasts are sprayed wet with a hose. Generally, the woman with the largest breasts wins.
[76] Brumberg, *Fasting Girls* 252.

They feature thin conventionally "gorgeous" models, whose images associate their overt happiness and success with, for instance, Diet Coke.[77]

The increased valuation of thin or emaciated female bodies coupled with ever-greater rates of obesity have created a fertile ground for the growth of problems with food and weight. The development of dieting culture has gone hand in hand with the rise of anorexia.[78] Rates of anorexia grew in frequency until 1970, when the standard of thinness was set. Current supermodels like Kate Moss are reported to weigh about ten pounds more than Twiggy did in the 1970s and to be at least two inches taller. The more voluptuous model Claudia Schiffer was forced to lose 15 pounds when she began modeling in the States to achieve the look necessary for American sales.[79] Authorities agree that the association of female thinness with sexual desirability and success in the media has caused the explosion of eating-disordered behavior among young women. For instance, a Los Angeles psychologist who treats eating-disordered teenagers comments on the impact of images of very thin women on television. His clients enjoy watching *Ally McBeal*, a popular television show about a single woman lawyer, who is portrayed by an emaciated-looking actress named Calista Flockhart. After viewing an episode clients are more resistant to therapy. The psychologist reports, "I have a number of kids in my practice who say, 'Why should I have to gain weight. [Flockhart] looks this way and she's successful?'"[80]

The popular singer Karen Carpenter's death in February 1983 due to complications from anorexia marked a highpoint of interest in the new disease. The combination of Carpenter's extremely clean-cut image—she sang songs

[77] Jean Kilbourne, "Still Killing us Softly: Advertising and the Obsession with Thinness," *Feminist Perspectives on Eating Disorders*, ed. Patricia Fallon, Melanie A. Katzman, Susan C. Wooley (New York and London: The Guilford Press, 1994): 395-418.
[78] "*Historisch ging die Verbreitung der Magersucht Hand in Hand mit der Durchsetzung der Selbstkontrolltechniken der Gewichtskontrolle, jedenfalls bis zu den siebziger Jahren des 20. Jahrhunderts.*" Habermas 153.
[79] Amy O'Connor, "Educating Claudia," *Self*, February 1999: 29.

that featured "moon dust" being "sprinkled in" her beloved's hair—and the reality of her decade-long battle with an eating disorder stirred the public imagination powerfully. A purging anorectic or "bulimarexic"—that is an extremely emaciated woman who doesn't just restrict her food intake but purges what little she eats—Carpenter regularly abused syrup of ipecac[81] to make herself vomit. This practice eventually proved fatal.

The meaning of anorexia has changed. Media attention to anorexia since the 1960s has led to the growth of group of "me-too anorectics," those for whom anorexia has become a model of deviant behavior.[82] Less psychologically disturbed than their forerunners, "me-too-anorectics" adopt the eating disorder as a much publicized—and hence glamorized—method of reacting to tensions implicit in modern constructions of feminine identity. However, only a small group of extraordinarily strong-willed individuals succeed at starving themselves. Because most people cannot bear fasting for long—a normal physiological reaction—they break their fasts, binge, and some become bulimic. For this reason many anorectics become bulimic, yet few bulimics develop anorexia.

Hence the popularity of anorexia has actually led to the increasing incidence of bulimia (and the binge-eating disorder). The real incidence of anorexia in Western countries has not risen since the 1970s, although the incidence of other eating disorders is on the rise.[83] As Americans have grown more accustomed to seeing images of extremely thin women in the media, anorexia may be becoming more lethal. The tolerance for emaciation leads to

---

[80] Karen S. Schneider, "Arguing her Case," *People Magazine*, 9 November 1998: 95.
[81] Ipecac is a purgative, commonly kept in American homes. As an antidote against poison, it works by making the user vomit profusely.
[82] Gordon 102-106; Habermas 155.
[83] Habermas 153-154.

anorexic patients' being diagnosed, treated, and hospitalized at ever decreasing weights.[84]

The propagation of slender female bodies remains the key factor in why women develop eating disorders. Yet it is important to note that the body ideal has not gone unaltered since Twiggy's time. Since the 1980s having a "toned" or "defined" looking body has become increasingly desirable. The popularity of fitness videos, exercise programs, and the introduction of a number of women's magazines with names like *Women's Fitness International, Health, Women's Sports Fitness,* and *Shape* document this trend. Rather than featuring recipes for chocolate cake and weight-loss diets in the same issue, as is still the preserve of more traditional women's magazines, these periodicals have articles on "getting tight" rather than getting skinny. Exercises are offered for working on specific muscle groups such as "abs" and "glutes." That the reader is expected to know what these muscle groups are marks an alteration in language usage that, perhaps, mirrors the change in body ideal. The new ideal is to emulate "lithe and luscious" Cindy Crawford rather than to resemble "anorectic runway ghosts."[85] This last comment highlights a new suspiciousness towards those who are perceived to be too skinny, and perhaps eating disordered. Significantly, Calista Flockhart, the actress mentioned above, has been accused of being anorexic.[86]

Conflicting body ideals for women exist in America today. The continued popularity of wet tee-shirt contests and the former *Baywatch* star Pamela Anderson suggest that the taste for full-figured women has never gone completely out of style. That Flockhart alternately represents an ideal to some and is accused of being too thin by others highlights anxiety about how slender

---

[84] Brumberg, *Fasting Girls* 256.
[85] Anne Taylor Flemming, "the new ideal: What makes a body beautiful?" *Women's Sports Fitness*, January/February 1999: 75.
[86] Flockhart insists in an interview: "'But I eat. I eat normally. I eat whatever I want, whenever I want. I *don't* have a messed-up relationship with food'" (Schneider 95).

women should be. Ideally this surplus of feminine ideals would lead to a greater sense of leniency about what makes women attractive. However, evidence suggests just the opposite: A recent *Psychology Today* survey suggests that body dissatisfaction is growing: 62% of women aged 13 to 19 report dissatisfaction with their weight; 67% of women over age 30 also dislike how much they weigh. More alarming still is the fact that 39% of women questioned in the study said that they would give up three years of their lives or more to be at their desired weight.[87]

Brumberg points out that the new fashion for muscle tone has not necessarily led to women feeling more physically empowered. Instead, the ideal of slender athleticism requires an even greater effort to fulfill:

> Instead of relaxing the imperative to lose weight and be thin, the pressure to control the body has been ratcheted upward by an even more demanding cultural ideal: a lean, taut, female body with visible musculature. This particular feminine icon—epitomized by Jane Fonda, Madonna, and the new Oprah—requires even more attention, work and control than the thin body desired by Carol Merano [a weight-obsessed girl from the 1960s].[88]

Common to Cindy Crawford, Pamela Anderson, and Calista Flockhart is that all three media icons are lean to thin. One assumes that they all work out and monitor their diets and their weight with care. Anderson, in fact, differs significantly from her ample-breasted counterparts in the fifties in that her figure is not nearly so hour-glass shaped as theirs were; it is more top heavy. Her large, surgically-enhanced breasts stand in improbable contrast to her small waist, thin hips, and long legs. Whatever body ideal a woman may now strive for, she will aim to be slender or thin—with or without visible muscles or breasts.

---

87 "A Very Revealing Picture: Psychology Today's 1997 Body Image Survey Findings," *Psychology Today*, January/February 1997: 34.

88 Brumberg, *Body Project* 123. Any person who enjoys exercising, including the author of this study, would argue that Brumberg's argument is one-sided here.

Since the beginning of the 1990s an anti-diet movement has grown up in America. This movement relies on research that suggests that the food deprivation involved in dieting actually leads dieters to gain weight over the course of time rather than to lose it, the so-called yo-yo effect. Some researchers suggest that the health risks of being overweight have been vastly exaggerated: relative physical fitness, and not weight alone, determines a person's overall health and longevity.[89] In turn, these theses have lead to a backlash in the medical community and dieting industry. Many argue that any justification of overweight is an invitation for individuals to kill themselves with overeating.[90]

The anti-dieting movement, the existence of advocacy groups such as NAAFA (the National Association to Advance Fat Acceptance), and new mainstream publications such as *Mode Style Beyond Size*, which fulfills all the functions of traditional women's fashion magazines while explicitly catering to readers sized 12 and up—all point towards a trend towards greater size acceptance in the States. However, the counter-evidence for the continued predominance of the valuation of thin bodies is overwhelming. One need only look at a conventional fashion magazine or watch a mainstream television show or movie to see that very thin, generally very young, models and actresses remain the ideal. The media makes it clear that being thin is of paramount importance to a woman's success, and being fat is sub-standard.[91]

---

89 Documenting the anti-dieting trend and the backlash that has followed it are the final chapters of Laura Fraser's *Losing IT: America's Obsession with Weight and the Industry That Feeds on It* (New York: Dutton, 1997). However, the author has a very strong anti-dieting basis based on her own experiences with dieting and bulimia.

90 In his article on obesity among America's poor populations Greg Critser quotes a physician from Los Angeles: "No one wants to overemphasize the problems of being fat to these girls, for fear of creating body-image problems that might lead to anorexia and bulimia. [...] the problem is that for every one affluent white anorexic you create by 'overemphasizing' obesity, you foster ten obese poor girls by downplaying the severity of the issue." "Let Them Eat Fat: The Heavy Truths about American 'Obesity'," *Harper's Magazine*, March 2000: 45; Stearns even goes so far as to suggest that a relaxation of standards of thinness since the mid 1980s has lead to a new weight explosion since then (134).

91 A recent study documents how much media images affected the likelihood of whether to American girls, aged 9-14, began to purge to control their weight: "Growing Up Today"

The ideal of slenderness and the attendant demonization of fat in American culture lead many women to restrict their diets rigidly. In turn, periods of self-starvation or extreme food restriction precede bingeing behavior, one aspect of bulimia nervosa.

1.2) Bulimia Nervosa and its History as Illustrated in Literature

According to DSM-IV the diagnostic criteria for bulimia nervosa are that bulimics repeatedly binge, which means that they eat far more than most people would or could in a short period of time (for instance, within two hours).[92] While bingeing they feel powerless to limit their consumption. In order not to gain weight they induce vomiting, abuse laxatives, enemas, diuretics, or ipecac. Some bulimics regurgitate the food they put in their mouths, that is, they chew it up and spit it out.[93] Alternately, they fast or exercise excessively to deter weight gain.[94] Binges and purges occur at least two times a week during a three-month duration. Like anorectics, bulimics are unduly concerned with their weight and body shape.

However, bulimics tend to be of normal or above average weight.[95] In contrast with anorectics, they maintain regular menstrual cycles. Conservative estimates suggest that bulimia occurs in 1% to 3% of adolescents and young adult women.[96] Yet occasional bulimic behavior has been reported in 40% of

---

(*Archives Pediatric Adolescent Medicine* 1999; 153:1184), as reviewed in "Purging: Peers and Media Influences," *Eating Disorders Review* (May/June 2000): 5.

[92] What is a "normal" amount is a matter of debate. A woman who chronically restricts her food intake may consider eating one Snickers bar a binge, whereas some bulimics consume 15,000 calories in one episode. Pierre J. V. Beumont, "The Clinical Presentation of Anorexia and Bulimia Nervosa," *Eating Disorders and Obesity: A Comprehensive Handbook* 156.

[93] Beumont 156.

[94] DSM-IV 549-550.

[95] Again the definition of "normal" weight is an imperfect one. While the bulimic may conform to the normal weight range for her height, her weight may be lower than what it would be if she did not use bulimic behaviors to control it. Beumont 155.

[96] DSM-IV 548.

college women.[97] Like anorexia, bulimia affects women ten times more commonly than men. Typically, bulimia begins later in life than anorexia, the usual onset being between 16 and 25 years of age. It is thought to be triggered by a young woman's first separation from home—for instance her going away to college—rather than puberty.[98] Dieting precedes bulimia just as it does anorexia. During a period of food restriction, the desire for food becomes overpowering. A binge follows, and the neophyte bulimic attempts to erase the effects of her "breaking" her diet by purging.

Bulimics frequently binge on sweet, high-calorie "junk food" in secret. They develop bizarre life-styles to accommodate their disorder.[99] Often without chewing, they consume over 10,000 calories during a binge—roughly five times what a person needs to eat during a day. Large quantities of fluid are consumed simultaneously in order to ease vomiting. And bulimics describe how they examine their vomit to check for the appearance of all the foods they have eaten.[100]

Considered easier to treat than anorexia, bulimia has been only too recently documented to know what its long-term effects are or how many women die from it. In the short run, bulimia causes ruptures in the stomach and esophagus and electrolyte imbalances. The abuse of ipecac may lead to heart failure and irregular heart rhythm. Recurrent vomiting destroys throat tissues and dental enamel, creates cavities, and makes the salivary glands swell, giving bulimics "chipmunk faces." Bulimics frequently develop what is called "Russell's sign," an abrasion on the back of the hand, caused by the teeth's damaging the skin when fingers are used to induce vomiting. Bulimia can go

---

[97] "Bulimia Nervosa," Explorations: Treating Eating Disorders: March 2, 1998 *Scientific American*, March 1998, 2 November 2002 <http://www.sciam.com/explorations/1998/030298/ eating/bulimia.html>.
[98] Gordon 26.
[99] Bruch, *Golden Cage* 89.
[100] Beumont 156. See also Hornbacher's description of using markers during a binge (*W* 61).

undetected for years, and bulimics suffer from relapses even after successful treatment and remain intensely concerned with their weight.

No classic description of the bulimic personality exists that compares with that of anorectics in *The Golden Cage.* This may be because bulimics comprise a heterogeneous group. Part of this heterogeneity rests on the fact that bulimia, more than anorexia, is a learnt behavior. Disturbingly, bulimics report that they learnt how to make themselves throw up from friends, sorority sisters, their mothers, or from movies, talk shows, Internet chat rooms and web sites as well as books about bulimia, which were intended to educate the public about the problem. Increasingly, women who have no severe psychological problems other than an extreme desire to lose or maintain their weights appear to develop bulimia.[101] They differ from the majority of American women only in the methods and degree of their weight-control concerns.

More often than anorectics, bulimics are characterized as having borderline personalities, meaning that their successful outer self masks an ugly, demonic interior. Bulimics tend to be sexually active, more socially outgoing, and impulsive than anorectics. Sexual relationships may be destructive.[102]

Frequently, bulimics describe their parents as neglectful. Whereas the anorectic perhaps reacts to too much parental involvement by refusing to eat, the bulimic acts on feelings that she was not loved enough by consuming vast quantities of food as a way of mothering herself.[103]

---

[101] Habermas 189-190.
[102] One study suggests that bulimics were three times more likely to have been sexually abused than other female members of the population. However, generally women with psychological problems appear to have been the victims of abuse: Robert L. Palmer, "Sexual Abuse and Eating Disorders," *Eating Disorders and Obesity*, ed. Kelly D. Brownell and Christopher G. Fairburn (New York and London: The Guilford Press, 1995) 231. Furthermore, sexual violence during dating has been demonstrated to increase the likelihood of bulimic behaviors, "Dating Violence Raises Risk of Abnormal Dieting," *Eating Disorders Review* 12 n 4 (July/August 2001): 8.
[103] Zerbe, *The Body Betrayed* 65.

Habermas goes farthest in interpreting bulimia as a societal malaise. According to him bulimics express problems inherent to being a woman now. Appearing to function superbly, the bulimic looks good, does well at work or school, and is well-liked. Yet she feels powerless to express negative emotions, particularly anger, and eagerly avoids conflicts. She would much rather take a pound of her own flesh than bite into others. In gorging she may indulge herself and indulge feelings of weakness; in ritualized catharsis she punishes herself for being weak and maintains her required ascetic appearance.[104]

To understand the pain of bulimia, I turn to poetry about this experience. An anonymous poem bears the title:

eating disorder

(for Aydin Aksoy)

measured spoonfuls
of melted ice cream
heaped carefully
methodically chewed
not like
handfuls of
"bulimic" and
"eating disorder"
stuffed in your mouth
hurling around your ears
borne by
graded glances suspect stares
to pull the puke out
or see right through you
just forget it
leave me alone
forget I have this physical [f]ailing
or hole hiding hygienic habit
that's nothing about
your thoughtless
ultimately uncaring unsubtle

[104] Habermas 182-184

and painful-to-even-look-at-or-acknowledge
"knowing" stare[105]

L. Schwartz writes in an untitled poem:

Dainty bites and delicate nibbles
promoting the face whose inside is crippled
by illicit feedings and well-hid self beatings
Each time that her hunger roars.

Mirrors will lie and people will too,
twisting reality and distorting truth
It's emaciation that causes elation
Each time her hunger roars.[106]

These poems illustrate the theme of deception central to bulimic existence. In "eating disorder" the "measured," "heaped, and "methodically chewed" public ice cream is contrasted with the unmeasured "handfuls of / 'bulimic'" food which is privately "stuffed in your mouth / hurling around your ears."[107] The "Dainty bites and delicate nibbles" of the second poem conceal "illicit feedings and well-hid self beatings."

Bulimic practices become synonymous with the narrators' dark interior lives; the speaker of L. Schwartz's untitled poem tells of "the face whose inside is crippled." In both poems the speakers express hostility towards those around them. Those who give the "'knowing' stares" referred to in the first poem are blind to what the speaker's bulimia is really about; their curiosity is experienced as "thoughtless / ultimately uncaring unsubtle." "[P]eople" in the second poem

[105] "eating disorder," *Eating Disorder Poetry Collection* 4 November 2002 <http://www.geocities.com/Wellesley/4220/edpoetry.html>.

[106] L. Schwarz, "Untitled," *Eating Disorder Poetry Collection* 4 November 2002 <http://www.geocities.com/Wellesley/4220/edpoetry.html>.

[107] The "measured spoonfuls / of melted ice cream / heaped carefully / methodically chewed" may be an allusion to T.S. Eliot's poetic description of the repetitive and monotonous quality of J. Alfred Prufrock's existence: "For I have known them all already, known them all— / Have known the evenings, mornings, afternoons, / I have measured out my life with coffee spoons; / I know the voices dying with a dying fall [...]." From "The Love Song of J. Alfred Prufrock" (1917) *T.S. Eliot: Selected Poems* (New York: Harcourt, Brace & World, 1934) 13.

"lie [. . .] twisting reality and distorting truth." The only truth is the inner one—the speaker's roaring "hunger" and the bliss that emaciation will bring her. Both texts emphasize the enormous gap between the bulimic's sense of reality and that of the individuals around her. The dichotomy between self-perception and the perception of others is symbolically played out in the bulimic's eating behavior. In public, she takes only "measured spoonfuls" or "delicate nibbles" of food. Privately, she gorges and purges and "beats" herself. A more explicit depiction of this process can be found in the following three-part poem by a writer who identifies herself as Sarah:

The Bulimic Experience; Today Will Be The Last

Sit and wallow.
Now get up to walk to the mirror and
force my eyes upon the raging beast
who has crawled into my soul.
Try hard to ignore her taunts.
Take a trip downstairs and
hope than no one will see the
fragile little girl
scratching away at my heart;
trying her hardest to get out.
It's clear; no one[']s looking.
Find more food.
More solace.
Now, carry myself to the chamber of torture…
~the bathroom~
Oh, no, someone might hear.
Try the bedroom.
Turn on the music so
i don't have to listen to myself
breaking into pieces.
Not too loud, though.
Must be alert to intruders.
All by myself now.
Now listen to and observe
the motives
Stuck with myself.

Kneel down to the alt[a]r I have built.
The alt[a]r of anguish.
~the garbage can~
—to release all that pain I just swallowed.
Bite after bite
of yummie pain,
tasty emptiness,
tantalizing loneliness.
Relief: its all gone now
So, now what?
I'll tell you.
Now you have to sit with yourself on the floor
with pieces of your soul, your heart,
your love scattered about.
Depleted.
Depleted, but so relieved.
Uh, oh!
I feel a tear cre[e]ping up.
Now another.
Damn! Here we go.
Why me, why this?
Cry, and cry, and cry.
No more. I will not do this anymore.
But, just in case I did not
get all that pain out,
better in[g]est 30 shame purging miracle workers.
~laxatives~
But, this is it.
I swear no more.

Next Day

Oh God, this agony.
Make this wretched pain go away.
I promise i will not take these again.
Just make this hurt go away

Later

Well, now it's all gone. Yesterday[']s pain is purged.
But, uh oh, I've just passed out.

~low electrolytes~
Better eat something small.
Don't want to have too much.
'Cause yesterday was the last.
Oh, no, I've eaten 50 calories!
May as well make it 100.
200,
300,
400,
500,
Damn! Too much!
What a pig!
No self control[]!
What a disgrace!
Oh, Man.
Stress.
Where's the food?
Just for today.
Let me eat.
Eat my way out of heartache.
And just one more time release.
But, I swear today will be the last...
~of Sarah.[108]

Though unpolished, this poem depicts how bulimia is experienced as an addiction. In each section, the speaker promises never again to binge. The first section closes with the words "But this is it. / I swear no more." The second section conveys a sense of what laxative induced pain can be and contains the oath "I promise I will not take these again." The third and final section concludes with a last ironic promise "And just one more time release. / But, I swear today will be the last... / ~of Sarah." Only with the annihilation of the poem's speaker can the cycle of filling and emptying the body be concluded.

Virtually every poem I have found on bulimia expresses the sentiment that the current binge will be the last one and the following purge will be the

[108] Sarah, "The Bulimic Experience; Today Will Be The Last," 6 February 1998 <http://users.neca.com/ cwildes/sarah.html>.

final cathartic release.[109] This all-or-nothing mentality, of course, encourages bulimia. To eat anything at all is to invite a binge as is illustrated in the "Later" section of the poem. Yet one must eat to survive. Hence food takes on a threatening quality.

The poem makes the importance of mirrors to eating-disordered individuals explicit. In the untitled poem above mirrors were depicted as being potentially duplicitous: "Mirrors will lie and people will too, / twisting reality and distorting truth." In "The Bulimic Experience" the speaker's vision of herself in the mirror works as the catalyst for her binge. Like the portrait of Dorian in *Dorian Gray,* the mirror described in this poem reflects a self too horrid to be contemplated for long. The image seen there embodies everything the bulimic hates. This includes the fat pig-like quality she describes herself as having with the words "Sit and wallow" and "the raging beast" in her soul that she sees in the mirror.

The manner in which the beastly eating disorder gains entry into the speaker's person—by "crawling" into her soul—emphasizes the animal's lowliness. This beast coexists in the speaker with "the fragile little girl" who "scratches away" at her heart. By taunting her, the beast appears to force the speaker to eat, while the presumably victimized girl tries "her hardest to get out." Yet it remains unclear who actually does the eating. Does the entrapped girl find "solace" in the food, or does the beast feed itself. At any rate, vomiting and defecating—with the help of laxatives—bring "tasty emptiness, / tantalizing loneliness. / Relief." Perhaps the conflict between the speaker's dichotomous

---

[109] To provide some point of comparison, I quote from two other poems about bulimia posted on a web site for eating disorder poetry: "How many times have you promised yourself / that it was the last time? / There does not exist[] a number high enough. / But the moment at hand is symbolic [. . .] the forthcoming orgy will be the last." Debbie Rose, "Thief in the Night," *Eating Disorder Poetry Collection* 4 November 2002 <http://www.geocities.com /Wellesley/ 4220/edpoetry.html>; "I gave myself one more day, / One more time, / Because I know I'll start tomorrow. / I ate everything I wanted with not restrictions, / Because I knew this was the last binge." Anonymous, "ONE MORE LAST TIME," *Eating Disorder Poetry Collection* 4 November 2002 <http://www.geocities.com/ Wellesley/4220/edpoetry.html>.

selves, the invasive demon and the helpless girl, has grown too large to remain confined within her body. Bingeing and purging has exorcised the conflict and left the speaker "Depleted, but so relieved."

Comparable to the speaker's divided vision of herself, is her ambivalent view of food. It is described both as "solace" and as swallowed "pain." Consuming food inevitably leads the speaker to the "chamber of torture" and "the altar of anguish." Imagery is Gothic. A petite, presumably innocent girl is compelled by a demonic beast to enter a torture chamber and worship at a Satanist altar. Localizing the urge to binge in an externalized demon, which has managed to penetrate the body, rids the speaker of responsibility. She is without volition, without the power to stop gorging, vomiting, and having diarrhea. The oaths the speaker takes in each part of the poem never to binge and purge again are empty.

The disturbing impression created by these poems is that the bulimic feels victimized by her eating disorder and food. She is unable to help herself or to be aided by others. In these poems existence is reduced to an interior dialogue between the overwhelmingly strong desire to eat and the weak and brutalized self. The volume of this dialogue is such that noise from the outside world becomes inaudible. Interests other than food, eating, and purgative techniques are rendered meaningless. They cannot compete with the internal drama.

The English psychiatrist Gerald Russell was the first to use the term "bulimia nervosa" in 1979, as an analogue to anorexia nervosa. Derived from the Greek words *bous* (ox) and *limos* (hunger), "bulimia nervosa" literally means a nervous ox-like hunger. Traditionally, "bulimia" was used to describe the condition of having an appetite as large as that of an ox.[110] Gorging and

[110] Brenda and William Parry-Jones, "History of Bulimia and Bulimia Nervosa," *Eating Disorders and Obesity: A Comprehensive Handbook* 145.

purging between courses was a pattern of behavior practiced by patricians in Rome. Seneca wrote: "They vomit to eat, and eat to vomit."[111]

In the twentieth century bulimia was initially thought to be an advanced phase of anorexia. For instance, Bruch speaks of "[a]norexic patients who indulge in binge eating."[112] Russell identified bulimia as a separate eating disorder during the 1970s. Anecdotal evidence suggests that purging techniques were used in the pre-Twiggy era as a method of weight control. In my own family Great Aunt May is reported to have regularly vomited after company dinners as early as 1910 as a method of weight control.

Two autobiographical poems by Denise Duhamel also testify to bulimia's existence before the seventies.[113] This set of poems challenges two misconceptions. Bulimics are not just young women—the speaker of these poems could be a grandmother. Bulimia was not invented after Twiggy. That the pampered and much-loved daughter of the first poem—with her "Three powders, each of a different fragrance, / on my vanity"—was initiated into bulimia by her mother is highly disconcerting. Even more alarming is the implication that the girl's mother was probably also bulimic. Who taught the debutante's mother about using purple feathers in the middle of the evening—her mother?

[111] Seneca, quoted in Gordon 12.
[112] Bruch, *The Golden Cage* 88.
[113] Denise Duhamel, "Feather, 1948"/"Finger, 1988." *Eating Our Hearts Out* 118-119.

Feather, 1948

My mother prepared me
for the party. I was coming out
in a long-waisted silk dress,
real pearls. Real flowers in my room.
Three powders, each of a different
fragrance,
on my vanity. I had everything –
although my mother did not make me
feel guilty or remind me of this.
Instead, she told me, her favorite
daughter,
"Here darling, put this feather
in your purse." The plume was a
purple
of royalty and courage. I stroked it
trying to imagine the bird
from which it was plucked.
"Dance and flirt. Drink
and eat as much as you want," my
mother said, her gaiety strained.
"But remember, we don't want you
getting fat.
Remember that you have your feather,
mid-evening, go to the bathroom,
and use it."

Finger, 1988

This morning the talk show host
said people like me
don't usually live this long.
Heart attacks over the toilet bowl.
Heart attacks right in the streets.
Finally in 1979, there became a name
for me, for what I do. Bulimic,
bulimia,
like Adam and Eve uttering tree,
sky, bird, flower. Like Adam
and Eve using verbs: uproot, bang
your head against a wall. My teeth
have been capped three times –
my dentist's confrontations
as tentative as a small child's tap
on his busy mother's shoulder
when he's afraid of her wrath.
The glands in my throat bulge
like beads on a necklace,
like two extra breaths, two extra
breasts, like elbows pushing to the
front
of a crowd. For forty years now,
everything has come to me
in groups: a cookie means bags
of cookies, ice cream, potato chips,
jars of mayonnaise. "No thanks" means
you hate me, I did something wrong,
I'm a terrible person,I hate myself,
I hate you.

The second poem "Finger, 1988" bears witness to the fact that one can live with bulimia for a long time without dying, even if talk-show hosts say otherwise. The poem also attests to the reluctance to confront bulimic women with their behaviors many individuals have. One wonders if the ineffectual dentist also heard the talk show on the day he recapped the bulimic's rotting teeth. One wonders if he does not have a wife or sister or daughter who battles with food herself.

The end of "Finger, 1988" concerns the bulimic speaker's shame at her uncontrolled eating. Other people's "No thanks" to offers of food are interpreted as verdicts on her eating excesses. These refusals lead the speaker to think "I did something wrong. / I'm a terrible person. I hate myself, I hate you." A similar sense of self-hatred is expressed in the poem "The Bulimic Experience," in which the speaker refers to herself as "wallow[ing]" like a pig and mentions the "disgrace" of her lack of self-control. The bulimic speakers of these poems associate their inability to limit their food intake with their unworthiness. Implicitly, they compare themselves unfavorably to those perfect women who never binge or break their diets. Their bulimia appears dirty, repellent, and vile to them and tends to be associated in their minds with their perceived overweight: "What a pig" comments "Sarah," the speaker of "The Bulimic Experience" after she has eaten just 500 calories, implying that her appetite matches her appearance in its porcine quality. An essay by Molly Jong-Fast comments on the bulimic's typical association of her eating disorder with overweight. Even for this daughter of the feminist writer Erika Jong, no amount of privilege or education could diminish her sense of being fundamentally damaged because she was "fat" and bulimic:

> During my illness, I'd walk down the street and in my mind believe that everyone who looked like me was confined to her own private prison—her body. Obsessive thinking was easy: Thin equaled happiness; fat

> equaled misery. The main flaw was not my polarized thinking, but my belief that my troubles stemmed from the fact that I was fat.[114]

This conflation of fat with the urge to eat and bulimia will be explored at length in *Wasted.*

Some of the buzz about bulimia began when Jane Fonda disclosed in a 1983 television interview that she had been a bulimic at Vassar College.[115] However, the late Lady Diana Spencer may have made bulimia famous. She was the leading proponent of awareness about the disorder. In her pre-divorce television interview with the BBC and in her published conversations with Andrew Morton, bulimia became synonymous with Diana's suffering within her marriage and the unfeeling Windsor family.[116]

The danger involved in celebrities promoting the pain of a condition they have suffered from is that the condition itself becomes identified with the famous person's glamour. Lady Diana and Jane Fonda embody ideals of feminine beauty. Their coming-out as former bulimics may well invite their admirers to copy their behavior.[117]

1.3) The Binge-Eating Disorder

Binge eating is listed within the EDNOS (Eating Disorder not Otherwise Classified) category of DSM-IV. Criteria for the Binge-Eating Disorder include binge eaters' consuming huge amounts of food within brief periods and feeling powerless over their binges. Binge eaters eat "much more rapidly than normal," although they are not physically hungry, and in private, because their consumption embarrasses them. Bingeing elicits feelings of

---

[114] Molly Jong-Fast, "A World Apart," *MODE Style Beyond Size,* May 1998: 70.

[115] Brumberg, *Fasting Girls* 18, 286.

[116] Andrew Morton, *Diana: Her True Story* (London: Pocket Books, 1992).

[117] Indeed the author of a book called *Responsible Bulimia* went so far as to say: "If such a health conscious female like Jane Fonda can use bulimia for several years, then perhaps it is just further evidence that bulimia is not necessarily the degrading, irresponsible practice which the eating disorder people would have us believe." As quoted in Gordon 114.

self-disgust and guilt.[118] The binge eater does not compensate for overeating by purging.

Whereas 90% to 95% of those who suffer from anorexia and bulimia are women, roughly a third of binge eaters are men. Binge eating occurs within 20% to 30% of patients who seek treatment for obesity, and is most common among the severely obese population. Binge eaters share still many similarities with bulimics: They are commonly co-diagnosed with depression; body shape and weight preoccupy them; they diet to try to control their weight, and periods of food restriction typically precede binges. They report feeling soothed by their compulsive eating. Sufferers have a history of extreme weight fluctuations and tend to have more difficulty losing weight and maintaining their weight loss than other dieters do. Binge eating contributes to obesity and its attendant health problems, including diabetes, high blood pressure and cholesterol levels, gallbladder and heart disease and some cancer types.[119] Also called compulsive overeating, the binge-eating disorder is not as well known as bulimia and anorexia. How much previously published research on obesity, which has been historically treated as a medical problem, may be applied to this psychological disorder remains unclear.

Since being obese and wanting to lose weight predispose women (and men) to the binge-eating disorder, it is vital to understand the problems obese individuals have in American society. It is a truism that fat is associated with lack of moral fiber and laziness. Even small children react to silhouettes of obese children by labeling them "lazy, dirty, stupid, ugly, cheats, and lies."[120]

Obesity is a class issue. Whether they be low-income rural whites from Kentucky or inner-city Latinos, poor Americans are far more likely to suffer

---

[118] DSM-IV 731.

[119] Marsha D. Markus, "Binge Eating and Obesity," *Eating Disorders and Obesity: A Comprehensive Handbook* 441-444.

[120] Albert J. Stunkard and Jeffery Sobal, "Psychosocial Consequences of Obesity," *Eating Disorders and Obesity: A Comprehensive Handbook* 417.

from obesity and its attendant ills such as diabetes. Obesity marks downward social mobility. By contrast a prerequisite of social and economic success in America is weight control: "In upscale corporate America, meanwhile, being fat is taboo, a sure-fire career-killer. If you can't control your own contours, goes the logic, how can you control a budget or a staff?"[121] Fatness becomes than a measure of class distinction. The lean own and operate the sources of fattening fast foods, the poor are targeted to consume them.

Since the poorest minority groups in American society tend to be the most obese ones, extreme overweight is also a racial and ethnic issue. Currently over-represented amongst Mexican Americans, African Americans and Native Americans, rates of obesity and severe obesity are also rising more rapidly in minority populations than in European American ones due in part to targeted marketing.[122] The horror of being doubly discriminated against for being dark skinned and obese is expressed by the character Leticia Musgrove in the movie *Monster's Ball* (2002). The mother of an obese boy, she explains her emotional efforts to keep her son from compulsively overeating as follows: To be black in America is bad enough, to be black and fat is unbearable.[123]

While weight is in great part a class issue in America it is in even greater part a gender one. Thin women are more likely to "marry up" than fatter ones. Fat women are more likely to be discriminated against on the basis of their appearance in employment, real estate, and college admission situations.[124] In a study on how the disabled accept their disability, the vast

---

[121] Crister 47.

[122] For current obesity rates see John P. Foreyt, "Weight Loss Programs for Minority Populations," *Eating Disorders and Obesity: A Comprehensive Handbook* 536-540. On increasing rates of obesity in minority populations, see Mary K. Stein, "Exploring Better Access to Care for Minority, Underserved Populations," *Eating Disorders Review* 12, n 4 (July/August 2001): 1.

[123] *Monster's Ball*, dir. Marc Foster, perf. Halle Berry, Billy Bob Thornton, Heath Ledger, Peter Boyle, Entertainment, 2002.

[124] Jeffery Sobal, "Social Influences on Body Weight," *Eating Disorders and Obesity: A Comprehensive Handbook*: "Among women, there is a clear inverse relationship between

majority of respondents reported that they would rather be deaf, dyslexic, diabetic, or have a heart disease than be obese.[125] Although all obese people suffer from discrimination, young women of the middle and upper class have the worst self-images. Whereas all Americans now grow steadily heavier during their lifetimes, white middle-class women gain weight more gradually during middle age than do men. This more gradual weight gain suggests that the pressure upon women to maintain a semblance of thinness is greater than that upon men.[126]

While organizations and laws exist to fight covert forms of discrimination against the overweight and obese, fat prejudice takes on insidious forms. One obese woman describes how she is routinely treated as invisible, for instance, by stewardesses who refuse to check to see if she has put on her seatbelt in the airplane.[127] Doctors may subject their obese patients to prejudiced treatment.[128] Betty Rose Dudley illustrates such discrimination brilliantly in a personal essay called "Fat Kills": When Dudley visits a thin doctor because of her persistent cough, she is met only with injunctions to lose weight and offered weight-loss pamphlets. Her cough and the possibility that she has lung cancer are steadfastly ignored.[129]

---

socio-economic status and weight, with upper-SES women being thinner than their lower-SES counterparts. [...] Heavier people (especially women) have a more difficult time attracting desirable marital partners" (75); Esther Rothblum assembles the facts on discrimination against fat women in an article bearing the witty title "'I'll Die for the Revolution but Don't Ask Me not to Diet': Feminism and the Continuing Stigmatization of Obesity," in *Feminist Perspectives on Eating Disorders*, ed. Patricia Fallon, Melanie A. Katzman, and Susan C. Wooley (New York: The Guilford Press, 1994) 53-76.

125 Albert J Stunkard and Jeffery Sobal, "Psychosocial Consequences of Obesity," *Eating Disorders and Obesity: A Comprehensive Handbook* 419.

126 Peter Stearns also notes that short men put on less weight in their adult lives than do their taller counterparts. Having a short stature represents such a social minus in American society that short men cannot afford to add to their social stigmatization by being overweight. By analogy, women can also not afford the double stigmatization of being women and overweight.

127 Natalie Kusz, "A Big Fat Secret," *Allure* July 1999: 70.

128 78% of obese individuals report being poorly treated by their medical care takers because of their weight. Stunkard and Sobal 418.

129 Betty Rose Dudley, "Fat Kills," *Fat!So? Magazine* 4 November 2002 <http:// www.fatso.com/big>.

Because the binge-eating disorder is "new" and relatively unstudied, few psychological profiles exist of typical binge eaters. The heightened language and condensed expressive means of poetry help to illuminate their experiences. The following poem, written by an author who refers to herself as Gaia, describes a woman's feelings before and during a binge:

The Angel That Feeds Me

I am sad.
In the bathroom I see my silver picture: Joint of pork,
flesh bulging out of tight, cutting string.
I go to the kitchen.
My angel is waiting for me, sitting on the table.
Butter coloured curls hang down to his waist,
marshmallow-pink cheeks, wet red lips like cut
strawberries.
"Come to me" he says.
I step into his arms, press my face against his flat
white chest, feel his velvet hair.
My angel smells of pastry and toffee, chocolate and
mint, creamy caramel.
"I will comfort you. I will give you what you need."
His voice is a thick syrup, nourishing me, filling the
hole that is my sadness.
I let him feed me.
I let him spoon ambrosia into my mouth, spoonful
after spoonful, on and on.
Soon the ambrosia starts to taste bitter and I close my
mouth. I tell him to stop but he continues forcing
food into my mouth.
I look at him and notice that his hazelnut eyes have
Darkened and sharpened to thorns. He has turned into
a demon.
I escape. I run away. I do not need him. I will not go
to him for comfort. I can live without his sweetness.
For days I am strong. I see him through windows,
hiding in the cupboards, holding out a plate of cakes
Then one day the sky is gr[a]y and I am sad and alone.
I go in search of my angel and step into his arms
again. Defeated[130]

---

[130] Gaia, "Me," 21 October 1998 <http://www.gurney.org.uk/eda/poetry.html>.

As in "The Bulimic Experience" the confrontation with her mirrored image triggers so much self-disgust in the speaker that she reacts by bingeing. The mirror reveals the outlines of her flesh, which the speaker likens to a fatty and unaesthetic "Joint of pork." The unappetizing image of the narrator's flesh, which sends her running to the kitchen, contrasts with that of the angel. With "[b]utter coloured curls" and "marshmallow-pink cheeks, wet red lips like cut / strawberries," he smells of desserts, and his "voice is a thick syrup." All the foods associated with the angel are sweet things that can be consumed rapidly during a binge, which do not require the preparation and cooking time of the more substantial joint of pork. The angel-cum-eating disorder is masculine. He invites the speaker to eat "sitting on her table" like a familiar friend or lover. He fills the "hole" made of sadness within her. Here the motif of lacking volition familiar from "The Bulimic Experience" recurs. Not the poem's speaker chooses to feed herself, but rather the angel feeds her. This angel fulfills stereotypical masculine and feminine love roles; he nourishes and comforts and fills the hole.

However, the gentle act of feeding alters when the angel refuses to stop. Spoon feeding turns into force feeding, and the angel is transformed into a demon. The gentle image of oral penetration is replaced by one of oral rape. Interestingly, eating disorders are repeatedly personified as dangerous supernatural creatures. I suspect that the moral imperative to diet is so powerful that many women feel that they do not have the right to actively feed themselves. The urge to eat must be projected onto some outside force, something or someone who tempts or forces them to consume food. The underlying issue is a sense of powerlessness. The speaker of "The Angel That Feeds Me" is unable to feel or satisfy her hunger. Instead, an externalized force foists food upon her.

In a poem by Kathy Anderson called "Surrounded" the speaker expresses her sense of vulnerability regarding food:

Surrounded

Even outdoors
she sees food everywhere

Strips
of sycamore bark
crunch
like potato chips
underfoot

Dog turds
on the grass
look just like
Tootsie Rolls

Belly tight
she tastes despair
rolling around
in her open mouth[131]

The title itself suggests ambushes and hostile takeovers. And this imagery is made explicit in the first stanza of the poem in which the speaker describes the seeming visual omnipresence of food.

However, the second stanza's "Strips / of sycamore bark / crunch" could be the beginning of a bucolic description of nature's beauties. Yet the pastoral moment is subverted with "like potato chips." The pedestrian crunch of peaceful footsteps through the woods is transformed into the act of masticating a fatty processed salty food. The contrast between the outdoor experience of walking and the indoor experience of eating would hardly be so crass if the speaker were to imagine the crunching sound of eating carrot sticks, for instance. In the second stanza potato chips overwhelm the image of sycamore bark on an auditory level.

In the third stanza the replacement of natural images by foodstuffs takes place on a visual level. Here nature's offering is a repellent one: "Dog turds / on the grass." Yet the speaker's other senses, for instance her olfactory one, are closed off, and the turds she sees are transformed into "Tootsie rolls." The repetition of opening dental and closing sibilant sounds in "Dog turds" and "Tootsie Rolls" suggests a closeness between these images that is underlined by their phonetic similarities. By bringing a dog's anus and a woman's mouth (the speaker's) into such close proximity, the speaker's disgust at her powerlessness to control her thoughts of food is expressed hyperbolically.

The "Belly tight" and "open mouth" of the final stanza are metaphors for the speaker's insatiable hunger. Rather than Tootsie Rolls or potato chips, she "tastes despair." The images of foods the speaker perceives in her surroundings fail to nourish her but instead render her insensitive to anything else.

In the following untitled poem, which was posted anonymously on the Internet, hunger is again experienced as being insatiable by the eating-disordered speaker:

> A hole so deep,
> It is all consuming.
> But lies empty in the v[a]in hope,
> That one day it will be filled[132]

The "hole" of the throat and stomach is a metonymy for the physical sensation of hunger. That this hole is "so deep" and that it "lies empty" expresses its limitless quality: No amount of food could possibly fill it. This personified hole has a life of its own: "It is all consuming." On the one hand the speaker disowns her appetite and negates her physical sensations. Rather than herself feeling hungry, the hole within her wishes to "be filled." She

[131] Kathy Anderson, "Surrounded," *Eating Our Hearts Out: Personal Accounts of Women's Relationship to Food* 161.
[132] untitled, 13 October 1998 <http://www.geocities.com/Wellesley/4220/edpoetry.html>.

does not consume food, rather the hole does. On the other hand the hungering hole is doomed to wait vainly, hoping "That one day it will be filled."

The poems "The Angel That Feeds Me," "Surrounded" and "A hole so deep" all concern the compulsion to eat that typifies both bulimia and the binge-eating disorder.

1.4) Sub-clinical Eating Disorders

Recent research suggests that those individuals who diet are subject to the same mood and behavioral changes as anorectics and starving people. During the Second World War a group of conscientious objectors was asked to reduce their food intake voluntarily so as to lose 25% of their body weight. Not surprisingly, the volunteers became obsessed by thoughts of food, mealtimes, and food preparations. Many became depressed and anxious and lost interest in all other activities besides eating. Those who were not able to maintain the strict diet, binged and felt guilty for having done so. Even after the men began to eat normally again, they remained preoccupied by food and their weight.[133] The importance of this study of the effects of starvation is its implication for chronic dieters. Dieters who eat less than 1,000 calories a day effectively starve themselves.[134] They become moody, anxious, depressed, and obsessed by thoughts of food.

When dieters overeat, they do not compensate by reducing their food intake afterwards. Rather, they become uninhibited, and eat more food rather than less. In other words, they binge. Dieters associate feelings and moral states with food, some foods are "good," others are "bad"; and dieters feel guilty when they eat "bad" foods. Like the eating disordered, chronic dieters tend to have a low sense of self-esteem and to be out of touch with their

---

[133] As summarized in Zerbe, *The Body Betrayed* 251-254.
[134] Zerbe, *The Body Betrayed* 252.

feelings and overly susceptible to external emotional triggers. However, it is not clear what comes first, the diet or the sense of low self-esteem.[135]

Restricting food intake even for a short time makes individuals want to overeat and may turn them into compulsive eaters or bulimics.[136] Most American women diet, and more women of "normal weight" diet than do their male counterparts.[137]

Because dieting is a precondition of eating disorders and common feature of American life, I include literary treatments of dieting in this study. These treatments come in two forms. Either they explore weight and shape control from inside the mind of the dieter, or they express rage at a society that keeps women down by keeping them desperate to be thin. The following poem by a writer named Shelly explores weight concerns as characteristic of modern femininity:

Becoming a Woman

Reclining on the matted futon, recuperating,
Its rumpled flannel drinks from my dewy skin.
I unravel my cramped back upon the bedding,
Each tender muscle collapsing (I can almost hear them sigh).
I eat the air like candy, lap it up like a panting dog.
Oxygen invades my lungs... over... and over.
The skin across my breast feels frail, as if with every breath,
a rib will tear through and expose the foul calories trespassing inside.
I explore and patrol this gymnast body like territory,
seeking rocky mountain hips and shallow valley abdomen.
Nike flashes me a sweaty smile from my steaming sneakers,
while Jane Fonda does her "cool down" on the 9 inch screen.

---

135 Janet Polivy and C. Peter Herman, "Dieting and its Relation to Eating Disorders, *Eating Disorders and Obesity: A Comprehensive Handbook* 85.

136 Shelley Channon and Andrew Hayward, "The Effect of Short-term Fasting on Processing of Food Cues in Normal Subjects," *International Journal of Eating Disorders* 9, No. 4 (1990): 451.

137 Colleen S. W. Rand, and John M. Kuldau, "Restrained Eating (Weight Concerns) in the General Population and Among Students," *International Journal of Eating Disorders* 10, No. 6 (1991): 706.

Sleep puckers up for its good night kiss,
Attempts to tuck my eyes into their velvety blankets.
Praying for slender dreams that satiate my hunger,
I stretch my arm to suffocate the light that casts ugly shadows.
The blood shot eyes of the clock frown a familiar fate...
An unplanned meal has put me past my bedtime once again.[138]

The title is self-explanatory. To be a woman in American culture is to worry about one's weight. The series of alliterative /r/ sounds in the first three lines help to create an atmosphere of exhaustion. The words "Reclining," "recuperating," "rumpled," and "unravel" are all initially produced in the back of the throat: a long distance must be traveled before they are out of the mouth. This lengthy process of articulation highlights what the words express—images of a tired undone body. With "rumpled" the post-workout body is likened to a once-pressed shirt or cloth that has been soiled, with "unravel" the speaker's sore back is metaphorically linked to tangled string. The speaker has no sense of accomplishment for the exercise she has done; she does not praise her body for its strength or agility but rather emphasizes its weakness, its need to rest after moving, and its frailty: her muscles are "collapsing," her skin "feels frail."

In the ninth and tenth line the body is perceived as hostile territory. Any deviation from the ideal of "rocky mountain hips and shallow valley abdomen" is sought out in order to be annihilated. Food, of course, is the enemy. "[F]oul calories" have been "trespassing" upon the thin body; the "unplanned meal" robs the narrator of her sleep. When calories are perceived as inherently evil, then they must be guarded against with constant vigilance. Dangers lurk of being infiltrated by food even when one sleeps. One must wish for "slender dreams that satiate," not images of fields of chocolate brownies, or one will be weakened and hungry when one wakes. The need to

[138] Shelley, "Becoming A Woman," 4 November 2002 <http://www.geocities.com./Wellsley/4220/ edpoetry.html>.

"patrol" the body for fear of its having gotten fatter and the association of food with moral states typify the normal dieter's psyche.

"Becoming a Woman" reiterates the sentiment expressed in the poem "Surrounded." The speakers of both poems battle against food. Only with heroic outputs of energy can the enemy—the superfluous calorie—be defeated. The sense of vulnerability to food these average dieters express is shared even by women whom American culture idolizes for their perfect figures. The model Claudia Schiffer reports: "'Sometimes I feel food is attacking me.'"[139]

The next poem by "Trish" is a critique of the culture that conditions some women to be, like the speaker of "Becoming a Woman," chronic dieters and others to become eating disordered:

CONFORM

I.
The people here have lost their individuality
have lost their shape.
They strain & strive toward one ideal.
A communism of the body.
Their minds work toward the on empty goal,
in a pursuit of nothingness.
They forge ahead blindly, powered by hunger
not understanding why.
Considering, momentarily the result of zero.

II.
They consume a feeling and draw on their life force prana.
They excrete venom from their lips while their arses remain dry.
Bright yellow urine
dehydrates their cells
and stagnates blood.
Distant insanity bites at their heels
chasing these people
who run on treadmills and fall behind.

---

[139] Amy O'Connor, "Educating Claudia," *Self*, February 1999: 29.

III.
These are patient people who meticulously
count units.
They bide their time,
starve off hunger and all its implications.
They chew the fat (Theirs)
screaming (in hushed tones)
of liberty, equality
fat free.
They refuse to dress their meals/
They call themselves Pritikin
but beyond pritikin is pure famine.

IV.
In the dark they run bony fingers
over bony arms
locating anatomical structures:
clavicle, scapula, ulna, humerus
which is not funny.
Upon locating the lumbar vertebra
they run to mirrors
and twist and turn to distinguish it from
their skin
which is limply and heavy
and draped across their frame
like a tent over poles.

V.
At the gym 2 or 3 sweatshirts
create the illusion
of slender perfection.
Beneath this lies a carcass.
They are floating away
defying gravity.
Their wrists slip through our stable grasp.
We question their isolation.
Then RESUME OUR OWN DENIAL.[140]

This poem takes its reader through a range of dieting and eating-disordered states. In the first stanza the relative normality of striving to conform to the

[140] Trish, "Conform," *Eating Disorders Poetry Collection* 4 November 2002 <http://www.geocities.com/Wellesley/4220/edpoetry.html>.

narrowly circumscribed ideal of the body beautiful is explored. In the last stanzas the extremity of deathly anorexia is illustrated.

In the first stanza we meet a striving uniform "people" bent on achieving the goal of embodying *the* body beautiful. So infatuated are "the people" with the propagandistic image of themselves as perfect bodies that they become mindless in their pursuit, "not understanding why." In the second stanza we find "the people" actively consuming themselves, using diuretics or eating a high protein diet, which makes their urine turn yellow. The "venom" they "excrete" is perhaps the diet book wisdom they have digested in the place of food. The "Distant insanity" might either be brought on by the diet pills they consume or by diet-induced hunger. The implication is that there is little to separate the normal dieter from the eating-disordered one.

The "people" of the first stanza are called the "patient people" in the third one. But these patient dieters who insist on their autonomy and their right to diet—"of liberty, equality / fat free."—are dangerously close to becoming the patients of eating disorder clinics. "[B]eyond [P]ritikin[141] is pure famine," the narrator insists. Beyond the structure and health that strict diet regimes promise is the specter of uncontrolled disordered eating and illness.

When the anorectic makes emaciation the key to her identity, she can only secure her self by verifying how thin she already is and by becoming even thinner. This thinking insists that every bone must be delineated. Flesh sinks away. The anorectics referred to in the fourth stanza as "they" resemble poorly constructed tents; their skin lies over their bones "limply and heavy / and draped across their frame."

The fifth stanza introduces the gym where "normal" dieters and "abnormal" anorectics meet to "run on treadmills" or otherwise torture their bodies. The image "of slender perfection" that the anorectic presents under her layers of sweatshirts is one normal dieters generally aspire to. Beneath the façade of perfection, however, "lies a carcass." "We," the readers, refuse to see how close the anorectic is to dying and "floating away."

1.5) Why Has the Incidence of Eating Disorders Increased?

There is no single cause for the increase and current prevalence of eating disorders. On this experts agree. However, researchers distinguish between several interrelated explanatory models: the medical one, the psychological-familiar model, and the cultural and feminist ones.

1.5.1) Physiological Explanations

Medical researchers argue that there must be a genetic or physical component involved in eating disorders. Otherwise, eating disorders would not affect so small a percentage of the general population, since all young American women are exposed to a culture that values thin female bodies while it effectively produces ever-fatter ones. The connection between disordered eating and depression caused by biochemical problems has been documented. Bulimia is very commonly treated with a variety of antidepressants, and anorectics are often prescribed Prozac.[142] However, the precise relation between mood disorders and eating disorders is not clear. It has not been proven whether the feelings of anxiety and depression experienced by many persons preceded their having eating problems. Not eating enough as anorectics and bulimics do makes individuals feel depressed and anxious.

---

[141] Nathan Pritikin's best-seller *Pritikin's Program for Diet and Exercise* (1979) espoused a very low-fat diet and exercise plan.
[142] Zerbe, *The Body Betrayed* 366.

Hence the mood disorder may be a symptom of the eating disorder and not a cause.[143]

Starving, gorging, and purging the body may be addictive behaviors that influence brain functioning. Bulimics describe feeling calm and safe after they vomit. They are also much more likely than anorectics to have problems with alcohol or drug abuse. The addiction model assumes that bulimics and binge eaters react uncontrollably to certain "toxic" foods, for instance sugars, and are unable to control their eating behavior after being exposed to these substances. Applying the 12-step program to food abuse, then, the bulimic patient or binge eater can avoid bingeing if she completely abstains from certain types of food.[144] The addiction theory is problematic in that it does not explain anorexia—except as an addiction to thinness—or distinguish between bulimia and simple binge eating.[145]

In the search for other physiological causes, one study documents chronic anorectics having had greater prenatal problems than other segments of the population.[146] Other studies note a higher incidence of eating disorders amongst identical versus non-identical twins, which would lend strength to the genetic hypothesis.[147] However, the influence that familial conditioning plays in the incidence of eating disorders amongst twins is not clear. Children of parents with eating disorders are more likely to have eating problems themselves, even when their parents are not their biological ones.[148] So the

---

[143] Peter J. Cooper, "Eating Disorders and their Relationship to Mood and Anxiety Disorders," *Eating Disorders and Obesity: A Comprehensive Handbook* 159-161.

[144] This notion of toxic food informs one popular autobiographical account of recovery bulimia. Caroline Adams Miller, *My Name Is Caroline* (1988; 1991).

[145] G. Terence Wilson, "Eating Disorders and Addictive Disorders," *Eating Disorders and Obesity: A Comprehensive Handbook* 166-167.

[146] Rita Bakan, C. Laird Birmingham, Elliot Goldner, "Chronicity in Anorexia Nervosa: Pregnancy and Birth Complications as Risk Factors," *International Journal of Eating Disorders* 10, No. 6 (1991): 631-645.

[147] Michael Stroiber, "Family-Genetic Perspectives on Anorexia Nervosa and Bulimia Nervosa, *Eating Disorders and Obesity: A Comprehensive Handbook* 214.

[148] On the effect that eating-disordered mothers have on their daughters' food and weight concerns, see Alan Stein, "Eating Disorders and Childrearing," *Eating Disorders and Obesity: A Comprehensive Handbook* 188-190; For evidence that eating disorders are

medical research is, at best, inconclusive. Medical models fail to explain the high incidence of eating disorders amongst certain socioeconomic groups versus others or the cause for the currently high incidence of eating disorders.

1.5.2) Psychological Theories

In 1895 Freud explained adolescent anorexia as a psychosexual disorder resulting from "a melancholia where sexuality is underdeveloped."[149] According to his view, the co-relation of anorexia and puberty shows that anorexia is a strategy some females use to combat the beginning of adult womanhood and the development of secondary sexual characteristics. That anorectics tend to participate in little sexual behavior as compared to their contemporaries confirms this view. Traditional psychiatrists have been quick to understand anorexia as a fear of impregnation that could be cured by the development of a healthy attitude towards adult female sexuality.

Freud has been repeatedly criticized for his tendency to see male psychosexual development as normative and female psychosexual development as abnormal. For him, a boy's growth centers on his recognition of having a penis and his mother's lack thereof. His Oedipal desire to be united with his mother is overcome by his greater fear of castration, which leads him to identify with his father's sex. The catalyst in a girl's development is by contrast her recognition that she does not have a penis and her need to develop a sexual identity based upon this lack. Although this view is generally regarded as one-sided and misogynist, latter-day Freudians still look for anatomical reasons for the preponderance of eating disorders in

---

learned behaviors rather than inherited ones, see the study by Crisp and Toms (1972) that Zerbe cites: An adoptive son and a foster daughter were raised by an anorexic man. Both children developed anorexia. *The Body Betrayed* 283-284.

[149] Sigmund Freud, *The Standard Edition of the Complete Works of Sigmund Freud*, trans. and ed. James Strachey, vol. 17, *An Infantile Neurosis and Other Works* (London, 1966) 106, quoted in Brumberg, *Fasting* 28.

females. One researcher suggests that the semi-concealed state of female genitalia, the loss of muscle mass and the weight gain during puberty contribute to a girl's ambivalent and unfocused sense of her own sexuality. A girl's becoming aware of her own genitalia may well occur when a boy touches her or when she visits a (usually male) gynecologist. Furthermore, sexual intercourse and pregnancy involve the body being penetrated by another being. Lactating is also not self-determined. Pubescence, pregnancy, childbirth, and lactation all involve more radical—and potentially alienating—experiences of the body than men experience. As a result, many girls feel uneasy with their pubescent bodies and nascent identities as mature women. This alienation leads some to focus all their negative feelings onto their bodies by starving, gorging, and purging. They externalize their sense of inner opacity in concrete bodily acts.[150]

The sense of want, which according to Freudians and neo-Freudians typifies female psychosexual development, is illustrated by the 1980 poem by Louise Glück, "Dedication to Hunger":

1 FROM THE SUBURBS
They cross the yard
and at the back door
the mother sees with pleasure
how alike they are, father and daughter—
I know something of that time.
The little girl purposefully
swinging her arms, laughing
her stark laugh:

It should be kept secret, that sound.
It means she's realized
that he never touches her.

[150] Lisa W. Cross, "Body and Self in Feminine Development: Implications for Eating Disorders and Delicate Self-Mutilation," *Bulletin of the Menninger Clinic* 57, Number 1 (Winter 1993): 46-68.

She is a child; he could touch her
if he wanted to.

2 GRANDMOTHER

"Often I would stand at the window—
your grandfather
was a young man then—
waiting, in the early evening."

That is what marriage is.
I watch the tiny figure
changing to a man
as he moves toward her,
the last light rings in his hair.
I do not question
their happiness. And he rushes in
with his young man's hunger,
so proud to have taught her that:
his kiss would have been
clearly tender—

Of course, of course. Except
it might as well have been
his hand over her mouth.

3 EROS

To be male, always
to go to women
and be taken back
into the pierced flesh:

I suppose
memory is stirred
And the girl child
who wills herself
into her father's arms
likewise loved him
second. Nor is she told
what need to express.
There is a look one sees,
the mouth somehow desperate—

Because the bond
cannot be proven.

4 THE DEVIATION
It begins quietly
in certain female children:
the fear of death, taking as its form
dedication to hunger,
because a woman's body
is a grave; it will accept
anything. I remember
lying in bed at night
touching the soft, digressive breasts,
touching, at fifteen,
the interfering flesh
that I would sacrifice
until the limbs were free
of blossom and subterfuge: I felt
what I feel now, aligning these words—
it is the same need to perfect,
of which death is the mere byproduct.

5 SACRED OBJECTS
Today in the field I saw
the hard, active buds of the dogwood
and wanted, as we say, to capture them,
to make them eternal. That is the premise
of renunciation: the child,
having no self to speak of,
comes to life in denial—

I stood apart in that achievement,
in that power to expose
the underlying body, like a god
for whose deed
there is no parallel in the natural world.[151]

Glück's poem offers the reader intense contradictory images of important periods in the speaker's personal history. The speaker's girlhood, her grandmother's early married life, her own sexual experiences, then her

[151] Louise Glück, "Dedication to Hunger," *Descending Figure* (New York: Ecco Press, 1980) 29.

puberty and the beginnings of her anorexia, and finally the narrative present are presented in successive order. In the first three sections of the poem the contradictory perceptions of the narrator and the persons she describes are given. In this manner an emotional distance is created between the narrated events and the reader.

"FROM THE SUBURBS" presents the poem's speaker and her mother's divergent visions of the speaker's girlhood. The mother, who is referred to in the third person, sees her husband and daughter's similarities with satisfaction. Returning to Bruch's observation about the lack of sons in the families of anorectics, we might surmise that this strong daughter with "her stark laugh" fulfills the function of an ersatz son. The narrator rapidly subverts this vision of happy 1950s suburbia with the words: "I know something of that time." The first-person voice introduces the ominous knowledge that the suburban idyll is suspect. The little girl's "stark laugh" masks her painful knowledge that her father refuses to touch her—that he has disowned her emotionally. Perhaps, she mimics her father's characteristics and not her mother's—which are not described—in an effort to win his physical affection by behaving like a boy.

The first stanza of the second section of the poem gives us the grandmother's first-person description of her life as a young married woman, in which she often waited at the window for her husband to return from work. Significantly, the mother in the first section of the poem and the grandmother in the second one are pictured as being indoors, the mother behind the back door and the grandmother behind the window. In these generations it was the woman's role to watch quietly within the confines of the house for the movements and noise of her returning spouse.

In the second stanza the speaker examines her grandmother's description of married life in a beneficial light. Envisioning how her grandfather appeared to grow larger in her grandmother's waiting eyes and how his hair seemed to glow in the evening light, she comments, "I do not question / their happiness." She goes on to picture how he "rush[ed] in" to give his wife a kiss filled with a "young man's hunger" and his pride in having initiated her sexually. The speaker does not question that the kiss "would have been / clearly tender."

The commentary "Of course, of course" that opens the next stanza would seem to summarize the positive reading of the newlywed's interactions: Yet the "of course(s)" work as a foil for the "Except" that follows them. The interpretation of the homecoming as just tender is shown to be simplistic. The grandfather might as well have placed "his hand over her mouth" and gagged her as kissed her.

The third section "EROS" describes the speaker's theory of what men experience in sex. Instead of directly describing a scene as in the poem's first section, she uses an infinitive construction and third-person voice to introduce a definition of masculinity: "To be male." Having sex is a way for men to re-enter the womb, to "be taken back / into the pierced flesh." The adjective "pierced" suggests that the flesh was perforated forcefully and painfully.

In the second stanza the speaker envisions the meaning of the sexual act from the female perspective. The desire for the man's embrace echoes the girl's desire for her father's touch. The longing for sex rests on the urge to physically demonstrate that a bond exists between the male lover (and the father before him) and the woman. This "bond" unlike the one to the first loved mother "cannot be proven."

Section 4 "THE DEVIATION" again presents a significant moment in the speaker's life from two perspectives. The beginnings of anorexia are examined from a general standpoint and then from a personal one. Anorexia begins, the speaker tells us using an, again, impersonal third-person voice, because girls are afraid of the death that becoming a woman represents to them: "Because a woman's body / *is* a grave; it will accept / anything." I read these lines in reference to the women's roles described in the first three sections of the poem. The girl longs for her father's embrace in vain; the grandmother waits for her husband to fill the house and her life: his kiss functions like the placing of a lid over the simmering pot of her own powers of articulation. In sex the woman is pierced by her lover's penis. Women are presented as passive, penetrated, and gagged in these images—as defective if you will.

The speaker goes on to describe her own burgeoning eating disorder. At 15 she regards her female flesh as "soft, digressive" and "interfering." To accept this flesh would be akin to putting a layer of "subterfuge" over the presumed honesty of the pre-menarche androgynous body. Functioning like those pretty pictures of the waiting bride and mother, the "blossom[ing]" flesh hides the ugly fact of female passivity. To "perfect" herself the speaker must rid herself of her concealing flesh. Here and in the final section of the poem, she likens this process to writing. Renouncing the flesh and working a poem are akin to the nature lover's desire to capture the bare possibility of "the hard, active buds" of a dogwood tree and thus make them transcendent. The attendant cost is that the buds will never bloom and the girl may die.

The hatred of female flesh that informs "The Deviation" has a different quality from that described in "Anorexic" and "For Ellen West." Here, flesh is regarded as a mask that detracts from the essential self, rather than as a symbol of dreaded maternity.

To read this poem in purely neo-Freudian terms would be to underestimate its richness. "Dedication to Hunger" can also be regarded as a critical commentary on the myths of women's happiness in a patriarchal cultural setting and on girls' alienation from their bodies, genitalia, and female identities. Yet the speaker displays a regard for the male body, which is reflected in her dubious "achievement" as an anorectic. She was "like a god" in her ability to make her fifteen-year old body eternally sexless. A disgust for female flesh informs the poem. That the body is regarded as being "pierced" by the penis in sex and not as actively engulfing or surrounding it illustrates a Freudian sense of female insufficiency.

Opposing Freud and Freudians, the psychiatrists Hilde Bruch in America and Mara Selvini Palozzi in Italy began to concentrate on the part that family dynamics play in the individual psyches of eating-disordered women during the 1960s and 1970s. Bruch's description of the overly controlling family of the anorectic has already been summarized. Palozzi went farther in seeing the anorectic's eating problems as symptomatic of familiar ills. Only when the marital ills between the anorectic's parents are addressed can the eating-disordered girl become well. Otherwise the family will continue to project all its problems onto the pathology of their daughter's eating. Changing family dynamics involves altering the unspoken alliances between family members and opening new lines of communication in "system therapy."[152] Addressing family dysfunction has become central to the treatment of the eating disordered.[153]

---

[152] "In my view the system of alliances constitutes the central and most serious problem facing the families of anorexic patients. It is the basis of a large number of secret rules that must never be mentioned or event hinted at, and that give rise to a whole series of distorted behavior patterns. However, as we shall see, it may be used to good effect by the therapist." Mara Salvini Palozzi, *Self-Starvation: From the Intrapsychic to the Transpersonal Approach to Anorexia Nervosa*, trans. Arnold Pomerans (1963; London: Human Context Books, 1974) 209.

[153] Typically, mothers are blamed for having treated their daughter as sources of emotional fulfillment and for not having allowed them to develop an adequate sense of self. Zerbe warns against the dangers of "mother blaming" by eating-disordered women and the clinicians who treat them, *The Body Betrayed* 74. Yet in another article she depicts the mother's neurotic need to live through the body of her daughter as a primary cause of body dissociation amongst eating-disordered women. Kathryn J. Zerbe, "Whose Body is It Anyway? Understanding and Treating Psychosomatic Aspects of Eating Disorders," *The Bulletin of the Menninger Clinic* 57, No. 2 (Spring 1993) 1 July 1998 <http://www.olmo.com/psychnet/zerbe.html>; on alternatives to "mother-blaming" in therapy, see also Judith Ruskay Rabinor, "Mothers, Daughters, and Eating Disorders: Honoring the Mother-Daughter Relationship," *Feminist Perspectives on Eating Disorders*, ed. Patricia Fallon, Melanie A. Katzman, and Susan C. Wooley (New York: The Guilford Press, 1994) 272-286.

One could also draw on the psychoanalyst Jacques Lacan's writings on mirroring to explain eating disorders as a search for signification. In *Life-Size*, *The Passion of Alice*, and *Wasted* the narrator's self-examinations in front of the mirror is a recurrent motif.[154] According to Lacan a child recognizes the form of itself in the mirror sometime before it is a year and a half old. This moment of recognition, in which the child begins to conceive of itself as unified and aware is simultaneously an example of false recognition, or, *méconnaisance*; what the child sees is only an image of itself and not its entirety; and, like the mythical Narcissus who falls in love with his own reflection in the water and drowns when he attempts to kiss his beloved, the child regards this seemingly unified image of what it sees with desire. Thus the child requires some other person or thing to mirror its existence, to show it that it exists.[155] The eating-disordered woman remains or returns to the "mirror phase" and a lack of individuation. She regresses to a preverbal identification with her body, which she uses to express herself rather than the symbolic order of words. Her attempt to achieve an impossible degree of thinness represents a desire to articulate herself as clearly as possible in the mirrored form of an outline of her fleshless bones. A Lacanian interpretation highlights the fact that eating disorders are the expressions of individual bodies. Becoming somebody—that is recognizing oneself as an individual and being recognized by others as a person—is not simply the result of outward pressures to become a functioning body within a highly disciplined socioeconomic system but also represents an important part of normal and abnormal psychological development.

The obvious objection to a Lacanian analysis of eating disorders is that such a reading would wholly ignore the significance of cultural pressures to

---

[154] Hornbacher describes how she never emerges from the mirror phase: "The 'mirror phase' of child development took on new meaning for me 'mirror phase' essentially describes my life" (*W* 15).

[155] Jacques Lacan, *Écrits: A Selection*, trans. Alan Sheridan (London: Tavistock Publications, 1977).

the development of anorexia, bulimia, and binge eating. Such an approach might get too caught up in individual psychological development and ignore the very real role that the media, the market economy, and the financially and socially dependent role of women and girls in our society play in the development and spread of eating disorders.

Another psychological model of eating disorders is the Jungian one. Marian Woodman's examines the psyches of anorexic and obese women to discover that these women do not experience femininity positively. According to Woodman, girls lack initiation rituals, which would give them a well-grounded sense of their adult female sexuality. Girls need to be introduced to the symbolic feminine experience by their mothers just as Greek girls were initiated into the Eleusinian Mysteries. These rites celebrated the birth of the goddess of the spring, Persephone, to her mother Demeter, goddess of the earth and the harvest. This essential feminine experience is a "life-affirming moment, a full feminine YES,"[156] revolving around a woman's embrace of her ability to give birth to her spiritual self or to a child. A good case can be made for the lack of empowering rituals to mark a girl's menarche in America. Menarche has been transformed from a privately experienced event marking a girl's ability to become pregnant into a public discussion of the advantages of various commercial products. The commercial stress on not staining or smelling—a strategy for selling personal hygiene products—has made menstruation a potential cause for embarrassment and divorced it from its relationship to female sexuality.[157]

While Woodman is certainly correct in her implicit criticism of culture's commercialization of menarche and the lack of spiritual rituals to demarcate adulthood, her analysis appears essentialist. She assumes that a

---

[156] Marion Woodman, *The Owl Was a Baker's Daughter: Obesity, Anorexia Nervosa and the Repressed Feminine* (Toronto: Inner City Books, 1980) 118.
[157] Brumberg, *The Body Project* 29-55. For a dramatic treatment of this theme, see Eve Ensler, "When I was Twelve. My Mother Slapped Me," *The Vagina Monologues: The V-Day Edition* (1998; New York: Villard, 2002) 35-40.

trans-historical, trans-cultural female nature or spirit exists, whose celebration may nourish individual women throughout the generations. Furthermore, she makes a direct analogy between physical and spiritual reproduction. There is a danger here of reducing the spectrum of female experience to female sexuality and reproduction

A Jungian orientation informs Kim Chernin's work on women's troubled relationship to food as well. For Chernin, anorexia is a response by the starving female soul to its lack of sustenance in patriarchal culture. Were girls to be granted a "reentry into the positive knowledge of woman's experience," they would not need to punish their bodies. They might then find—"Joy, ecstasy, a feeling of worship, powerful emotion, passion, pleasure in the body, kinship with nature, a knowledge of the animal self and all that unspoken music of existence this soul would sing."[158] The connection between female hunger and female embodiment is described by one of Chernin's own poems:

The Hunger Song

Hungering, I
go out, I
go ravening into the woods
feed me, I cry
to the trees, desire
rising driven
in me like
a sap and falling
into my body again
I enter into the world
eating the snow, this

[158] Kim Chernin, *The Obsession* 198; See also Noelle Caskey, "Interpreting Anorexia Nervosa," *The Female Body in Western Culture: Contemporary perspectives*, ed. Susan Rubin Suleiman (Cambridge, MA: Harvard UP, 1986). Caskey adopts a Jungian outlook to examine anorexia as an expression of Western culture's fear of feminine fat with its implications of fertility and as a communicative disorder based on a daughter's psychic incest with her father and over-identification with her animus.

is my breath, I
say air of us feeding
me look
at this acorn I made
Love, to know you
like this, flesh
bound as I am, you
in your ecstasy
branching, I
in my green thoughts
growing up
out of the snow.[159]

Chernin's poem makes an analogy between a woman's hunger and her lack of a connection to nature. "[R]avening" suggests both that the speaker has been made raving mad and ravenously hungry in the domestic world. Solace from culture is sought in the woods. Spiritual sustenance is the "air of us" created by the exchange between the woman and the oak tree. The union between the speaker and the tree is physical, as exemplified by the ambiguous "look / at this acorn I made / Love, to" as well as spiritual. She, "flesh / bound" joins the tree's "ecstasy / branching" in her "green thoughts." Woman unites with and is sustained by nature.

The poem could be read as a variation of the myth of Daphne and Apollo. Daphne, a young nymph, fled from the god Apollo's amorous chase. She begged her father the river-god to save her and was transformed by him into a laurel tree. In this poem the woman escapes from the indoors and longs to be united with the tree. "The Hunger Song" also represents a novel twist on the traditional literary coupling of woman with nature. In this poem it is not the male narrator who seeks escape and spiritual solace in a feminized nature, but a female who chooses to be satisfied by the tree. This is presumably the "kinship with nature" and "knowledge of the animal self." Again, I want to point out the risk of simplifying experience by looking for its apotheosis in

[159] Chernin xxiii.

the natural and animal. Women and men are cultural animals. No one key to feminine experience may be found in natural imagery.[160]

1.5.3) Eating Disorders as Cultural Ills and Expressions of Gender Problems

A number of commentators compare hysteria to contemporary eating disorders to demonstrate that the latter are symptomatic of cultural tensions. Such a view regards illness as a cultural construct and considers how power relations are reflected in sickness. Specifically, female dependency is reproduced in women's disorders and is legitimized by medical discourse. As anorexic girls express the unstated problems of their individual nuclear families, hysterics and bulimics express the hidden ills of their respective cultural milieus.

The illness called "hysteria" was diagnosed as early as in 1900 BC. Ancient Egyptians and ancient Greeks, after them, both believed that the uterus floated around in the female body and caused illness and distress during its migrations. From the beginning hysteria was associated with deviant sexuality and was treated with ghastly physical means, including the application of leeches to the vulva and cervix.[161]

Hysteria became epidemic in the late nineteenth century. The term was used to describe a whole battery of behaviors, including extreme displays of violent emotions, fainting, contortions, and real or imagined physical pains. The adjective "epidemic"[162] is key here because this modifier is so commonly used to describe the current incidence of eating disorders. Significantly,

---

[160] On man (and woman) as a cultural construct, see Clifford Geertz, "The Impact of the Concept of Culture on the Concept of Man," *The Interpretation of Cultures: Selected Essays* (New York: Basic Books, 1973) 46-54.

[161] Mark S. Micale, *Approaching Hysteria: Disease and its Interpretations* (Princeton, New Jersey: Princeton UP, 1995) 19.

[162] Claire Kahane, *Passions of the Voice: Hysteria, Narrative, and the Figure of the Speaking Woman, 1850 –1915* (Baltimore: Johns Hopkins UP, 1995) 7.

hysterical symptoms were reported almost exclusively in women and seemed to have occurred more frequently in the middle class than amongst the poor.[163] The parallels to eating disorders are obvious.

The incidence of hysteria grew in an era when anxieties about women's sexuality and behavior were strong.[164] The late nineteenth century was marked by the greater participation of middle-class women in the public workforce. Simultaneously, women married later, and birthrates declined so that the biological role of woman as baby makers and nurturers became more ambivalent. Urbanization led to the increased possibility of women acting without the surveillance of their families, neighbors and religious leaders. Worry about women's increased independence was met by inventing illnesses and sound medical reasons for women to remain sequestered in the safety of the middle-class home.[165] New ideological controls also arose to limit women's potential freedom. The late nineteenth century gave rise to an intensification of the division between men and women's proscribed roles. This division rested on both the popularity of poems like Coventry Patmore's "The Angel in the House" (1854), which idealized a wife's suffocating

---

[163] The French neurologist Jean-Martin Charcot was instrumental in hysteria's being recognized as a psychologically rather than a purely medically or spiritually determined illness. In an interesting parallel to the first medical descriptions of anorexia, Charcot recommended removing the hysteric from her home environment to ameliorate the cure. Although Charcot was criticized for stage-managing his patients hysterical fits, his work was, nonetheless, instrumental to Freud's understanding of hysteria, and hence anorexia. Freud developed a "talking cure" for hysteria, in which traumatic sexual experiences—Freud changed his mind about whether these experiences were real or imagined—may be exercised in intensive therapeutic sessions between the analysist and the analysand. Hysteria then is the mother of modern psychoanalysis. On the history of hysteria, see Kahane 1-13; Micale 19-29; On Charcot's medical theater of hysteria, see Habermas 177-178; and Elisabeth Bronfen, *The Knotted Subject: Hysteria and Its Discontents* (Princeton, NJ: Princeton UP, 1998) 174-240.
[164] Brian Turner, *The Body and Society* 103, 107-108, 112-114.
[165] Analogous to hysteria, agoraphobia—the fear of the market place—was first diagnosed in the late nineteenth century. The fear of open places and strangers kept middle-class women, who could potentially work, at home. By lending justification to the division of men to the public world and women to the private sector, the discovery of agoraphobia also answered fears about women's independence and vulnerability in the brave new world. Turner 107-108.

domesticity, and the pseudo-scientific foundation of Darwin's doctrine of a separate evolution of the sexes. Medical discourses on hysteria contributed to cementing the separate gender spheres: women were warned that work outside the home and education would lead to disease, reduced attractiveness, and even the end of civilization.[166]

On the individual level hysteria provided nineteenth century women with a deviant model of behavior. Hysterics could express unacceptable emotions—aggression or overt sexual desire—and be excused from domestic duties. The infantile emotionalism of hysterical women and their physical weakness contributed to furthering women's dependence. Every newly identified hysteric made the case for the necessity of women remaining cloistered at home stronger, and every new case of publicized hysteria could become fodder for the discursive mill on women's inherent weakness. The dissemination of hysteria occurred in medical discourse and through plays and novels, in which hysterics served as sympathy figures. Habermas suggests, for instance, that Flaubert's *Madame Bovary* (1857) provided a model of hysterical behavior for readers. Emma Bovary reacts to the discrepancy between her visions of romance and the reality of her narrow bourgeois life by demonstrating a series of hysterical behaviors—fainting, lack of breath and appetite, panic attacks, depression—and eventually by committing suicide. Emma's hysteria provided readers with a rendering of how the tensions inherent in nineteenth-century middle-class life played themselves out in one woman's destiny.[167]

Hysteria disappeared in the twentieth century.[168] Cultural conditions changed so that the illness no longer expressed societal ills and gender

---

[166] Kahane 4.

[167] Habermas 175, 177.

[168] Not according to Elaine Showalter, who in *Hystories: Histerical Epidemics and Modern Culture* (New York: Columbia UP, 1997) reads contemporary phenomena such as anorexia and bulimia, recovered memory of childhood incest, Satanic ritual abuse, and chronic fatigue syndrome as culturally-propagated forms of hysteria and discovers a pattern to how these "epidemics" are discovered, publicized, and cashed in on: "Hysteria

troubles. In late capitalism men and women have become performing selves. Conspicuous consumerism and the aging of the population in Western industrial societies have made us vitally concerned with appearances and "keeping face."[169] The pressure to look good as a way to show that one is good is re-enforced by medical and pseudo-medical injunctions to diet and exercise in order to be healthy and to live longer. The body is treated as a commodity whose value may be calculated on the basis of the discipline and care with which it is maintained. Women's worth, particularly, is measured in their ability to correspond with inflexible models of physical desirability. Eating disorders, the argument goes, like hysteria before them express and reinforce patriarchal relations.[170] Women obviously now enjoy more public privileges than they did in the age of hysteria. Yet they remain underrepresented in real possessions of power, continue to be paid less for performing the same work as their male counterparts, and are have limited control over their bodies. Economic, financial, and political gains which women have made in the last thirty years have been offset by a standard of beauty so difficult to achieve that women are weakened and de-politicized in doing so.[171] The obsession with keeping thin keeps women busy, while they

---

not only survives in the 1990s, it is more contagious than in the past. Infectious diseases spread by ecological change, modern technology, urbanization, jet travel, and human interaction. Infectious epidemics of hysteria spread by stories circulated through self-help books, articles in newspapers and magazines, TV talk shows and series, films, the Internet, and even literary criticism. The cultural narratives of hysteria, which I call ***hystories***, multiply rapidly and uncontrollably in the era of mass media, telecommunications, and e-mail" (5).

[169] Turner summarizes Erving Goffman's *The Presentation of Self in Everyday Life* (Anchor, 1959; Harmondsworth: Penguin, 1990) in his discussion of the "performing self" (110-114).

[170] Brian Turner, whose theory I have been re-reiterating here, speaks only about anorexia. However, I think his theory can be generalized to include bulimia and other eating disorders: "All disease is disorder—metaphorically, literally, socially and politically" (114).

[171] In her most powerful analysis Naomi Woolf depicts a horror scenario in which the best and brightest young men of the Western world slowly commit suicide by starving themselves to death. Positions of power remain vacant, and institutions invest everything they have in order to save these young men and their own futures. Her message is clear; because golden girls and not golden boys are destroying themselves in front of the public

are effectively locked out of the avenues of power. Furthermore, eating disorders reinforce misogynist attitudes and practices in medicine, as new ways for women to be sick are discovered and documented and treated by—mostly male—practitioners.[172]

On an individual level eating disorders then have replaced hysteria as a model for deviant feminine behavior. The media fascination with anorexia and to a lesser degree bulimia has made these disorders famous. Anorexia and bulimia are publicly associated with beautiful, white, rich women and girls such as Jane Fonda, Lady Diana, and Victoria, the Princess of Sweden.[173] And the anorectic embodies the cultural values of slenderness, self-control, and competition.[174] In Steven Levenkron's novel *The Best Little Girl in the World* (1978) the anorexic protagonist, a would-be dancer, is described as making a pile of magazine pictures of fashion models with the "fattest" at the top and the thinnest at the bottom. She throws the pictures away successively as she succeeds in becoming thinner than the featured models.[175] In her memoir Marya Hornbacher describes the effect of seeing the film version of this novel on patients in an eating disorder clinic. So envious were these women of the appearance of the actress who had had to starve herself to play the leading role that they vowed to become even thinner than her (*W* 43). Nurses who treat anorexic girls sometimes envy their self-control and emaciation so much that their ability to care for these patients is

---

eye eating disorders continue to go unnoticed or are combated with only superficial means. *The Beauty Myth* (New York: Anchor Book, 1991) 179-181.

[172] Turner 222-224.

[173] On 29 November 1997 the Swedish Royal Family admitted that the then 20 year-old Princess Victoria was suffering from anorexia, after the princess had appeared at a ball, looking unnaturally thin in a sleeveless dress. Lasse Granestrand, "*Kronprinsessan får hjälp*" (Crown Princess Receives Help), *Dagens Nyheter* (largest morning paper in Sweden) 29 November 1997: A5.

[174] Gordon 130.

[175] Steven Levenkron, *The Best Little Girl in the World*, (1979; Harmondsworth: Puffin, 1995) 16.

compromised.[176] Eating disorder clinics may function like prisons in that their inmates learn better and more effective ways to practice the behaviors that brought them to these institutions.[177]

Alternately, anorexia may be seen as a form of resistance to condoned feminine behaviors. According to Susan Bardo women use anorexia as a way to protest against conforming to traditional feminine roles. Anorectics publicly demonstrate their being self-contained and without wants. In this they react to a culture that—as a result of its Platonic and Christian traditions—devalues the body and favors the intellectual, and associates women with voracious, dangerous physicality. Ironically, anorexia feeds the cultural conditions that create the illness: The anorectic—and the bulimic, binge eater and chronic dieter—fears her hunger as a dangerous lack of control. In her pursuit of her ideal of slenderness she becomes too weak to pursue anything else and is consumed by the hunger she wants to control.[178]

Some alternative theories on the etiology of eating disorders also concentrate on gender issues. Sandra Lee Bartky suggests that male and female power relations get played out on the field of the female body. Corseting, clitoridectomies, binding feet, and the limiting of access to contraception and abortion are some obvious examples of this. Western women's bodies are forced to be more docile than men's are in terms of their shape, movements, and forms of ornamentation. Bartky draws on Foucault's

---

[176] "Female nurses who care for anorexic patients are particularly vulnerable to these competitive feelings; 'how does she do it' is not an infrequent comment that follows a contentious interaction with a patient" (Gordon 105); "Judging by the number of women I've talked to who have gone through hospital-setting treatment, it is fairly common to have nurses who have eating issues of their own. They are certainly a source of serious irritation to their patients, who often find it difficult to listen to advice from women talking out of both sides of their mouths. It seems reasonable that hospitals should carefully screen nurses slated for rounds on and eating-disorder unit" (*W* 147).

[177] "There is nothing so welcome to the anorectic or bulimic, much as she protests and howls, as a world wherein everything, everything, revolves around food.

And there is nothing so wonderfully conducive to eating disorders as treatment" (*W* 145); See also Gordon 103.

[178] Susan Bordo, "Anorexia Nervosa" 89.

work on the history of punitive methods and techniques in *Discipline and Punish: The Birth of the Prison* (1979) to show that surveillance no longer comes from an external source of authority, but has been internalized in every culturally adept female body. In *Discipline and Punish* Foucault suggests that the method for surveying inmates has been gradually transferred from the prison warden to the individual, who now acts as his or her own warden.[179] Making an analogy between the alteration of penal techniques and the metamorphosis of body disciplines, Bartky argues that Victorian corsets have been replaced by an internal standard of slenderness. Dieting practices, injunctions to move in a graceful, feminine way, and to ornament oneself in a pleasing manner all lead to the circumscription of the female body. This reduced female body is too weak to fight against her enforced docility.[180]

Another causal model of eating disorders draws a comparison between the stigmatization of sexually nonconformist women in the 1940s and 1950s and weight prejudice towards overweight women today. The "fallen woman" of the earlier era who expressed her sexuality outside of marriage met with social reprobation and lost her status as marriageable. Today the obese woman meets with social outrage and disgust for her lack of control. This condemnation is reflected in the phrase "she's let herself go," which is used to describe a woman who has gained a considerable amount of weight. This phrase is not applied to men. On a metaphoric level both the pregnant single woman and the fat lady burst out of the britches of social convention.[181] Society punishes fat women for failing to discipline their appetite for food as it once condemned "loose women" for their nonconformist sexuality. Modern

---

[179] Michel Foucault, "Complete and Austere Institutions" from *Discipline and Punish: The Birth of the Prison*, trans. Alan Sheridan (New York: Pantheon Books, 1979) in *The Foucault Reader*, ed. Paul Rabinow (New York: Pantheon Books, 1984) 217.

[180] Sandra Lee Bartky, "Foucault, Femininity, and the Modernization of Patriarchal Power," *Feminism & Foucault: Reflections on Resistance*, ed. Irene Diamond and Lee Quinby (Boston, Northeastern UP, 1988) 77.

[181] Rosalyn Meadow and Lillie Weiss, *Good Girls Don't Eat Dessert: Changing Your Relationship to Food and Sex* (New York: Harmony Books, 1992).

Hester Prynnes are forced to wear baggy jeans rather than a scarlet letter to denote their moral failings.

Some of the poems on bulimia, binge eating, and chronic dieting printed above confirm this theory. The untitled poem, beginning with the phrase "Dainty bites" mentions "illicit feedings." In conventional usage the adjective "illicit" describes sexual or criminal activity, not eating practices. Consuming food appears to have replaced sex as the covert activity, which the female speakers of these poems need to think and talk about. Images of food appear to be inescapable in the poem "Surrounded." A nagging concern with how much eating is acceptable informs the comparison between "measured spoonfuls [...] methodically chewed" and food "stuffed in your mouth / hurling around your ears" in the poem "eating disorder." The types of food the speakers of these poems refer to are exclusively "unhealthy" ones. The poems "eating disorder," "Feather, 1948 / Finger, 1988," "The Angel that Feeds Me," and "Surrounded" mention ice cream, bags of cookies, jars of mayonnaise, pastry, toffee, chocolate, and Tootsie Rolls. These "illicit" foods are the ones eating-disordered women gorge on and normal dieters "break" their regimens with. For the speakers of these poems the "good woman" is the one who does not eat at all or who has her appetite and food consumption under complete control.

The variety of explanations for eating disorders demonstrate that no is no single cause for them. Cultural tensions regarding consumption and control over the female body are expressed in anorexia, bulimia, binge eating and chronic dieting. The media perpetuate images of unrealistically thin women who appear to embody success, happiness, and desirability. Women and girls appear to be acutely vulnerable to American culture's aggressive promotion of snack foods and the ascetically thin female body. Expressed in the poems quoted above, this vulnerability is explored in depth in the novels and the memoir I discuss in chapters three, four, and five.

II Perspectives on Literary Accounts of Eating Disorders

As Tilmann Habermas effectively argues in his history of anorexia, the increase of the incidence of eating disorders has grown in proportion to the fashionableness of the thin female body. In America, where the social pressures to be thin are matched in intensity by market pressures to eat fatty, over-processed foods, the atmosphere is ripe for all manner of food-related problems. As has been demonstrated in the comparison of hysteria to eating disorders, women and girls as dependent members of society are particularly vulnerable to those disorders that reflect and express broader cultural tensions.

The spread of illnesses among the most powerful socioeconomic group in the United States has led to the proliferation of commentaries on these phenomena. Just as there has been an explosion of medical texts to describe and delineate forms of eating disorders, so there has been an expansion of high- and low-brow literary texts to explore the eating-disordered experience. What is the relation between literary accounts of eating disorders and the culture in which they are written?

Answering this question necessitates a short detour into modern literary theory.

2.1) Reading Literature within Its Cultural Context

Speaking very generally, there has been a trend in literary criticism during the last twenty years to read texts within context, that is, with an eye to the worlds in which they arise and in which they will be received. Contrary to Russian formalists and new critics, critics nowadays rarely treat literary texts as inviolable objects that, on the basis of their extraordinary use of language or metaphor, enjoy an existence apart from the everyday world. In the wake of feminist and post-structuralist theories, criticism has become more political and more specific. Insights of post-colonial critics have radically challenged the privileged position of the Anglo-European white, middle-class reader, and the canon he and his forefathers created. The literary canon is now recognized to be a construction, based upon limited aesthetic and social judgements. Hence the canon and the receptions of individual literary works are subject to change. [1]

This general trend is reflected in the methods and goals of cultural studies, which attempts to combine the traditional critical interest in close reading and literary history with an attention to the fuzzy, mutable world outside of the text. One of the fathers of this critical practice is Raymond Williams. Williams has challenged traditional Marxist theories that insisted on the economic foundation of culture with the idea that no single principle determines cultural developments:

> [...] no mode of production, and therefore no dominant society or order of society, and therefore no dominant culture, in reality exhausts the full range of human practice, human energy, human intention (this range is not the inventory of some original 'human nature' but, on the contrary, is that extraordinary range of variations, both practised and imagined, or which human beings are and have shown themselves to be capable).[2]

---

[1] See, for instance, Jane P. Tompkins's challenge to those who excluded the socially relevant yet sentimental text *Uncle Tom's Cabin* from the canon of American literature, "*Uncle Tom's Cabin* and the Politics of Literary History, *The New Feminist Criticism: Essays on Women, Literature, and Theory*, ed. Elaine Showalter (New York: Random House, 1985) 81-104. "The very grounds on which sentimental fiction has been dismissed by its detractors, grounds that have come to seem universal standards of aesthetic judgment, were established in a struggle to supplant the tradition of evangelical piety and moral commitment these novelists represent. In reaction against their world view, and perhaps even more against their success, twentieth century critics have taught generations of students to equate popularity with debasement, emotionality with ineffectiveness, religiosity with fakery, domesticity with triviality, and all of these, implicitly, with womanly inferiority" (82).

[2] Raymond Williams, "Base and Superstructure in Marxist Cultural Theory," *Problems in Materialism and Culture* (London: Verso, 1980); reprinted in *New Historicism and Cultural Materialism: A Reader*, ed. Kiernan Ryan (London: Arnold, 1996) 26.

According to Williams, culture does not remain constant over any longer period of time but undergoes a constant flux between its emergent, dominant, and adversarial elements.[3] Exchange occurs between popular/emergent and elitist/residual expressions of culture. In a continuous state of change, then, culture can be seen as dialogue between newer and older elements, which is subjectively experienced by its members.[4] Dominant culture continuously attempts to adopt emerging trends.

In the twentieth century the line between clearly definable elite and popular cultural elements has become blurred. This process can be illustrated in the realm of fashions in clothes: High-brow designers look to the streets for inspiration for the next new expensive garment. The in-your-face, nearly-falling-off baggy pants of the Philadelphia street youth—which in turn apes convicts' beltless uniforms—is transformed by the up-scale designer into the midriff-baring, hip-hugging pants and skirts currently displayed by supermodels.

Like other leading literary theories of the past two decades, cultural studies does not assume that there is an absolute correspondence between the context of the literary work and the work itself. With new historians and cultural materialists, cultural studies theorists assume that the human is a cultural construct. Adopting the insights of the anthropologist Clifford Geertz and the philosopher-historian Michel Foucault, among others, students of cultural studies doubt the existence of a transcendent human essence. Rather, they assume that humans are shaped by their cultural settings and individual circumstances. Since literary texts are not transcendent reflections of the core of humanity but cultural products, it is fruitless to separate them from non-literary texts. Depending on how one sees it, textual analysis becomes quite anecdotal or

[3] Williams 26.

[4] The Russian philosopher and literary theorist Mikhail Bakhtin asserted that literary texts are by nature polyphonic. Every utterance produces a variety of meanings and arises out of a dialogue between conflicting social voices. Literary works are multi-leveled and "heteroglot,"

very inclusive: for instance, new historians treat a relatively unknown travelling merchant's account of how his fellow Englishmen destroyed an African village in 1586 as a valuable commentary on how Christopher Marlowe went about constructing his characters.[5] Similarly, the decision by *Vogue*'s editor to print an image of Hillary Clinton on the cover of the December issue because she was looking "*amazing*" (read "thin") provides insight into the culture in which eating disorders and literary accounts of them arise.

Catherine Belsey elucidates the cultural studies approach in her demand that English departments use tools for explicating literary texts to disclose the formal properties of non-literary texts and objects:

> More than any other discipline, English has been concerned with the study of signifying practice. Traditionally we have not only analysed meanings (philosophy does that too), and we have not only been concerned with social relations (history and sociology are too). Supremely, English departments have attended to the formal properties of texts, their modes of address to readers and the conditions in which they are intelligible. Cultural history needs to appropriate and develop those strategies, putting them to work not in order to demonstrate the value of the text, or its coherence as the expression of the authorial subjectivity which is its origin, but to lay bare the contradictions and conflicts, the instabilities and indeterminacies, which inevitably reside in any bid for truth. We need only extend the range of texts we are willing to discuss, to put on the syllabus [...].
>
> That 'only' is there to cheer us up, to make it all sound easy. I'm not sure how easy it is. But if we can interpret Shakespeare, we can surely learn to interpret fashion, and music–and privies. [6]

In this study I follow Belsey's lead by including many different kinds of cultural phenomena in my description of the etiology of eating disorders. Psychology, media, economics, and sociology and various discursive forms are all considered. By providing a large field of data, or "cultural facts," I hope to

---

involving subversive as well as dominant voices. Mikhail Bakhtin, *Problems of Dostoevsky's Poetics,*" trans. R.W. Rotsel (Ann Arbor, MI: Ardis, 1973).

[5] Stephen Greenblatt, *Renaissance Self-Fashioning* (Chicago: Chicago UP, 1980) 193-194.

[6] Catherine Belsey, "Towards Cultural History – In Theory and Practice," *New Historicism and Cultural Materialism: A Reader*, ed. Kiernan Ryan (London: Arnold, 1996) 89-90.

establish cultural patterns based on as broad a survey of relevant information as possible.[7]

Although cultural critics pay attention to the importance of material context, they are aware that the context and the subject itself are to a degree indefinable. To quote from Antony Easthope's description of cultural studies: "[...] text and context always slide past each other. Although texts are always read in contexts and within institutions, they always exceed any given context of reading with the power to engage other readings in other contexts."[8] Any attempt to observe a culture represents an objectification of the same and implies the exclusion of other—perhaps contradictory—elements. This study, for instance, concentrates on the phenomena of eating disorders and their literary representations within the context of American women's attitudes towards weight and food; it ignores a variety of other potentially relevant cultural subjects and contexts.[9]

In attempting to establish a social pattern of fat phobia coupled with fattening eating habits, I run the danger of overlooking contradictory phenomena. As mentioned above some evidence of increasing "fat" acceptance belies the dominance of the cult of thinness. This study operates on the premise that despite efforts to fight discrimination against overweight individuals, having a slender body remains an extraordinarily powerful and potentially punishing cultural value for women.

---

[7] "What should in my view most distinguish Cultural *Studies* from such individual readings is that in cultural analysis, meaning is conceived in terms of social patterns of interpretation, which locate any given reading within a larger distribution of other people's different readings." Alan Durant, "Facts and meanings in British Cultural Studies," *Studying British Cultures*, ed. Susan Bassnett (London, 1997) 32.

[8] Antony Easthope, "But what *is* Cultural Studies?" *Studying British Cultures*, ed. Susan Bassnett (London, 1997) 15.

[9] For instance, 5% to 10% of those who suffer from eating disorders are men, and discovering the reasons some men fall prey to these strongly gender-identified illnesses would throw light on Americans' relationship to food and consumption. Other culture-bound syndromes that predominantly affect women could be studied in conjunction with eating disorders, such as cutting, depression, and the chronic fatigue syndrome.

Furthermore, the position of the practitioner of cultural studies is subjective and unsteady. Like the construct called "man" the critical observer is in a constant process of fashioning himself or herself and being fashioned by his or her society.[10] To describe the text and the society around it, the cultural critic must be conscious of her or his limitations. The author of this study is an American who has lived outside of the United States for more than a decade. There is a danger of missing the newest shifts of the geological plates of culture when one does not live on top of the fault lines. Practitioners of cultural studies attempt to balance the foibles of their own subjectively determined powers of observation with an awareness of reception; the issue of whom literary accounts of eating disorders are intended for and who reads them needs to be addressed.[11]

In its diversity and the multiplicity of its sources cultural studies much resembles the American Unitarian Church, in which one may have Catholic, Protestant, Jewish, Agnostic, or Atheist beliefs but still belong. In particular, American cultural studies represents a diverse interdependent field that embraces popular cultural studies, sex and gender studies, regionalist studies, technology studies, ethnicity studies, African-American studies, media studies, among many other subjects. American cultural studies asks questions of what it means to be American, what the myths and scripts are that inform American identity, and searches for the points of conflict within that identity along the

[10] I borrow the term "self-fashioning" from the leading light of new historicism, Stephen Greenblatt, although it has been criticized by cultural materialists for smacking too much of historical pessimism. See Alan Sinfield, "Cultural Materialism, *Othello*, and the Politics of Plausibility" from *Faultlines: Cultural Materialism and the Politics of Dissident Reading* (Oxford: Clarendon Press, 1992) in *New Historicism and Cultural Materialism: A Reader*, ed. Kiernan Ryan (London: Arnold, 1996) 70-71.

[11] "Awareness of the empirical reader must include the person who's doing the cultural analysis, their own investment, how they are seduced by their own work. Cultural studies should always compel attention to subjectivity in terms of the assumed position and point of view of the practitioner. What is the *look* of the sociologist, anthropologist, ethnographer or expert in cultural studies when examining forms of social activity, British horror films of the 1960s, say, or transvestite prostitutes in Rome?" Easthope, "Cultural Studies?" 17.

lines, of sexual preference, gender, race, class, and ethnicity.[12] American cultural studies has been influenced in equal parts by the anti-elitism and post-Marxism of its more ideological British cousin cultural materialism, by the challenge to historical inquiry made by new historicism and post-colonialism, and by the deconstructive and post-modernist understanding of text. Whereas British proponents of cultural criticism often espouse a neo-Gramscian approach to culture and suggest that bourgeois values are perpetuated through economic production and consumption, American proponents commonly adopt a Foucauldian notion of discourse as constituting culture and creating cultural subjects, without any clear cut economic cause and effect.[13] American theorists such as Steven Mailloux advocate a form of rhetorical cultural criticism in which the reception of works such as *Huckleberry Finn* are interrogated in terms of tropes and narratives in order to determine what makes them literary.[14] Others propose more politicized readings of literary texts and cultures on the basis of race or other forms of alterity.[15] Whatever their ideological or political

---

[12] Neil Campbell and Alasdair Kean, *American Cultural Studies: An Introduction to American Culture* (London and New York: Routledge, 1997).

[13] Compare, for example, Catherine Gallagher's and Jeremy Hawthorn's contrasting statements of their reading approaches. Gallagher states: "Although there has been a certain amount of controversy over just what the new historicism is, what constitutes its essence and what its accidents, most of its adherents and opponents would probably agree that it entails reading literary and nonliterary texts as constituents of historical discourses that are both inside and outside of texts and that its practitioners generally posit no fixed hierarchy of cause and effect as they trace the connections among texts, discourses, power, and the constitution of subjectivity." From "Marxism and the New Historicism," *New Historicism and Cultural Materialism: A Reader*, ed. Kiernan Ryan (London: Arnold, 1996) 45. By contrast Hawthorn states: "I started this book by declaring—or confessing—my Marxism. I remain convinced that any serious theory of history needs some conception of the relative strength enjoyed by the myriad possible forces and influences which can direct and determine the path of human society." From *Cunning Passages: New Historicism, Cultural Materialism and Marxism in the Contemporary Literary Debate* (London: Arnold, 1996) 226.

[14] Steven Mailloux, "Rhetorical Hermeneutics as Reception Study: *Huckleberry Finn* and 'The Bad Boy Room'," *Reconceptualizing American Literary/Cultural Studies*, ed. William E. Cain (New York and London: Garland Publishing, 1996).

[15] I mention just two articles whose titles illustrate their having been written from a clearly-articulated cultural position: Cornel West's "The Postmodern Crisis of Black Intellectuals," *American Mythologies*, ed. Marshall Blonsky (New York, Oxford: Oxford UP, 1992) 689-705; and Angie Chabram-Dernesrsesian's " I Throw Punches for My Race, but I Don't Want

framework, cultural critics agree that culture represents a manifold text and process and that an informed reading of a literary text depends on an alertness to context. As Fred Inglis puts it: Cultural studies "is the theory of open-mindedness, and of the honest, even gleeful recognition of the fragmentation of both world and theory which has been generalized as postmodernism."[16]

2.2) Metaphors of Hunger, Society, and Literature: Maud Ellmann's *The Hunger Artists: Starving, Writing, and Imprisonment* and Leslie Heywood's *Dedication to Hunger: The Anorexic Aesthetic in Modern Culture*

This is not the first study to examine a variety of literary texts on eating disorders within the context of contemporary culture. Other studies include Maud Ellmann's *The Hunger Artists: Starving, Writing, and Imprisonment* (1993) and Leslie Heywood's *Dedication to Hunger: The Anorexic Aesthetic in Modern Culture* (1996). I want to describe these studies and discuss how my own reading of eating disorders as cultural artifacts differs from them.

Ellmann prefaces her discussion of the connection between prolific writing and self-starvation with some observations on contemporary American culture. An Irish woman, she reports on the transformation of her leftist formally anti-war American colleagues between the 1960s and the 1970s. In the pattern of the actress-activist turned fitness expert, Jane Fonda, Americans now fight battles against food additives and hidden fats rather than against the jingoistic foreign policy of Richard Nixon. The measure of one's moral fiber, Ellmann asserts, is now calculated by the amount of healthy dietary fiber one takes in. This likening of dietary vigilance to moral worth goes back to a traditional American fear of gluttony and greed. Americans' fascination with achieving

---

to Be a Man: Writing Us—Chica-nos (Girl, Us)/ Chicanas—into the Movement Script." *American Mythologies*, ed. Marshall Blonsky (New York, Oxford: Oxford UP, 1992) 81-103.

perfect bodies finds its equivalent in the great and growing number of texts about the body. Particularly scholars "west of the Rockies"—where the health craze is presumably in greater flower than elsewhere in the States—are guilty of clutching on to the body as a last concrete material entity about which they may write and theorize:

> Indeed, the theorization of the body has become the academic version of the "workout." In criticism, the cult of the body has arisen in defense against poststructuralism, and especially against the fear that "history" and "real life" have been overlooked in favor of a dangerous Gallic fascination with the signifier. In this context the body has come to represent the last bastion of materiality [...].[17]

This assessment of American scholarship on the body and American body fetishism precedes Ellmann's description of the significance of hunger and self-starvation for the Irish, a topic clearly closer to her heart. The Irish, according to Ellmann, have a long tradition of using self-starvation to political ends. A medieval Irish man could fast on the doorstep of the man who owed him money or had injured him in some way as a recognized legal means of forcing him to address the plaintiff's grievances. Similarly, the Irish Hunger Strikers used self-induced fasts as a method of drawing media attention to their plight and trying to get the Thatcher government to recognize them as political prisoners rather than as "common" criminals in 1981.[18] This brief comparison of the history and meanings of self-starvation in the U.S.A. and Ireland lends credit to Ellmann's observation that hunger has a rich variety of meanings and is culturally dependent: "[...] in order to interpret self-starvation it is necessary to explore the cultural milieu in which the ritual occurs."[19]

---

[16] Fred Inglis, *Cultural Studies* (Oxford and Cambridge: Blackwell, 1933) 227-228.
[17] Maud Ellmann, *The Hunger Artists: Starving, Writing, and Imprisonment* (Cambridge, MA: Harvard UP, 1993) 3.
[18] Ellmann, *The Hunger Artists* 12, 71.
[19] Ellmann 7.

This statement might lead the reader to expect that a synchronic study of literary accounts of hunger, arising out of the Irish and American cultures respectively, will follow. Instead, Ellmann goes on to conduct an ahistorical exploration of the metaphor of hunger and writing. Her thesis is that writers starve to write. The more a writer fasts, the fatter the book he or she will produce. This pattern holds true, whether the authorial body is a fictional one, as in the case of Clarissa Harlowe from Samuel Richardson's novel of the same name (1747-8), or an actual one, as in the case of the Hunger Striker Bobby Sands. While Clarissa's body begins to dwindle away after she has been raped and is in confinement, her communications become steadily more prolific. Similarly, the Hunger Strikers, for whom correspondence was forbidden, wrote more and more *comms* (communications) to each other and to individuals outside of prison as their fast escalated into self-starvation: "Like Clarissa, their starvation generated a peculiarly prolific and rapacious literature, where words rushed in to fill the emptiness that food might occupy."[20]

After exploring the connection between bloated texts and emaciated authors in works by Keats, Yeats, and others, Ellmann adds another component to her analysis of metaphorical relations. She reiterates Foucault's thesis that the concept of individual selfhood was invented during the seventeenth and eighteenth centuries, just as orphans, criminals, and the insane were being incarcerated and institutionalized for the first time in history. Hence discursive practices of the self coincide with the inception of disciplinary institutions: "To be a person is to be a prison, this historical coincidence suggests."[21] Ellmann completes her exploration of "*dis*embodiment [of] writing and starvation as the arts of discarnation"[22] with the claim that imprisonment strengthens the relationship between loquacity and fasting. She sees this as a feature of literary texts, whether they are contemporary American, such as Mary Gordon's *Final*

[20] Ellmann 83.
[21] Ellmann 94.

Payments (1978) or contemporary South African, such as *Life and Times of Michael K* (1983), or from the Victorian English period, such as Emily Brontë's *Wuthering Heights* (1847). In effect, Ellmann's thematic analysis of self-starvation runs completely counter to her opening claim that hunger must be viewed within its cultural context.

Nonetheless, Ellmann's theory that texts grow voluminous while authorial flesh diminishes bears scrutiny. This thesis is illustrated by Ellmann's analysis of *Final Payments*. Isabel, the American Catholic heroine, seeks to exonerate her guilt for her father's death and for an affair with a married man. She does so by making amends with the person she hates most—the conniving housekeeper, who had hoped to become her widowed father's second wife until Isabel had her fired. After a confrontation with her lover's wife, Isabel decides to live with the housekeeper. She proceeds to eat herself into a state of obliviousness and passivity, while the housekeeper displays overt hostility towards her. Only when Isabel begins to communicate with the outside world again does she stop bingeing. She recognizes that she must first lose the flesh she has insulated her feelings with before she may resume communications with her lover. In Isabel's case being hungry and being able to express herself appear to be correlated states.

As I wrote in the introduction, more novelistic accounts of anorexia are available than of bulimia or binge eating. This fact seems to lend credence to Ellmann's claim that a wealth of words exists where there is a lack of flesh. However, it is not clear whether the connection between the wealth of literature on female self-starvation rests on an inherent coupling of words and weightlessness or on the cultural fascination with thinness.

Whereas the central thesis of Ellmann's study is skinny writer = fat book, the main idea of Leslie Heywood's examination of the connection between anorexia and cultural aesthetic is skinny woman = skinny text. The contrast

---

[22] Ellmann 4.

between these two equations provides an interesting commentary on the metaphorical richness of images of flesh and text in Western culture.

The poem "Dedication to Hunger" provides one of the central examples for Heywood's thesis. Heywood reads the fourth and fifth stanza of the poem as a metaphor for American culture (printed in chapter II, section 2.5.2 above). The speaker of the poem compares her youthful desire to rid herself of female flesh with her artistic aims as a poet. Heywood believes that the desire to pare words down to spare perfection results from Western culture's denial of the value of feminine fat, subjectivity, and irrationality. She writes:

> The convergence between "perfecting" the body and perfecting a structure of words marks a dense set of cultural assumptions about language, gender, subjectivity, and identity that stand as a constitutive problem in the lives of many women who struggle to keep "legs attached to [...] hip" while living with the awareness that they "could wake up any day and find [themselves] in pieces." That act of writing has given me some freedom from the grip of anorexic cultural scripts, and I will feel this work is successful if it inspires others to write their own versions.[23]

The second sentence of the quotation brings the most interesting and problematic aspect of Heywood's study of cultural anorexia into focus. She uses autobiographical experience to illustrate how the pervasive anorexic code affects individual women's lives. Thus the fact that she was raped at sixteen by her track coach, had anorexia, adopted a "masculine" critical voice in her academic work, and was kissed inappropriately by a professor are experiences that she understands to be exemplary for all women in patriarchal culture.

Heywood's profoundly autobiographical style may strike the reader as megalomaniac. Her aims are programmatic: She wishes to reform academic practices to include fleshy subjective "feminine" voices and to destroy those cultural scripts that make women anorexic. For instance, she wants to combat

---

[23] Leslie Heywood, *Dedication to Hunger: The Anorexic Aesthetic in Modern Culture* (Berkeley: California UP, 1996) xiii.

the "anorexic logic" of academia that relegates many students, most of them women, to a position of frustrated "self-abasement."[24] This self-abasement results from their not being able to master the dominant form of academic debate, a form "that is articulated in terms of conquest, domination, or simple one-upmanship."[25]

This combination of terms sounds like a summary of the leitmotifs of the post-colonial critique of the discourse and practices of imperialism.[26] Heywood voices resistance to dominant forms of discourse, which she associates with the denial of non-linear, fleshy, feminine experience. In a, perhaps, exaggerated attempt to be politically correct Heywood includes African Americans, homosexuals, Latinos, Asians and the poor in her definition of potential anorectics—those who deny the bodily self, those who suffer from a "poverty of self-definition."[27] This global definition of anorexia can be criticized for its lack of specificity and for its implicit condescension to those African Americans, gays, lesbians, and Asians who do not consider themselves "anorexic."

Heywood begins her book with a cultural critique in which the abnegation of flesh is traced back to the philosophy of Plato, Descartes, and Hegel, and the psychology of Freud. These thinkers argued for the superiority

---

[24] Heywood, 58.

[25] "[...] we need to change the paradigm that dictates education in general—the ways of reading, writing, and thinking about ideas—so that women and men who are uncomfortable articulating themselves according to male models can really feel they have entered the academy as more than masculine imitations, more than Hegel's "impotent shadows." Heywood 58.

[26] For seminal texts on the discursive objectification of the foreign and exotic other, see Edward Said's *Orientalism* (London: Routledge & Kegan Paul, 1978): "In a quite constant way, Orientalism depends for its strategy on this flexible *positional* superiority, which puts the Westerner in a whole series of possible relationships with the Orient without ever losing him the relative upper hand" (6); and Gayatri Chakravorty Spivak, "Can the Subaltern Speak?" from *Marxism and the Interpretation of Culture*, eds. C. Nelson and L. Gross (1988) in *Colonial Discourse and Post-Colonial Theory: A Reader*, ed. Patrick Williams and Laura Chrisman (New York: Harvester Wheatsheaf, 1993) "The clearest available example of such epistemic violence is the remotely orchestrated, far-flung, and heterogeneous project to constitute the colonial subject as Other. This project is also the asymmetrical obliteration of the trace of that Other in its precarious Subject-ivity" (76).

[27] Heywood 33.

of the ratio to sensuous bodily experience, and anticipated or adopted the Judeo-Christian equation of woman with sin. Heywood follows the path of this "anorexic logic" into the present and discovers the imperative to deny female flesh in cultural artifacts as diverse as Nike advertisements for sporting goods, the film *Silence of the Lambs* (1991), Imagist poetry, and modernist prose. In the first chapter she offers a sophisticated analysis of how Nike advertisements directed at women appear to encourage a sense of positive individual embodiment but really sell the idea that self-actualization can only be attained by conforming to a uniform ideal of slenderness. Implicitly, such advertisements suggest that the ideal can only be achieved through the purchase and use of a variety of Nike sporting goods.[28]

Via a reading of Glück's "Dedication to Hunger," Heywood moves on to examine the anorexia she understands as informing modernist poetry. Most significantly for her thesis, Heywood observes how the speaker in Glück's poem compares purging herself of flesh with her poetic activity. The speaker perfects her writing as she once tried to perfect her body: "I stood apart in that achievement, / in that power to expose / the underlying body, like a god / for whose deed / there is no parallel in the natural world." For Heywood, Glück's equation of physical anorexia with mental perfection and godlike power represents a common cultural construct:

> By connecting masculinity, activity, and aesthetics on the one hand and femininity, passivity, and bodily flesh on the other, Glück calls attention to a narrative we all have too readily accepted. The fierce detachment of the narrative voice is the expression of an equally fierce pain, which comes from what the logic of renunciation has encouraged us to will into our flesh, what it has encouraged us to shape our bodies into. In accepting the cultural narrative that makes bodily renunciation heroic and masculine, we try to make ourselves more powerful, "godlike," in a way that destroys us.[29]

---

[28] Heywood 31-34.
[29] Heywood 48.

Heywood finds the roots of this "cultural narrative" in the poetry of T.S. Eliot, William Carlos Williams, and Ezra Pound as well as in Franz Kafka's and Joseph Conrad's prose. She equates these authors' stylistic strategy of paring away unnecessary fluff from their imagery with a hatred of female flesh and a profound fear of emotion and ambiguity. Hence Kafka's description of his need to diet in order to write and Pound's characterization of himself as delivering *The Waste Land* by Ceasarean section—by stripping it of excess—are read as indications of how modernist writers have informed the current cultural distaste for feminine fat and textual surplus.[30] Heywood's commitment to this line of reasoning leads her at times to articulate statements, which—if one can retain one's sense of humor—read like parodies of so-called female irrationality. One example is her argument: "The 'great books' that have provided us with our cultural heritage and 'meaning' have also given us anorexia." The logic of this statement is that if great books inform the cultural heritage and if this culture is anorexic, then great books have created anorexia. I hope that the second chapter of this study has convincingly argued that the causes of anorexia and other eating disorders are myriad and complexly interrelated.

According to Heywood, the West Indian novelist Jean Rhys and her character Antoinette/Bertha from *Wide Sargasso Sea* (1966) provide an antidote to the white, male, misogynist modernist poet. Heywood argues that women are relegated to "nonbeing" in our male-identified culture, just as Antoinette was forced to disappear into the attic of Thornfield Hall, and Rhys was neglected as a dangerous and powerful voice in literature. Like the contemporary anorectic, who makes misguided attempts to realize herself by renouncing her flesh, Antoinette burns down Thornfield Hall in an effort to free herself from her person and her environment.

---

[30] See Heywood's discussion of Kafka's journal entry from 3 January 1912 (71) and of Pound's letter to Eliot about the birthing process of *The Waste Land* (85).

I certainly agree with Heywood that an anorexic aesthetic determines preferences for the female body in contemporary American culture. Obviously, perpetual dieting and compulsive sport activities belong to this cultural obsession with thinness. However, I cannot share Heywood's conviction that "anorexic logic" extends to all art forms, discursive practices, and inter-gender relations.

One of the problems of her study is that it advertises itself as post-structuralist but persists in a logical dualism regarding the use of "masculine" and "feminine." In Heywood's argumentation, the feminine is consistently associated with fleshiness, subjectivity, underdogs in discursive practices, and with authenticity. The masculine, by contrast, is associated with the rigorous logic that denies fleshy subjectivity. As Heywood writes about the "The Fire Sermon" section of *The Waste Land*: "Eliot's urge to 'trim the fat' from bodies, textual or otherwise, is a desire to cut out and discard this extra, to reject the feminine as body to affirm the masculine body."[31] This is problematic for two reasons. One, as in Jungian studies of anorexia discussed in chapter two, essential femininity is associated with bodily experience and masculinity with a linear logic that abnegates the somatic. Two, the so-called feminine always wins in the contest for authenticity. By implication, only literary works in which no paring away occurs are positively subjective and feminine. By this account one would have to question not only the worth of modernist works by white male authors, but also that of the non-canonical "Dedication to Hunger," which was obviously written with a selective eye and ear. As the author of *The New York Times* review of Heywood's book argues, if Eliot's trimming the fat involves an abnegation of the feminine and the subjective then so does even Rhys's art: "By this logic, however, all art is anorexic—and misogynistic. After all, all art is

[31] Heywood 89.

about selection and choice, all art is about making some sort of order out of chaos." [32]

The present study aims to go beyond Ellmann's and Heywood's analyses of literary disorders and modern culture by offering an overview of a far wider range of both poetic and prose texts and performing a more far-reaching analysis of their cultural functions. Like Heywood I concentrate on American culture as a basis for understanding contemporary literary treatments of eating disorders. Yet I do not rely on one central metaphor to illuminate the relationship between eating disorders and literary texts. I strongly disagree with the thesis that the aesthetic of modernism has led to the proliferation of anorexia.

Contrary to Ellmann and Heywood I want to demonstrate how literary accounts of eating disorders comment upon cultural patterns at large. I argue that these accounts belong to the genre of "confessional" literature. The confessional style was evident in the manner in Heywood's use of her personal history to illuminate larger theoretical constructs. Challenging traditional values of distance and impersonality in theoretical writing, her work provides an illustration of the trend toward confessionalism in American critical theory.

2.3) Writings about Starvation and Gorging as Forms of Confession

The term "confessional" was coined by M.L. Rosenthal in 1959 to describe the autobiographical quality of Robert Lowell's writing in *Life Studies* (1959). Rosenthal stresses the embarrassingly personal nature of Lowell's self-revelations: "His speaker is unequivocally himself, and it is hard not to think of *Life Studies* as a series of personal confidences, rather shameful, that one is honor-bound not to reveal."[33] Later Rosenthal used "confessional" to describe

[32] Michiko Kakutani, "Fear of Fat as the Bane of Modernism," *New York Times*, 12 March 1996: 15 (C).
[33] "Poetry as Confession: *Life Studies* by Robert Lowell," *The Nation*, 10 September 1959; reprinted in M.L. Rosenthal, *Our Life in Poetry: Selected Essays and Reviews* (New York: Persea Books, 1991) 109.

the work of Sylvia Plath, Anne Sexton, W.D. Snodgrass, and John Berryman as well. The term has come to descriptive for the work of many poets of the sixties whose writing probed their negative psychological experiences.

In succeeding works such as *The Modern Poetic Sequence: The Genius of Modern Poetry* (1983), Rosenthal elaborates on his definition of "confessional writing." In regard to Robert Lowell, his key example, he writes:

> The shift to confessional poetry from writing like this [from Auden's "Sonnets from China"] is a simple one: to the attempt to present the poet's own naked self and unrationalized, uncensored actual feelings and behavior. [...] The chaos of the psychic situation becomes the ground of a reoriented art in which the beset self is the testing-ground and embodiment of all human possibilities. The terrors, pains, early miseries, regrets, vexation, and lassitudes that Wordsworth suffered are now the main proofs of one's existence; the degree of their intensity confirms their (and our) reality. The artistic problem is to make a genuine poetry out of the language of untrammeled self-awareness [...].
>
> The passion for this sort of disturbed awareness is characteristic of the modern sensibility in many ways—reticence and social "decency" sacrificed to acutely observant frankness [...].
>
> We are talking about poetry, of course, not gossiping about Lowell. The problem we have been discussing generates a certain resistance to confessional poetry, which cannot succeed unless it gets beyond merely talking about oneself. If the details of one's private life become something more, poetically, the reason will be the affective language resonating, through the poem. In the process "oneself" (Robert Lowell, the Irish poet Austin Clarke, Allen Ginsberg, W.D. Snodgrass, Sylvia Plath, John Berryman, Anne Sexton) operates like any other dominating symbol in the work. That is, "I" becomes something other through the medium that absorbs its association; it becomes a magnetic cohesive center for all the emotional and subjective currents running through the work.[34]

The most important points of this characterization of confessional poetry are as follows: 1) The naked, uncensored self is at the center of the poem; in the word "naked" the importance of bodily detail is expressed. 2) The individual's psychological state is the background of the artwork and demarcates the limits of human experience. This artistic sensibility contrasts with T.S. Eliot's theory of the universality of the poetic work, which may be achieved only if the artist's immerses himself in cultural tradition.[35] Here the particularity of individual experience is the measure of all things. 3) The use of "affective language" determines whether the text is literary or not. 4) Due to psychic pain or physical duress the confessional poet presents a subjectively distorted vision and is solipsistic. 5) The confessional poet's solipsism and his need to reveal intimate details of his personal life mirror wider societal trends. In this last observation Rosenthal predates Foucault's characterization of modern man as a confessional animal in *The History of Sexuality* (1980).

That we live in a culture of compulsive confession may be seen in the media's attention to the foibles of public figures. The press demands that a public personality confess his or her wrongs and be punished or forgiven. Much public scorn was directed towards Queen Elizabeth and Prince Charles because they did not grieve openly enough after Princess Diana's death or publicly admit that they had treated her shabbily. Two standards of public behavior came into conflict with respect to perceptions of the Royals' behavior. According to the stiff-upper-lip school of behavior, one should express violent emotions such as grief in private. According to the Oprah-Winfrey-talk show school of decorum, no emotion is an emotion unless it is expressed publicly and violently.

In the United States outrage at the media for over-reporting the Lewinsky scandal was matched by a seemingly insatiable desire for more details. The celebrity-interviewer Barbara Walter's televised questioning of Monica Lewinsky in March 1999 enjoyed "superbowl" ratings and revealed, in case

---

[34] M. L. Rosenthal and Sally M. Gall, *The Modern Poetic Sequence* (New York and Oxford: Oxford UP, 1983) 393-394.

[35] "What is to be insisted upon is that the poet must develop or procure the consciousness of the past and that he should continue to develop this consciousness throughout his career.

What happens is a continual surrender of himself as he is at the moment to something which is more valuable. The progress of an artist is a continual self-sacrifice, a continual

anyone did not already know, that Lewinsky had suffered from a depression, has always struggled with her weight, and had had an abortion.[36] *Monica's Story* (1999), co-authored by the Lady Diana biographer Andrew Morton, promised to give the former White House intern the celebrity status of the beautiful dead princess.[37] The logic of confessionalism is one of infinite regression. The farther one delves into the juicy details of visceral life—preferably that of a celebrity—the more truth about that individual shall be known. The confession of bodily details may confer short-lived celebrity on ordinary individuals such as Monica Lewinsky. In the aftermath of her public testimony every tape-recorded word about her relations with Clinton was made the object of endless speculation and interpretation. Hence one *New Yorker* reviewer wrote about Lewinky's various confessions: "Every morsel of scandal language—'creep,' 'pulkes,' 'knee-pads,' 'schmucko'—has been parsed as thoroughly as 'The Fairie Queene.'"[38] The public searches such testimony of the banal for insight into the essence of Lewinsky and Clinton's liason. The act of testifying itself seems to make events more meaningful.

A recent German novel comments on the pressure to tell one's story in America in fictional terms. *Briefe aus Amerika* (Letters from America, 1999) describes the experiences of a young German academician, who unwittingly begins a romance with the president's daughter while he is teaching at a prestigious university:

> I think, therefore I am. The sentence is absolutely false and contrary to every reality as far as the individual person is concerned. Today the sentence would have to read: I tell my story, therefore I am. The world tells my story, therefore I am all the more, no matter whether the story is true or

---

extinction of personality." T.S. Eliot, "Tradition and the Individual Talent," *Twentieth-Century Literary Criticism: A Reader*, ed. David Lodge (1919; London: Longman, 1972) 73.

[36] Mark Hosenball and Barbara Kantrowitz, "Ready for Her Close-Up," *Newsweek*, 15 March 1999: 20.

[37] Carla Power, et al., "Monica Madness," *Newsweek*, 22 March 1999: 89.

[38] David Remnick, "Our Lady of Secrets," *The New Yorker*, 8 February 1999: 23.

> completely fictitious. The greater the others' notions are, as long as they are about me, the greater my story will be, the greater I myself will be, therefore, I am, I thought, and I bought countless numbers of newspapers and read my story in them. [39]

A voyeuristic interest in the secrets, illnesses, sexual peccadilloes, and deviant behavior of public figures can be documented in a perusal of magazines such as *People Weekly* or any celebrity tabloid. The interest in what was once considered too personal to print appears endless. Christopher Lasch suggests that narcissistic culture has turned into a culture of shamelessness, that "the only thing forbidden in our culture of exposure is the inclination to forbid—to set limits on disclosure."[40]

The compulsion to testify is noticeable in many avenues in American life. It has become something of a medial trope for American sports figures to confess to having abused their wives or drugs or alcohol, to do some public penance—be briefly incarcerated or pay a large fine—and then to return to athletic glory. Many poems cited in the previous chapter were quoted from web sites. Such sites fulfill the need many individuals have to testify about their ills and pains.

In American social theory and literary criticism, autobiographical criticism is taking on more and more relevance. In part this movement away from the values of impersonality and distance stems from the feminist motto of the seventies that personal experience is the basis for informed political action

[39] "Ich denke, also bin ich. Der Satz ist völlig falsch und gegen jede Wirklichkeit, soweit sie den einzelnen Mensch angeht. Heute muß es heißen: Ich erzähle meine Geschichte, also bin ich. Die Welt erzählt meine Geschichte, also bin ich um so mehr, egal ob sie nun wahr oder frei erfunden ist. Je größer die Einfälle anderer, solange sie nur mir gelten, desto größer ist meine Geschichte, desto größer bin ich selbst, also bin ich, dachte ich, und kaufte unzählige Zeitungen und las darin meine Geschichte" [trans. mine]. Joachim Zelter, *Briefe aus Amerika* (Stuttgart: Ithaka Verlag, 1998) 143-144.

[40] Christopher Lasch, "For Shame: Why Americans Should Be Wary of Self-Esteem," *New Republic*, 10 August 1992: 29, quoted in Madeleine Sorapure, "Representing Shame," *Writing Lives: American Biography and Autobiography*, ed. Hans Bak and Hans Krabbendam (Amsterdam: VU UP, 1998) 106.

and, hence, that the bodily life has a place in theoretical practice.[41] As overriding explanatory systems such as Christianity and Marxism have been challenged, smaller and less global ordering systems have replaced them. No longer does some grand anonymous objective mind make the text at hand accessible to the reader but a single situated critic. Thus the post-colonial critic Gayatri Spivak writes of having to place her identity in a variety of contexts: as a woman, as an Indian, as an ethnic Hindi, as a professor of color.[42] Stephen Greenblatt finishes his account of the Renaissance creation of self with an anecdote about how he was interrupted while reading Geertz's text on cultural relativity on a plane. This anecdote leads him to express his own problematic need to believe in his own autonomy and ability to actualize himself despite his increasing awareness of his cultural relativity.[43] Laura Fraser prefaces her mud-slinging exposé of the American weight loss industry with an account of her own battles with her weight and resultant bulimia.[44] An attestation of one's personal stake in a topic has become a reflex in much academic writing.[45]

I want to differentiate between confessional writing and the informed use of the authorial "I." I see the two as unrelated. The first foregrounds the body as anecdotal evidence for the writer's commitment to his or her subject. The body—to return to Ellmann's argument—is the "last bastion of materiality"

---

[41] Diane P. Freedman, "Autobiographical Literary Criticism as the New Belletrism: *Personal Experience*," *Confessions of the Critics*, ed. H. Aram Veeser (New York and London: Routledge, 1996) 8.

[42] Gayatri Chakravorty Spivak, "Lives," *Confessions of the Critics*, ed. H. Aram Veeser (New York and London: Routledge, 1996) 205.

[43] Stephen Greenblatt, *Renaissance Self-Fashioning*, 255-257.

[44] Fraser's dieting career, which began when she was in kindergarten and ended in bulimic excess, made her want to write about the hypocrisy and duplicitous methods of the American dieting industry. Laura Fraser, "Introduction in Dietland," *Losing It: America's Obsession with Weight and the Industry that Feeds on It* (New York: Dutton, 1997) 1-15.

[45] This trend has been contested. Note the ambivalence surrounding the usage of the word "confessional" in the following announcement for a call for papers. The author asks: "How does a 'scholar' and critic write the autobiographical essay that explores his/her identify while being more than 'merely' confessional? How do we negotiate the 'confessional' aspects of our own life-story in our academic lives and identities?" Kim Wells, "CFP: Autobiography, the Scholar, and The Essay," 8 April 2000 <http:// www-english.tamu.edu/egsa/icol/>.

critics can hold on to.[46] Avoiding the first-person singular in academic texts so as to appear unbiased or to avoid a discussion of the selection process involved in making one's argument may be an obfuscating and dated practice. One can be held more accountable for one's thought and selections if one refers to one's research process in the first person.[47]

Describing American culture's abundance of personal testimony may sound moralistic. It echoes James Atlas's condemnation of confessional literature as "dwelling on the sordid excesses of the self."[48] Instead, I wish to ask what the roots of current confessional practices are and why these forms of expression have become so popular.

Michel Foucault argues in *The History of Sexuality* (1980) that confession has gone from being an exclusively Christian practice to being the leading psychological, medical, and literary one: "Western man has become a confessing animal," he asserts.[49] Foucault demonstrates how confessional techniques have contributed to the development of the modern subject. Disciplinary techniques used in producing productive and disciplined "docile

[46] "Like a naked body intruded into a group of clothed ones, an allusion to the public, private life we have in common is overwhelming: the sign itself packs so much of a wallop that it obliterates what it means to illustrate or indicate. If intruding the body, the banal, the bit of familiar scandal, or the merely personal was once a useful political strategy that served to dramatize and correct the pretensions of 'formal' or 'male' or 'traditional' academic discourse, it now threatens to foreclose thought. It also contributes to the political atmosphere of invasiveness, staged confession, and 'outing,' the insistence on the sexual or sociological fact of life that blots out everything else." Rachel Brownstein, "Interrupted Reading: Personal Criticism in the Present Time," *Confessions of the Critics*, ed. H. Aram Veeser (New York and London: Routledge, 1996) 37.

[47] "My advice to authors is to step out from behind the curtain and write in a straightforward style that identifies the real author of an article as he or she moves through each of the stages of an investigation. It is not easy to develop a voice that is identifiable and consistent, but authors who do so will become known for the quality of their communication, as well as the quality of their scholarship. Writing in an accessible style will also enhance the peer-review process, as reviewers can more accurately assign responsibility for major decisions in a piece or work and raise appropriate questions." Gary Natriello, "The Author's Voice: Revealing the Person behind the Curtain," *Teachers College Record* 99, no. 4 (Summer 1998): 620.

[48] James Atlas, "Confessing to Voyeurs," quoted in Sorapure, "Representing Shame," 106.

[49] Michel Foucault, *The History of Sexuality: Volume 1: An Introduction*, trans. Robert Hurley (New York: Vintage Books, 1980) 59.

bodies"[50] are based on the notion that the body of the insane person, the criminal, or the diseased individual can be broken down into measurable discrete parts.[51] The body itself becomes a form of signification. This measurable body requires the interpretive gaze of the psychiatrist, criminologist, or the doctor to be deciphered and understood.

A vital contribution to the process of interpreting deviance is provided by the individual's confession of insanity, crime, or disease—in other words of secrets of the body. Disclosures of bodily weakness, particularly of sexual nature, were the traditional subject of religious confessions. Beginning in the sixteenth century, confession was transformed from a technique for disciplining the conscience to the leading mode of discipline in child rearing, medicine and psychiatry.[52] Increasingly, the external controls on individuals through figures of authority have been transferred to the individual, who has learnt to monitor him- or herself constantly and to report on this process to doctors and psychiatrists. By willingly confessing to some form of transgression against accepted behavior codes, individuals serve to uphold the status quo. And their confessors may take voyeuristic pleasure in the confessed deviance.

In writings by eating-disordered women the revelation of fleshy weakness also represents the central theme. Foucault describes this revelation process as the leitmotif of modern literature:

> Whence a metamorphosis in literature: we have passed from a pleasure to be recounted and heard, centering on the heroic or marvelous narration of 'trials' of bravery or sainthood, to a literature ordered according to the

---

[50] Michel Foucault, "Docile Bodies" from *Discipline and Punish: The Birth of the Prison*, trans. Alan Sheridan (New York: Pantheon Books, 1979) in *The Foucault Reader*, ed. Paul Rabinow (New York: Pantheon Books, 1984) 180.

[51] "And by that very fact, clinical experience sees a new space opening up before it: the tangible space of the body, which at the same time is that opaque mass in which secrets, invisible lesions, and the very mystery of origins lie hidden." Michel Foucault, *The Birth of the Clinic: An Archaeology of Medical Perception*, trans. A.M. Sheridan Smith (New York: Vintage Books, 1994) 122.

[52] Foucault, *History* 68.

> infinite task of extracting from the depths of oneself, in between the words, a truth which the very form of the confession holds out like a shimmering mirage.[53]

Whereas Foucault regards sex and deviant sexuality as the primary subject of modern confession, the weakness of the flesh is construed in texts on eating disorders to be one of uncontrolled appetite rather than sexual desire. Foucault also argues that the proliferation of discourse about abnormal physical and psychological behavior has contributed to the establishment of new institutions to treat "abnormal" individuals, such as asylums, clinics, orphanages, and prisons. Confessional techniques then contribute both to the classification and generation of new types of deviance and to the growth of institutions to correct and control these abnormalities.

In the extended narratives discussed in this study, being hospitalized in one of these new types of institutions, the eating disorder clinic, plays a significant role. The experiences the anorexic or bulimic woman has there are not necessarily healing but they are profound. Hospitalization provides the narrative frame of the novels *Life-Size* and *The Passion of Alice*. Being admitted to the hospital at 52 pounds represents the end of the events that Hornbacher relates retrospectively in *Wasted: A Memoir of Anorexia and Bulimia*.

If one accepts Foucault's theory that discourses produced at a given time serve to justify the *epistemé* (knowledge system) out of which they arise, one might argue that the narratives described here help to legitimate the existence of eating disorder clinics and the creation of new kinds of therapies to treat the ever-expanding repertoire of eating disorders. The disclosure of the narrator's sin, disordered eating, and her realization that her obsessive thoughts and ritualistic behavior concerning food and her body have been self-destructive, are

---

[53] Foucault, *History* 59.

brought together in these lengthy confessions in which the clinic and therapeutic discourse play central parts.[54]

In an amplification on and a critique of Foucault's analysis of confession, the sociologists Mike Hepworth and Bryan Turner have pointed out the following: 1) Confession belongs to the system of Western beliefs that rests on the notion of individual responsibility, guilt, and redemption. 2) It is important not to concentrate exclusively on deviant individuals in an analysis of confession—as Foucault does— because confessional practices serve primarily as a form of social control. Private conscience is linked to the public or divine order when the criminal confesses his or her crime to the police, when the patient confesses his or her ailment to a medical authority, or when the penitent individual confesses her sin to a priest. Confessions are generally made to authority figures and have some public consequences. If one applies this insight to literary confessions, the question of how confessional texts are received and by whom becomes central: Literary absolution may only occur if a sympathetic reader responds to the confession, hence giving it significance. 3) The Christian practice of confession has been adopted in Freudian psychoanalysis in the belief that there is an intimate connection between physical illness and the need to do penance for some wrong:

> [...] spiritual confession has traditionally and persistently been connected with physical and mental healing. [...] The notion that illness is produced by guilt for transgressions of moral regulations and that confession will simultaneously restore health by restoring group membership appears to be a perennial component of western culture.[55]

---

[54] For Foucault's most elaborated discussion of how discursive practices operate, see *The Archaeology of Knowledge*, trans. A.M. Sheridan Smith (New York: Harper Colophon, 1972). One has to be careful about interpreting narratives on eating disorders as supporting the disciplinary institutions they describe. More like Ken Kesey's *One Flew Over the Cuckoo's Nest* (1962), the novels and memoir described here are extremely critical of these institutions and the authority figures who have power there.

[55] Mike Hepworth and Bryan Turner, *Confession: Studies in Deviance and Society* (1982) 84.

Confessional practices inform many psychological practices: By uncovering the ugly secrets of the past some truth of self will be revealed and the pain of the secrecy or denial may be overcome. This is the tenor of the advice given to women in one self-help guide, which counsels readers to surmount their problems with food by delving into the bodily secrets of the past:

> Many women have had to reveal secret horrors of molestation, rape, and incest so they could be free of the humiliation and self-loathing secret-keeping brings. [...] As a woman finds the center of herself in this journey toward wholeness, she encounters her deepest pain: the pain of abandonment and isolation, of feeling unworthy and inept, of unrealized dreams and missed opportunities, of physical or emotional abuse, of the loss of loved ones or failed marriages, and the pain that comes with being female in a world that does not honor the feminine.[56]

The notion that informs this type of psychological inquiry is that painful events, particularly those that affect the body, are more significant to the creation and evolution of the self than joyous or non-bodily ones. In modern psychology and in much contemporary writing, the revelation of secrets, particularly bodily ones, stands at the center of experience.

Regarding prose fiction, the genre of "confessional" writing has been documented in various ways. Peter Axthelm published an account of "modern existentialist confessional" novels in 1967, which concentrates on the importance of Dostoevsky's *Notes from the Underground* (1864) to the genre. According to Axthelm the confessional novel is characterized by several criteria, the most important of which is the "hero's" perception and presentation of himself as sick or in some manner unbalanced.[57] Contrary to the Promethean hero, the confessional one does not rebel against his circumstances but regards

---

[56] Anita A. Johnston, *Eating in the Light of the Moon: How Women Can Let Go of Compulsive Eating through Metaphor and Storytelling* (Secaucus, N.J.: Birch Lane Press, 1996) 134.

[57] Axthelm's exclusive use of "hero" and masculine pronouns reveals that his text is, at least sociologically and linguistically, dated.

himself as the source of his painful condition: "His suffering originates not in the chaos of the world but in the chaos within the self, and for him the only possible order or value must be found in self-understanding."[58] The hero's confession usually transpires in a small room, or cell, reminiscent of the church confessional. This insight recalls Ellmann's thesis that incarceration is conducive to voluminous expression. Experimental methods are used to portray the confessional process, journalistic style or the police interrogation. The confessional novel differs from the stream-of-consciousness novels of Joyce and Faulkner in that the selection process is made evident in the prose; the hero relates the painful events of his past in the order of their relative importance to him. The narrative voice is often ironic. This irony helps to maintain distance between the author and the hero. Furthermore, doubles are often introduced as mirror figures to the hero. Lastly, the narrative structure copies that of religious confession and Augustine's *Confessions*: Through purgation in the form of the narration of painful life events absolution may be achieved. For the confessional protagonist, this absolution has nothing to do with faith or religious repentance. Rather, a heightened level of self-perception is achieved.

I adopt several of Axthelm's criteria to describe confessional writing. In the extended narratives discussed here the narrators are identical with the suffering self, the object of narrative interest. No division exists between the implied author and the protagonist as in the novels Axthelm describes. Similar to the confessional novels he studies, irony plays an important role in *Life-Size*, *The Passion of Alice,* and *Wasted.* Hornbacher satirizes the society that encouraged her to become so ill and pokes fun at her own unhealthy attitudes. About her idealization of illness and emaciation, she wryly comments: "Dying is also very exciting. It's a pity I didn't notice it sooner."[59]

---

[58] Peter Axthelm, *The Modern Confessional Novel* (New Haven: Yale UP, 1967) 9.
[59] Hornbacher, *Wasted* 244.

Yet the *doppelgänger* plays a far less important role in these texts than in the ones Axthelm analyses. Instead, actual mirrors and the process of seeing one's own reflection are central interests. Self-worth is determined on the basis of what the eating-disordered woman thinks she sees. If she believes she looks fat she binges (like the speakers of "The Bulimic Experience" and "The Angel That Feeds Me") or is full of self-loathing (like the narrator of *Wasted*). If she believes she appears thin, she feels reassured of who she is (Josie of *Life-Size* and Alice of *The Passion of Alice*).

Rosalind Coward takes a different tack than Axthelm in her exploration of confessional writing. In an article on the abuse of the word "feminist" in the marketing of women-centered fiction she calls those novels "confessional" in which female experience is reduced to libidinal adventure. Coward notes that many novels were being advertised in the 1970s and 1980s as being "feminist" because they related how middle-class women emerged from the home, had their consciousness raised, and experimented sexually. In these novels erotic self-discovery constitutes narrative epiphany. Best-selling novels like Marilyn French's *The Women's Room* (1979) and Lisa Alther's *Kinflicks* (1976) were reputed to "change lives" and were called "feminist" because they allegedly revealed some universal truth about feminine experience:

> A dominant element in contemporary fiction has been that of the 'confessional' novel – the structuring of the novel, and the significant events of the narrative, around the voice of a principal protagonist describing her/his life [...]. For this structure has increasingly been characterized by the absolute centrality given to the experience of adolescence and young adulthood. In particular the experiences of this period have come to be almost synonymous with sexual experience.
> [...] But where women have been, and are, the central focus of the novel, a variation occurs. That variation is that the only space where knowledge or understanding for women is produced is across sexual experience—love, marriage, divorce, or just sex. [...] Indeed, it could be argued that the emergence of this particular form of 'women's writing,' with its emphasis on sexual experience as the source of significant experience, might have

> the effect of confirming women as bearers of sentiment, experience, and romance (albeit disillusioned).[60]

Written almost twenty years ago, Coward's description still bears true for many women's novels in which sexuality is treated as the defining experience. The sexual act stands at the center of narrative events as an ordering principle, as love or marriage form the center of more traditional romance fiction. Novels in which the heroine's growth occurs when she comes to realize herself sexually—put more blatantly, when she learns how to have a multiple orgasm—remain popular and represent a niche in the novel market. In much fiction marketed specifically to women, Virginia Woolf's claim that the truth of female experience can only be told if the truth of the female body is written about honestly[61] is turned into a form of fetishism. Testimony of sexual experience is held to be relevant; the non-visceral remains ignored.

Unlike the novels that Coward describes, narratives about eating disorders pay less attention to sexuality. Instead, eating concerns and bodily obsession represent primary interests.[62] The initiation experience is masticatory rather than sexual; it involves the protagonist's first bizarre abuses of food.

---

[60] Rosalind Coward, "Are Women's Novels Feminist Novels?" *The New Feminist Criticism: Essays on Women, Literature, and Theory*, ed. Elaine Showalter (1980; New York: Random House, 1985) 232-235.

[61] Virginia Woolf, "Professions for Women," *Virginia Woolf: Women and Writing*, intro. Michèle Barrett (1931; London: The Women's Press, 1979). "To speak without figure she [the woman novelist] had thought of something, something about the body, about the passions which it was unfitting for her as a woman to say. Men, her reason told her, would be shocked. The consciousness of what men will say of woman who speaks the truth about her passions had roused her from her artist's state of unconsciousness. She could write no more. The trance was over. Her imagination could work no longer. This I believe to be a very common experience with women writers—they are impeded by the extreme conventionality of the other sex. For though men sensibly allow themselves great freedom in these respects, I doubt that they realize or can control the extreme severity with which they condemn such freedom in women" (61-62).

[62] Hornbacher writes that the eating-disordered woman's relation to her sexuality is at best problematic: "Sex and women with eating disorders are strange bedfellows. We approach it in different ways. Some women avoid it like the plague, much more than I did. Some women seek it out as a source of marginal intimacy, an oasis of companionship in a desert of isolation. Others, like me, use it as power, but that's a little different [...]. Some women, as

Since Rosenthal's time "confessionalism" has been used as an umbrella term to characterize self-referential and self-revelatory literature. It usually has negative connotations. James Atlas, for instance, calls confessional writing "autopathography" rather than autobiography, "not the story of a life but the confession of deviancy, of a trauma, an ordeal, and addiction."[63]

Carolyn G. Heilbrun suggests that critics reserve the term for texts they do not wish to address seriously, most often those written by women. Personal detail from a woman's pen tends to be treated as "disgustingly autobiographical," whereas that from a male writer is more rapidly extolled as being universal.[64] Other theorists note that any attempt to convey "intimate personal feelings" in texts about women's lives tends to be denigrated by male critics as being too limited in interest.[65] Heilbrun acknowledges that the recent "flood" of publications detailing women's traumas may have negative ramifications.[66] Yet she argues that this flood has occurred because women historically lacked the opportunity to tell such stories. Motifs first voiced in poems by writers like Plath and Sexton now find expression in memoirs and autobiographies by women: "[...] 'confessional' poetry of the female kind has passed from immediate view, that anguish has now found its place in the autobiographical memoir."[67]

At any rate, an interest in illness and disability marks recent writing about women's lives. Audre Lorde's *Cancer Journals* (1980) about the author's mastectomy, Lucy Grearly's *Autobiography of a Face* (1994) concerning Grearly's facial disfiguration due to cancer, and Isabel Allende's *Paula* (1995)

---

we laughed about it in the hospital, use it simply to burn calories, but then there's the bummer of having to be naked and seen in the flesh" (*W* 226).

[63] Sorapure 106.

[64] Sorapure 39.

[65] Linda Wagner-Martin, "*Still* Telling Women's Lives," *Writing Lives: American Biography and Autobiography*, ed. Hans Bak and Hans Krabbendam (Amsterdam: VU UP, 1998) 295.

[66] Carolyn G. Heilbrun, "Contemporary Memoirs: Or, Who Cares Who Did What to Whom?" *The American Scholar* (Summer 1999): 37.

[67] Heilbrun 41

about the coma and death of the author's daughter—are cases in point. These texts represent part of a larger interest in the experience and particulars of illness. America is often described as having a disease-of-the-month mentality. The media treats illnesses like heroic battles and those who suffer from them like brave soldiers. For example, a recent *People* cover features the headline:

> At America's colleges, tens of thousands of young women are risking their health and their lives in a desperate desire to be thin. Here is a look at the crisis, and at the chilling personal stories of four who are battling back.[68]

Note how the imagery suggests catastrophe: Women "risk" their lives; their desire is "desperate"; the situation represents a "crisis" against which some, implicitly heroic, individuals are "battling back." When actual wars are lacking play, the media produces illnesses to dramatize.

The texts discussed in the following chapters lie somewhere between narratives about physical illness and personal accounts of psychological disorders. Like many tales of sickness, the basic story line is illness, worsening of illness, crisis, and possible recovery. The sufferings of the body are explored as in works about physical debility. However, the state of the narrator's mind and her being hospitalized for her illness are also of concern. To a degree then the narratives I describe here are literary descendants of Sylvia Plath's *The Bell Jar* (1963), an autobiographical account of Plath's mental breakdown, suicide attempt, hospitalization, and recovery.

An intimate examination of the disturbed self motivates these poems, novels on, and literary memoirs of eating disorders. Telling these stories seems to be a form of redemption or healing.[69] The key to the psychological self appears to be gained through a minute perusal of physical pain and deviance.

---

[68] Cover, *People Weekly*, 4 December 1999.

[69] And, indeed, story telling may well represent an effective form of healing. As Showalter writes in *Hystories*: "Literary critics especially know that narrative can be healing, and that the act of telling one's story may be therapeutic even when it is fictional. The writing cure, the

Some literary accounts of eating disorders insist on their didactic purpose. Maya Hornbacher writes programmatically, "I would do anything to keep people from going where I went. This book was the only thing I could think of" (*W* 7). This passionate statement of purpose echoes Heywood's manifesto—to help women free themselves from the cultural script of anorexia as she has done. Authors assume that their testimony of personal pain will be the best preventative for the readers' experiencing similar woes.

Comments from readers of literary accounts of eating disorders suggest that these texts do help some women not to engage in eating-disordered behavior.[70] However, significant evidence shows that the dissemination of information about eating disorder leads to their proliferation.[71] Paradoxically,

---

acting cure, the dancing cure, all forms of creativity and art, are effective, meaningful forms of self-help" (204-205).

[70] Amazon.com currently lists 257 reader reviews of Hornbacher's text. These reviews—worthy of an extended textual analysis in themselves—present a heated debate between readers who judge the book to be helpful or harmful. Compare the following: A reader from UK, "Ipecac and everything - didn't she do well!, September 24, 2001": "Many people who have had an eating disorder will know just how addictive reading about other people's eating disorders can become. When I was ill I thought the *Eating Disorders Newsletters* my mother used to get deserved to be World Classics. These days, in the advent of *Wasted*, *Life-Size* and re-issue and re-issue of *The Best Little Girl in the World*, anorexics have the best ready-made reading list they could ever hope for. The first two are even well written - anorexia porn at its very best! Hornbacher may believe that she wrote this work for purely altruistic reasons but I find this unconvincing. To truly want to recover is admirable but it always involves a sense of loss. Might as well record the glory and squalor of the past, just in case no one notices you should you become normal."; Sienna, "Saves Lives, June 9, 2001": "This book is written in a way where even if you don't have an eating disorder, you could question. Meaning, it is written in a way where anyone can understand the torment that this woman went through and helps those that do not suffer understand why and how it can happen to anyone. It's truth and uncensored memories haunt you while you read, and this haunting can save people's lives that do suffer from anorexia and/or bulimia. It is written beautifully with words that flow through your mind with curiosity and sadness. I recommend it to anyone who has ever known someone with an eating disorder, suffers themselves, or just revels in fearless people who reveal their lives through literature in hopes to de-glamorize this concept of being thin." Both reviews are from *Amazon.com. Customer Reviews Wasted*, 4 November 2002 <http://www.amazon.com/exec/obidos/tg/stores/detail/-/books/0060930934/customer-reviews/3/ref=cm rev_next/ 104-4996524-6277528?show=-submittime>.

[71] Hornbacher describes how a novelistic account of anorexia contributed to her idealization of anorectics and the development of her bulimia (*W* 43); Laura Fraser describes how she got the idea to try to make herself throw up from an Ann Lander's advice column on the same subject. *Losing It: America's Obsession with Weight and the Industry That Feeds on It* (New

Wasted may teach the reader how to induce vomiting more effectively than she already knew how. Just as the Hornbacher picked up new tricks for destroying her body during every hospitalization, some readers may experience her memoir as presenting a great buffet of abusive behaviors from which they may choose. One clinical psychologist actually warns parents not to allow *Wasted* to enter their homes. She states that the book is potentially more dangerous than pro-eating disorder websites and reports that it has been banned in the eating disorder treatment center where she works.[72] Significantly, Hornbacher's memoir is marketed with a cover featuring her slim body. While the title *Wasted* highlights the irretrievable loss of life energy that went into creating this form, for those who are susceptible to the fascination with thinness, what may speak louder to them is the image of the thin=attractive=enviable author.

In summary, I call those texts "confessional" that describe the experiences of a narrator who is ill and whose illness causes her vision to be profoundly distorted. The relation of shameful events determines the narrative structure of confessional writing. Furthermore, illness provides the key to the confessional narrator's identity. Either she fetishizes her body or her eating disorder or both. Moreover, confessional texts are written with a sense of intended agency. The three extended texts discussed below and many of the poems quoted above demand that the situation of eating-disordered women be recognized and that the conditions that make them sick change.

York: Dutton, 1997) 5; Richard Gordon also attests that the flood of autobiographical accounts of eating disorders contributes to their proliferation. *Anorexia and Bulimia* 106-109.

[72] Kathleen Robinson (Licensed Clinical Psychologist), "A How To Book For Those Who Want An Eating Disorder, May 3, 2002": "As a psychologist with a hospital based eating disorder treatment facility, I am writing to warn all parents that this book should not be allowed to enter into their homes. This is an instruction manual that glamorizes eating disorders and will give your child that extra motivation to become an anorexic or bulimic. I appreciate what the author tried to do; however, this book is one of the only banned books on our inpatient units due to the damage it has done and continues to do. If your child has this book, PLEASE inquire further. If you thought that pro-eating disorder web sites were damaging, then you should be afraid of *Wasted*!" From *Amazon.com. Customer Reviews* *Wasted*, 4 November 2002.

Part II

III Jenefer Shute's *Life-Size*
A Socially Critical and Confessional Account of an Anorectic's Hospitalization

This chapter begins the analysis of prose writings on eating disorders with an introduction of Jenefer Shute's *Life-Size*. The novel is described in culturally critical terms with respect to influences on the protagonist's burgeoning eating disorder, including medial images, the conflation of thinness with wealth, the male gaze and the cultural icon Barbie (4.1). Furthermore, *Life-Size* is analyzed as a confessional novel on the basis of the narrator's disturbed sense of self and her distorted vision of others (4.2); the site of her confession is also scrutinized. The aesthetic and potentially attractive qualities of this confession of anorexia are also examined. Finally, this chapter compares *Life-Size* to Margaret Atwood's *Lady Oracle* to highlight the difference between a confessional and a humorous postmodern treatment of eating disorders (4.3).

Published in 1992, Jenefer Shute's *Life-Size* was the first in a series of confessional novels concerning eating disorders to appear in the last decade of the twentieth century. The novel was received favorably and won an award from the 1993 Feminist Book Festival.[1]

The first paragraph of the novel reveals its central themes:

> I'm lying here, just occupying space, drifting in and out of a dream, when I hear something clattering and rumbling down the hall. I know what it is; my jaw and stomach muscles tense, but otherwise I remain exactly as I am. Why should I move? The trolley stops outside the door with a faint tinkle of crockery; after a brief knock (giving me no time to respond), she comes in, smiling and pert, brisk and trim in her white tunic and pants. (Trim, but don't think I don't notice the almost-sagging buttocks, the incipient droop of the upper arm). (*L-S* 1)

---

[1] The medical humanities web site of New York University also recommends the novel for its treatment of anorexia. Felice Aull, "Shute, Jenefer P. Life-Size," 4 November 2002 <http://endeavor.med.nyu.edu/lit-med/lit-med-db/webdocs/webauthors/shute145-au-.html>.

The novel begins in medias res. A description of the narrator's body and her physical inertia, presented in a first-person voice in the present tense, is the first image to meet the reader. This body and its experiences will dominate the action of the novel. Appropriately, the initial description of the body stresses the speaker's sense of her lightness. This lightness is of a physical and psychological nature; Josie weighs under 70 pounds at the beginning of the novel; disjointed, circular, and obsessive, her thoughts all concern the maintenance of her very low weight. The progressive verbs that describe the narrator's physical being also denote her sense of mental buoyancy: "lying here," "occupying space, drifting in and out of a dream" give the reader the sense that the speaker is floating above rather than dwelling in her thoughts and feelings. These verbs signifying lightness are set off in contrast to what the speaker hears "rumbling and clattering down the hall." The use of present tense progressive verbs to describe the trolley in a parallel construction emphasizes the heaviness, loudness, and definition of the approaching object in contrast to the speaker's internal state. Building tension, the speaker does not yet reveal the identity of the thing she hears but describes only her reaction to it, how her body becomes awake and active and no longer floats. A Gothic mood is established: the heroine appears to be under some duress, threatened by forces surrounding her.

The Gothic quality of many texts describing eating disorders became apparent in the readings of poems about bulimia and binge eating. The desire to eat is experienced by the speakers of these poems as resembling a monster; the poems' speakers describe their feelings of being surrounded by food, threatened by calories, and overwhelmed by the gaping hole of hunger within them. Likewise, Josie perceives food and those who would make her eat it to be demonic. Like many Gothic heroines she feels threatened by her surroundings and is in fact enclosed within the hospital walls. She vacillates between feeling rationally superior to those around her and terribly lost and disoriented. In the latter state she resembles Gothic heroines from Ann Radcliffe's Emily to the heroines of Victoria Holt's novels in their wanderings through nightmarish worlds. As will become apparent in the following discussion Josie tends, like many Gothic characters, to have a polarized image of herself as well: Either she envisions herself as a leaping ballerina or a terribly fat and clumsy monstrosity.[2]

The rhetorical question, "Why should I move?" highlights the speaker's ambivalent reactions to the approaching object: on the one hand, she wishes to be invulnerable to the threat it presents, and, on the other hand her body has already reacted to it defensively. The next sentence reveals the identity of this threatening entity—a trolley covered by plates and cups, presumably full of food. From the picture of the thin self-contemplative woman and the blurb about content on the cover of the novel, the reader knows that the speaker does not fear being poisoned but being fattened up. (The paragraphs that follow further describe the speaker's first encounter with food in the novel, one that inspires her with fear, hostility, and disgust). The brief knock, which the speaker experiences as too fast to respond to, reiterates the sense that the speaker has been forcefully awakened from a pleasant dream state to be confronted by loud and hostile entities, food and people. The characterization of the visitor's appearance and clothes that follows tells the reader two things: one, the visitor is a nurse and hence the speaker is a patient and in some manner sick; two, that the speaker is highly concerned with weight and is critical of those who are not—to her mind—sufficiently thin ("don't think I don't notice the almost-sagging buttocks, the incipient droop of the upper arm").

The introductory paragraph sets the scene and establishes a sense of dramatic tension: what will happen when the speaker has to eat some of the

[2] In the introduction to a study of the female Gothic in literature, Julian Fleenor describes this genre as being characterized by: 1) a nightmare atmosphere—often an enclosed space—with which the Gothic heroine is in conflict, 2) the heroine's terror or fear of her surroundings, and 3) her dichotomous thinking about others and herself as good or evil. Julian Fleenor,

food on that tray? *Life-Size* begins with the twenty-five-year-old Josie's admittance into an eating disorder clinic or unit of a hospital and describes her anorexic mindset in the opening chapters. This includes detailed accounts of the excruciating care with which she eats miniscule amounts of food,[3] the manner in which she divides foods into "good" and "bad," the minute examinations of her body, and the painful seemingly masochistic lengths with which she tortures her body for any hint of fatness. The reader is given a vision of the narrowness and the obsessive quality of Josie's thoughts; she thinks exclusively about her weight, her body, and her self as a product of the former two.

During the course of her hospitalization Josie puts on mental and physical weight. At the end of the novel she can feel the depth of her sadness and is in the process of learning how to cohabit with her foreign heavier body. Josie's gradual recovery represents the primary narrative strand of the novel. Equally important are the interspersed flashbacks to Josie's childhood and adolescence, as well as intertextual references to advice from women's magazines and diet books, to quotations from an anthropological text on food and eating, and to diagnostic materials used in the hospital.

The story told in flashbacks is compelling and dramatic: As a fifteen-year-old Josie went on her first diet, from which she never recovered, since each weight loss was accompanied by the desire to solidify and overtrump it. While Josie relearns to eat in the narrative foreground of the novel, she teaches herself to starve in the secondary narrative strand, told in a chronological series of flashbacks. This second narrative story culminates in her eating ground-up glass, which she mistakes for "shaved ice or sugar crystals" (*L-S* 218). Josie

---

"Introduction: The Female Gothic," *The Female Gothic* (Montréal, London: Eden Press, 1983) 3-28. See also the discussion of the Gothic mood in Hornbacher's *Wasted*, chapter V.

[3] An example of this is the following: "Slowly, delicately, precisely, I cut the piece of toast into halves, then quarters, then eighths, then sixteenths, and daintily convey each piece to my mouth, allowing three minutes between bites. Then, in the same way, I eat exactly half the slice of cantaloupe, panicking for a moment: how can anything so heartrendingly sweet and juicy, so intensely orange and alive, have so few calories?" (*L-S* 18).

refers to this climax of her efforts to force her body to live without food throughout the novel in a somewhat elliptical fashion before the event is narrated realistically at the end of chapter seventeen.

3.1) The Makings of an Anorectic
The Media

From a cultural studies perspective one of the most interesting aspects of the novel is its examination of texts that helped contribute to the heroine's anorexia. Beginning in chapter five, diet and behavioral advice given in women's magazines is printed in italicized form in juxtaposition with the narrator's description of her feelings about her burgeoning adolescent body. Initially, she is confident that her body will grow to look more like the "other bodies"—the idealized images in magazines. And she has the assurance—given by the wisdom of magazine advice—that, if she does not naturally become beautiful, there are steps she can take to transform herself:

> [...] there were measures, I knew, that I could take. One could always take measures, to measure up.
> I studied the magazines.
>
> *When it comes to being beautiful, half the fun is learning how.*
>
> *Keep yourself in check.*
> *Be some Body.*
>
> *Get frequent trims.*
>
> *Stand tall, glance down. If you see your navel, you need tummy firming.* (*L-S* 64)

These brief admonitions to improve one's physical self, written by magazine editors, reveal much about American culture and the myth of female beauty. Like the constitutional right to personal happiness, the idea that every woman can be potentially beautiful if she only works hard enough informs American popular culture. The adolescent, mirror-obsessed Josie believes that by faithfully following all of the advice she reads, she will inevitably turn out to be gorgeous. Josie's plan to "measure up" by following magazine advice is executed in part so that she will be as unlike her fat mother as possible. This fat mother is perceived as an abysmal failure, who cannot hold her husband's attention due to her obesity (*L-S* 63). Interspersed with descriptions of Josie's unhappy mother and Josie's feelings of hatred towards her is the recurring admonition—taken straight from *Mademoiselle* or *Seventeen*—to claim one's right to happiness by perfecting one's figure: Chapter five ends with the prescriptive that is repeated three times over: "*The secret word is* Body."

The Association of Thinness with Wealth and Status

Josie's dreaded mother who is "[t]rapped in her private padded cell" (*L-S* 63) stands in direct contrast to Josie's friend Amanda Jane, the heroine of her pre-anorexic years. With her golden skin and naturally long, lean limbs Amanda Jane embodies the ideal. After a several months' separation Josie is invited to spend a month at Amanda's family's beach house. Josie's first impressions are of the differences, which have seemingly grown greater, between Amanda Jane and herself. Amanda has grown taller and even thinner; her clothes are understated versus Josie's "garish" wardrobe that has been taken "fresh from this month's *Seventeen*" (*L-S* 88). Whereas Josie wears a skimpy one-piece suit that requires constant tugging, Amanda Jane wears a demure bikini. Amanda reads *Vogue* rather than *Seventeen* and protects her skin from the sun rather than "irradiat[ing]" (*L-S* 90) her pimples in the sun as Josie does. Most importantly, Amanda Jane has internalized cultural messages, lacking in Josie's upbringing, about the differences between how the sexes should approach and consume food. Amanda "never, ever ate dessert" (*L-S* 91). She, like her mother, knows that "'It's nice to be slender, dear'" (*L-S* 89). And she, unlike Josie, does not need to be admonished not to eat the hors d'oeuvres that are prepared by women but not intended to be eaten by them.

Just after the scene in which Josie is rebuked by Amanda and her mother for eating "like a man," a text passage taken directly from a women's magazine follows, which reiterates the lesson of how to eat like a "proper" girl. The advice for how to pack a picnic lunch for a woman and a man, respectively, is reprinted without comment:

> *Delight him, but don't undo your diet.*
>
> *How?*
>
> *Pack a bilateral lunch.*

His	*Hers*
2 slices baked ham: 290	*1 slice baked ham: 145*
1 cup barbecue beans: 220	*2 dill pickle wedges: 30*
1 dill pickle wedge: 15	*2 teaspoons mustard: 20*
2 tablespoons creamy mustard sauce: 115	*½ cup coleslaw: 55*
½ cup coleslaw: 55	*1 7-inch bread stick: 50*
1 buttered roll: 125	*8 ounces diet soda: 1*
3 spiced crab apples: 85	
8 ounces lime soda: 105	
Total calories: 1,010	*Total calories: 301*

(*L-S* 89-90)

Since it is estimated that women expend approximately 2,065 worth of calories per day in energy as compared with the 2,462 calories that men expend, the total caloric amounts listed above are striking. The diet advice proffered above would suggest that men should eat over 3,000 calories a day—if their breakfasts and dinners are comparable to their lunches—and, by the same logic, women should eat under a thousand calories a day. Only obese individuals should consume less than a thousand calories per day in short-term medically supervised programs: yet the above is offered as a general strategy to women.[4] As pointed out above every woman on a diet includes the majority of American women. Hence a recipe for food deprivation and its attendant behaviors, including bingeing and obsessive thinking about food, is offered as general diet advice.

That Josie first internalizes the lessons of feminine eating behaviors at her wealthier friend's family beach house underscores the connection between affluence and slenderness in America. As documented above slenderness is perceived as a mark and a privilege of affluence and success in the States.

Amanda Jane's family's wealth is disclosed to the reader in a number of details: Amanda Jane leaves public school to attend boarding school, whereas Josie has to win a scholarship to attend the private Deerborne academy (*L-S* 66); Amanda Jane does not date boys her age but assembles a hope chest for when she will get married—another sign of affluence expressed in more traditional sexual mores for girls; finally, Amanda Jane's family's wealth stands in contrast to the economic uncertainty of Josie's family; Josie's father is unemployed for at least half a year, and it remains unclear whether he was fired or resigned from his job at AminCom. These distinctions represent subtle class nuances, of course. For Josie's family, with their maid, their habit of drinking coffee in the living room, and their mother's compulsive spending habits is by no means poor. However, the connection is made in Josie's and the reader's mind between wealth and Amanda's "lanky and lean" body, which does not "mutate[]" in puberty as Josie's does, "into a pimply, potbellied, pendulous-breasted sow" (*L-S* 59). With a mother and an upbringing like Amanda Jane's, one learns to eat in a restrained "feminine" fashion: no hors d'oeuvres, no dessert, no second helpings.

---

[4] Thomas A. Wadden, "Very-Low-Calorie Diets: Appraisal and Recommendations," *Eating Disorders and Obesity: A Comprehensive Handbook*, ed. Kelly D. Brownell and Christopher G. Fairburn (New York and London: The Guilford Press, 1995) 485.

Curiously, Josie does not adopt Amanda Jane and her mother's restrained eating style while she is visiting them. Rather, she stuffs herself during her month at the beach house as though to assert her identity in contradistinction to "Manda's," and she grows "plumper and more hideous by the day" (*L-S* 91). Whether Josie punishes her flesh in this manner to demonstrate defiantly that her mother has failed to teach her the necessary lessons of femininity remains unclear. Just as likely, she reacts out of a sense of despair of her ever being able to resemble Amanda, despite her having followed all of the advice on being beautiful.

What initiates Josie's first diet is not the example of Amanda Jane and her mother but the chance remark of an admired boy on her having a "chubby" waist.

Influence of Male Condemnation on Josie's Anorexia

At a party at which she feels miserable, Josie encounters a rough boy whom she entitles Sweatso. Even during her pre-anorexic life she identifies other people according to their bodily characteristics. Sweatso asks her to accompany his friends and him to another party. Out of a desire to be near "Ice Blue Eyes," one of Sweatso's friends, she joins them. At the party at which no one talks, she imagines that she is, or is actually, violated by Sweatso and another youth:

> A common fantasy among young women, so I'm told (the motorcycle gang—how banal). Mine are all pretty classic; Herr Doktor Professor Frog, I mean Freud, would recognize the lot. Dr. Eighty-Bucks-an-Hour was armed with a list (fantasies: domestic, suburban, exotic) when, a year or so later, he labored at—mother's behest—to convince me that, of course, I'd imagined it all. (All of it, all). (*L-S* 102)

This curious passage highlights one of the novel's central features: the narrator is unreliable.[5] She skips from event to event, interprets the same event

[5] The concept of the "unreliable narrator" was developed by Wayne C. Booth in his seminal work *The Rhetoric of Fiction* (1961) to describe those narrators whose actions or words do

variously, and reiterates the telling of traumatic events in an obsessive fashion. Her hostility towards the psychiatrist who treats her, whom she refers to derisively as Herr Doktor Professor Frog and Dr. Eighty-Bucks-an-Hour, renders her voice ironic; we suspect she means the opposite of what she literally says. The emphatic repetition of "I'd imagined it all. (All of it, all)" suggests that she did in fact experience the traumatic events she alludes to. The credulous, sympathetic reader initially believes that she was sexually violated by the motorcycle gang. However, what the narrator relates later calls this reading into question. She writes: "So perhaps what really happened was this": and then tells how the admired Ice-Blue-Eyes said, "A little chubby there, aren't we?" (*L-S* 102) when he reached out to hold her waist to keep her from falling off his motorcycle. That Josie later describes in detail how she lost her virginity to her first boyfriend underscores the fact that she, at least, was not raped by Sweatso and his friend.

Ice-Blue-Eye's chance comment initiates a bout of self-abuse in the narrator: she stares at the image of her body in the mirror obsessively and touches her waist where he had touched her to feel the "palpable, rubbery bulge" (*L-S* 103). This event precedes Josie's first diet, a diet that does not end until she has been hospitalized at less than seventy pounds. The male gaze and male condemnation make Josie wish to remake herself completely. Ice-Blue-Eyes's comment is predated by her father's remark about her figure in a bikini that "*Playboy* likes them plump"(*L-S* 54). Josie chooses not to appear in a bathing suit again until she weighs less than ninety pounds. Even after she has become emaciated, Josie imagines that others perceive her as fat. When her married professor ignores her after they have slept together for the first time,

---

not correspond with the norms of the work's "implied author." Booth's concept has been critically re-examined in the German language text *Unreliable Narration: Studien zur Theorie und Praxis unglaubwürdigen Erzählens in der englischsprachichen Literatur,* ed. Ansgar Nünning (Trier: Wissenschaftlicher Verlag Trier, 1998). For an overview see Greta

she assumes that he has been repelled by what she perceives to be her overweight and muses: "The problem was my body" (*L-S* 189). She does not even entertain the thought that he may feel remorseful for having begun an affair with a student or may have been shocked by her extreme underweight. Josie's sense of identity rests on how she thinks others, particularly men, perceive her body. On the rare occasions when she does experience desire, her pleasure lies in her awareness that the man touching her can feel how thin she is.[6]

Barbie: Icon of Idealized Womanhood

Other critical insights into American culture are offered in *Life-Size* when the narrator refers to her history with Barbies and their affect on her body image. As a girl Josie found an idealized image of the female form in her Barbie doll:

> Barbie, you were so slender and firm, with a tiny, jointed waist that never spread. Your breasts pointed up and forward, perfectly symmetrical, unmarked by the rude red eye of a nipple, and your straight thighs met in a demure beige plastic Y, smooth, sealed and uncleft. (*L-S* 57)

Later, she comments on her fear of going to a graduate school located far away from her lover, the married professor, by asking "But what were my options?" and then enumerating career choices for Barbie from 1959 to 1983 without comment (*L-S* 198-199). Over a span of twenty-four years Barbie's careers have remained centrally motivated by her having a forum for displaying her body and wardrobe. Hence Josie's very traditional thoughts about not wanting to be

---

Olson, "Reconsidering Unreliability: Fallible and Untrustworthy Narrators," *Narrative* 11, No. 1 (January 2003): 81-97.

[6] See, for instance, the description of Josie's sexual experiences with her first boyfriend: "I enjoyed prompting his passion and was proud to feel his hands urgently outlining my new bones. (But there was still too much softness there, in the belly and the thighs: I wanted to be perfectly hard, offering no purchase)" (*L-S* 137); and the description of her last sexual encounter with a weight-obsessed graduate student: "Although I was somewhat aroused, it was mainly by the feeling of his feeling me, and by knowing, from my own obsessive explorations, exactly what his hand encountered" (*L-S* 32).

separated from her lover are presented in juxtaposition with Barbie's traditional preoccupations with choosing a career on the basis of clothes.

Introduced in 1959, the Barbie doll remains forty years later one of the most popular toys in Western culture.[7] While her career choices have occasionally been in male-dominated fields—she was depicted as a medical doctor in 1973—Barbie's overwhelming concern has remained the presentation of her face and figure. The majority of her occupations being in the fields of fashion and design reflect this. As a model, a ballerina, a stewardess, an aerobics instructor, and a designer, Barbie has had ample opportunity to display her figure, which includes feet set permanently in a position to wear stiletto heals, enormous gravity-defying breasts that lack nipples, a tiny waist and hips, and disproportionately long legs. Despite the promise given by the fashion magazines Josie reads that anyone can "measure up" if she works and diets hard enough, no woman, even with the help of plastic surgery, can measure up to Barbie's impossible standard of beauty. Yet Barbie dolls remain cultural icons, and many eating-disordered narrators describe how important playing with these dolls was to them.

3.1) Confessional Aspects of *Life-Size*

Life-Size may be described as confessional, because the narrator's distorted view of herself determines the scope of the novel and the surreal manner in which she views food, bodies, and life. Josie's central preoccupation is to explain herself and her alternating feelings of grandiosity and self-abasement. The testimony of illness becomes a metaphor for healing: the more Josie reveals about the genesis and the horrifying excesses of her anorexia and the more the reader learns about her illness, the healthier she becomes. The pursuit of self-understanding takes place on the field of the body. The attempt to verify her

---

[7] Sharlene Hesse-Biber, *Am I Thin Enough Yet* 28.

existence by measuring her body is revealed in Josie's obsession with looking at her reflection in mirrors, performing body inventories, and measuring herself. The novel is also confessional because its disclosure of intimate information about the self occurs from within a prison-like enclosed space—Josie's room in the hospital. Moreover, the use of "affective language"—to borrow Rosenthal's term—determines the novel's aesthetic quality. The skillful intertwining of narrative strands and text types, the complex causality of Josie's anorexia, and the speaker's articulate voice mark *Life-Size*'s formal superiority to many autobiographical accounts of anorexia.

Josie's Distorted Sense of Self

The distorted sense of identity, which Rosenthal says marks the "the beset self" and Axthelm, the "afflicted and unbalanced" confessional hero,[8] manifests itself in Josie's alternating views of herself as deeply troubled or as superhuman. On the one hand Josie is terrified by the possibility that she may appear ugly and fat to others. On the other hand she perceives herself as being vastly superior to them. The latter attitude is revealed in her desire to become "pure consciousness" in contradistinction to the fat fleshy, desirous mass of habitual consumers around her:

> I never feel hungry and despise those who do, whose lives are governed by the peristaltic pulse. Never have they learned to ignore that gaping maw: its slightest twinge sends them running to the trough. From the day's first mouthful to the last at night, their lives are one long foraging. In the morning, hunched over their desks, they munch on soft dough; at noon, they herd out en masse, meat-hungry, to feed; midafternoon, in a circadian slump, they crave sugar; arriving home, they root in the refrigerator's roaring heart and eat upright before an open door. And all this before the serious eating begins, the ever-to-be-repeated hours of shopping and chopping and mixing and cooking and serving only to wolf down the result in seconds and greet it the next morning transformed into shit.

---

[8] Peter M. Axthelm, *The Modern Confessional Novel* 9.

> But I've freed myself from this compulsion. When I wake, I'm empty, light, light-headed; I like to stay this way, free and pure, light on my feet, traveling light. For me, food's only interest lies in how little I need, how strong I am, how well I can resist—each time achieving another small victory of the will: one carrot instead of two, half a cracker, no more peas. Each gain makes me stronger, purer, larger in my exercise of power, until eventually I see no reason to eat at all. (*L-S* 7-8)

The adjectives Josie uses to describe herself "free and pure, light" reveal her sense of superiority as compared to the bound, impure, and heavy feeders around her. The verbs she uses to characterize their eating habits, including "munch," "root," and "wolf down" all stress the animal-like nature of their actions. Other people's interest in food goes unabated, forcing them into ceaseless active pursuit of foodstuffs—a pursuit whose meaninglessness is revealed in its end, the transformation of food into waste. Josie's rejection of food, by contrast, is seen by her as an act of empowerment: She speaks of "gain," of becoming "stronger" and "larger"—all words that denote increased size, strength and power. Starving the body through the implementation of rigid willpower strengthens the narrator's sense of her own invincibility. This sense of empowerment is, paradoxically, won by her losing weight, by her becoming ever thinner and smaller and physically powerless.

However, Josie's periods of feeling invincibly strong and superior are often interrupted by her sudden insights into her weakness and ugliness. After the nurse discovers that Josie has hidden part of a meal she has been served, Josie describes her sense of how she must appear to her "keeper" (*L-S* 6): "lying here flat in a faded robe, my fragile limbs sticking out like a grasshopper's, my skin a dry grayish white, netted with veins, my fingertips and nails blueberry-hued, the crook of each arm a purplish mess dotted with bloody pinpricks" (*L-S* 14). As at so many times Josie's sense of whether she is vastly more powerful and superior to others or much weaker than them is determined by how she thinks her body looks.

Searching for Selfhood in Mirrors and Measurements

Josie's body and its relative fatness or thinness represent the text's focal point. Her identity depends on whether she sees herself as obese or as emaciated. Lacking is some space in between. To gauge her identity Josie requires constant references to herself and ways to measure her volume.

As poems like "The Bulimic Experience" and "The Angel that Feeds Me" reveal, confrontations with one's reflection in the mirror are central to the eating-disordered woman's experience. For those who binge, the perception of oneself as fat initiates periods of uncontrolled consumption. For Josie, what she believes she sees in the various mirrors that make up her world determines who she is. Eleven scenes in the novel describe Josie's intense relationship with the mirror, which began during her adolescence, when she started to scrutinize the changes taking place in her body, and culminates in her love-hate relationship with her reflected image as an adult anorectic. Whereas other women in her ballet class also look at themselves in the mirror, Josie is obsessed by the mirror-paneled walls there:

> I need a mirror. I have no idea what I look like, because what I look like depends on which mirror I'm looking in. In the ballet studio, all four walls are paneled with mirrors, but each is slightly different, so I always stand in front of the one that elongates me, Modigliani-like. The next panel, which I avoid, compresses me into a troll. [...]
>
> I sit in the corner where the mirrors meet, my back to the rest of the class, the soles of my feet meeting like hands in prayer. And I stare, without blinking, straight ahead, as if meditating on something mysterious. (I could never bring myself to join their idle chatter: how would I ever break in? what would be the 'natural' thing to say?) Aloof, on a higher plane altogether, I stare straight ahead—at my reflection, at the reflection of that reflection.
>
> [...] I can't eat another mouthful until I've weighed and measured myself, until I've looked at myself in all the positions I've developed, like an inverse bodybuilder, to display each part. (*L-S* 41-42)

Josie's addictive need to see her own reflection is revealed in the first and last sentence of the above quotation. In the hospital without the opportunity to study her mirrored reflection, she has no sense of her identity at all. Yet as the second sentence shows, Josie's identity is unstable. Every mirror reveals something new and informs Josie that she is obese and monstrously ugly or acceptably, even delightfully, thin.

The search for self in the mirror takes on the aspect of a spiritual quest. When Josie regards herself in the reflection of the mirrors adjoining each other in the corner of the ballet room, she is "on a higher plane altogether." With prayer-like posture, unblinking eyes, and silent mouth, she contemplates the mystery of her reflected self. She has the sense of being as "clean and pure" as the speaker of the first poem on anorexia printed in Chapter II above, which begins "I'm in control." These passages illustrate the religious character of the anorectic's vision of herself: the reader is reminded of the fasting saints of the middle ages and those "fasting girls" who tested the limits of their bodies' ability to be sustained by transcendental manna rather than earthly food during Victorian times.

The same mirror may even reflect different selves. Josie initially fails to recognize herself in the mirror during a meeting with her treatment team in the conference room: At first she sees the "face of an old woman [...] with shadowy, sunken cheeks and deep grooves around the mouth." After recognizing this face as her own she "adjust[s] the tilt of [her] head" to transform the image into a "face of exquisite delicacy, ethereal, haunting" (*L-S* 70). More than mere altars to the pursuit of a perfected self, mirrors prove threatening when they reflect undesirable images. Alternately, they may be used as sites for transforming the self.

How does Josie's experience of mirrors differ from that of other women in an appearance-obsessed culture? Josie reflects that all women regard mirrors with a mixture of shame, horror, and nervousness.[9] In her study of literary accounts of women and mirrors from the past 150 years, Jenijoy La Belle surmises that mirroring represents a process in a woman's assertion of her own identity that occurs during her whole life. Women look both for themselves and for "the other" in their perusals of mirrors. Recognizing the importance of their looks, they verify their identities in their cultural surroundings by looking in the glass. They also invent themselves anew in these sessions.[10] La Belle reads many modern texts on women's interactions with mirrors as assertions of female identity that transcend the traditional division between mind and body.[11]

What La Belle describes differs considerably from Josie's experiences of mirrors. For Josie no sense of identity between her body and herself is possible: either she objectifies her body as a perfect artistic creation of which she is immensely proud or she perceives it as a horrifying fat monster. The sight of herself can make her "want to run screaming from the room" (*L-S* 179). Josie has no sense of phenomenological unity with her body, fat or thin. She tries to control and perfect her body but finds herself being mostly controlled by it. Depending on how much flesh she thinks she sees, Josie admires or despises herself. This pattern proves true for other eating-disordered women as well.

Another form of mirroring occurs when Josie performs her daily body checks. Taking physical inventories of her emaciated body with its bones and hollows quiets her sense of anxiety. Typical anorexic behavior, this process was described in the fourth stanza of the poem "Conform" above, in which the speaker describes the anorectic's anxious surveys of her bones—"clavicle,

---

[9] "Everyone has her own gesture: tugging at the bottom of a T-Shirt, looking over a shoulder to hitch tights up and leotard down, pressing a palm against a tummy glimpsed in profile, rearranging a neckline to show clavicles or cleavage. Everyone has her own costume, ritualistically designed, a palimpsest in whose layers you can read the history of that body's imperfections" (*L-S* 178-179).

[10] Jenijoy La Belle, *Herself Beheld: The Literature of the Looking Glass* (Ithaca and London: Cornell UP, 1988) 2.

scapula, ulna, humerous."[12] Josie describes her daily confirmation of her self and her emaciation as a "ritual" and an "inventory" (*L-S* 9). She moves from her hipbones to her wrists and elbows, then to her thighs, hips and buttocks, and finally to her collarbone, ribs, and vertebrae—moving up and down the body like a sculptor, molding the image of the model into the proper proportions. Again, this inventory has the appearance of being a process of self-creation. The inventory is performed daily to verify how far Josie has gone in accomplishing her goal of becoming fleshless: "Just the bones, no disfiguring flesh, just the pure, clear shape of me" (*L-S* 9-10).

Yet another form of verifying her worth occurs when Josie weighs herself. In her pre-hospital life she performed this rite twenty times a day and had strict rules that were associated with it. If she gains weight, she has to lose; if she has lost weight, she also has to lose. The "miniature stage" (*L-S* 159).

Josie's Distorted Sense of Other People's Bodies and Food

The centrality of Josie's preoccupation with her body extends to her distorted vision of others' bodies and food. Existence, for her, consists of what she perceives as the relative fatness of the people and things that surround her. Just as she pictures her own history as a series of photos of her more or less fat body, so she recalls her boyfriends and lovers as a series of variously colored and shaped penises. Bodies impact Josie rather than personalities. She consistently describes Suzanne, the nurse who is instrumental to her recovery, in terms of her body. The initial paragraph of the novel describes how Josie perceives the nurse solely as an overweight body: "don't think I don't notice the almost-sagging buttocks, the incipient droop of the upper arm." In chapter two

---

[11] "When women look at themselves in mirrors, they participate in a largely ignored panoply of body/self interactions programmatically excluded from the metaphysics of masculine self-presence." La Belle 171. See also La Belle 171-185.
[12] See Chapter I, section 1.3) above.

Josie is astounded by Suzanne's "enormous, looming breasts and a fleshy fold under her chin" (*L-S* 27). Soon thereafter, she describes Suzanne's arm as "meaty and tight, like a sausage" (*L-S* 31). When angry at Suzanne, she refers to her mentally as a "freckled cow" (*L-S* 69). Not insignificantly, Suzanne's flesh is compared to food, to sausages, and indirectly to meat, to a cow. Even when the nurse has become a full-fledged person to Josie and she no longer refers to her with monikers such as "Miss Pert," "Squeaky," or "Ms. Squeak" but with her given name, Josie remains preoccupied by her weight. During an emotionally charged scene in which Suzanne and Josie argue about whether an orange slice is a garnish or not, Josie characterizes Suzanne as standing "with her hands on her not insubstantial hips." For Josie no intensity of emotion can overtrump the importance of the body to identity, whether it be her own or another person's.

Particularly female flesh repels her. The sight of a pregnant woman or a fat woman eating is the most obscene image she can imagine. Overweight women inspire nothing but scorn in Josie, as is reflected in her descriptions of them: A fellow graduate student is a "plump, overpainted parakeet" (*L-S* 221); a "lumpy lesbian" (*L-S* 202) lives downstairs from Josie during graduate school; she is amazed by the ugliness of the "slovenly padding" of a woman whom she sees with her affectionate lover on the bus: "how could she let a man touch her—never mind (I tried to imagine) exposing that flabby flesh to his sight?"(*L-S* 203). Everything related to female sexuality, including menstruation, breasts, and pregnancy disgusts her. Josie cannot fathom the nurse's interest in her periods.[13] After a meal of a "whole tomato and a whole orange," she is unable to complete her morning inventory of her body because she feels as though she is pregnant: "beached whalelike" with "heavy, sagging breasts scored with

[13] "Who, given the choice, would really opt to menstruate, invite the monthly hemorrhage—a reminder that the body is nothing but a bay of blood, liable to seep or spatter at any moment?" (*L-S* 5); "Normal physiological functioning. Growth and bleeding and hunger and decay. A long, slow rotting; meat going bad" (*L-S* 226)

stretch marks" (*L-S* 30). Similarly, after a meal consisting of one apple and a one-inch cube of cheese, Josie anxiously performs her inventory, thinking "I'm pregnant already, pregnant with matter that will soon be me" (*L-S* 48). Conversely, she feels envious of another patient's "tiny, chaste waist" (*L-S* 48). The idea of leaving the hospital awakens the following associations in Josie's mind: "Discharge: ugly word, gynecological word, cottage cheesy" (*L-S* 220).

Josie's distaste for female flesh stems in great part from her relationship with her despised obese mother. When she feels fat, she imagines her mother's body: "Dense and polluted, this immense mass of flesh swells like dough as I lie here; raising my hand to the light, I see only my mother's fat paw" (*L-S* 30). Later in the novel she suffers from feelings of self-loathing after she has gained weight. Performing her daily inventory, she imagines that the image of her mother has been imposed over her once meager body:

> My chin feels as if it's developing a little pad, right under the point, though she says I'm imagining it. But I can feel it, I can even see it, so familiar from its former residence on my mother's face. On the outside of each thigh, a pinchable piece has pushed out (bruised rotten from pinching it, hard, all day). No amount of leg-lifting—dog-at-the-hydrant-style—seems to help, though I have flapped both limbs till they seized. What's happening is that my true nature is re-emerging, inscribed in fat for all to see: corrupt, slothful, insatiable. (*L-S* 123)

For Josie, her mother embodies a monstrous version of her true obese self. Like Mr. Hyde for Dr. Jekyll or his portrait for Dorian Gray, Josie's mother—with her insatiable appetites for food and consumer goods—is Josie's demoniac *doppelgänger*; She represents a part of Josie that she would desperately like to destroy. Hence she has many fantasies about hurting her mother. But she also fears that this hungry *doppelgänger* is far stronger than the thin self she has worked so hard to achieve. Like Victor Frankenstein with his Creature, Josie fears that if she ever relaxes her stance of vigilant readiness, her monstrous mother will be waiting and ready to destroy her. In a scene that is repeatedly referred to throughout the novel, which is apparently an exaggeration of a violent argument Josie and her mother once had, Josie imagines her mother dragging her across the floor, wanting to kill, roast, and eat her.[14] When Josie does eat, she gorges on food until she loses consciousness, thus demonstrating a lack of self-control that resembles her mother's insatiability. When she binges Josie perceives herself as a "ravening monster [...] huge, with a crammed, bloated maw, hands full of food, half-chewed matter drooling from a never-empty mouth, lumbering insatiably towards everything, everyone, in my path" (*L-S* 175). As in Dr. Jekyll's case, it becomes a matter of life or death for Josie to determine who shall gain control of her body: the obese monster or the controlled rational self, who works on "perfecting [her] emptiness" (*L-S* 52).

Josie's identification of her bottomless hunger and fat with her monstrous mother recalls poems on binge eating and bulimia that associate eating disorders with demons and witches. Moreover, her conflation of fat with her consuming mother and with the threat of a pregnant belly shows that Josie imagines that obesity may overtake her from within and from without. In both cases demoniac fat intimately relates to female flesh and sexuality.[15]

Josie's distaste for female flesh in general, and particularly for her fat mother's, finds an analogy in her perceptions of food. Recurrently, foods that Josie considers "bad," read fattening, are associated in her mind with women's

---

[14] "She's dragging me by the hair, my skin is coming out in handfuls, the carpet is burning my skin off my elbows, she's trying to gouge my eyes with her other hand, with my teeth and nails I flail at her ankles, missing and screaming, screaming and screaming, the fire engine is at the door, false alarm, yes but what *is* the smell? *In a sample of sixty cannibal societies, about thirty-five percent roasted the meat, regardless of whether it came from kin or from strangers.* It's the roast, officer (my daughter, skinned and burning); sorry to have bothered you. *Out of twenty-six cannibal societies who ate only their relatives, only two actually boiled them. The cannibals not only unpredictably roasted or boiled relatives and strangers alike; they also baked them, smoked them, or ate them raw.* Next time, gag her as well. I will, officer, I will." (*L-S* 24-25). See *L-S* 67, 80-81, and 148 for other descriptions of this scene.

[15] Despite Josie's obvious distaste for the mature female body, it would be simplistic to suggest that her eating disorder is motivated by a fear of adult female sexuality. Josie's attitude towards sexuality is complex: she is able to experience arousal as something positive

bodies. During a binge she contemplates the doughnuts she has just bought as follows: "But could I really eat these lewd-looking pastries, powdered like a plump woman's flesh, in public?" (*L-S* 171). Butter is "lewd," chewing is "obscene"—both adjectives that Josie associates with overweight or pregnant women. Having been given another chance to try to eat voluntarily before she is artificially fed, Josie is allowed to choose foods she will not have to consume; these are "[m]eat, fish, eggs, and the opaque white or bluish white liquid secreted by the mammary glands of female mammals for the nourishment of their young" (*L-S* 73-74).[16]

During the course of her ten-year radical diet Josie learns a variety of ways to make foods appear inedible to her. She separates foods into categories of good and evil. Diet advice is remembered and applied whenever possible. On the two occasions when she is confronted with a menu containing cheese, Josie recalls the diet mantra: "[*c*]*heese is the hardest food to digest and it contaminates everything you eat it with*" (*L-S* 12, 38). Similarly, when she is served salad she remembers the dietary advice: "*It's possible to slow yourself down by eating too much salad*" (*L-S* 10, 164). Furthermore, Josie associates types of food with unappetizing things they resemble so as to render them inedible: hence lentil soup becomes diarrhea (*L-S* 164) and chicken a corpse in her mind (*L-S* 4). Just as people resemble foods to her, so foodstuffs take on anthropomorphic qualities in Josie's mind: She pictures a glass of milk as being "beaded with sweat" (*L-S* 2); she wants to kill the egg she has been served, before it kills her; and she attributes malevolent intentions to a potato: "It's plump, complacent, daring me to eat it" (*L-S* 126).

Contrarily, Josie reads the Food Section of the *New York Times* as food pornography, fantasizes about vanilla and strawberries and cream (*L-S* 3),

---

and to think of the female body with pleasure, for instance, when she thinks of the image of Amanda's long tanned limbs (*L-S* 188).

[16] Although Josie is disgusted by fat in general, she shows no such obsessive interest in men's bodies and flesh as she does in women's.

dreams about food while she is in college, and describes inanimate objects using food-related metaphors. Josie envisions the hospital's corridor as "a stretch of shiny avocado floor" (*L-S* 44).

This conflation of images reveals the narrator's skewed vision of herself and her body. Everything she perceives is reduced in her mind to food, bodies, fat, bones, and the edible and inedible.

Testifying in an Enclosed Space

Another confessional aspect of the narrative is that it takes place in a setting that is typically used for making personal testimonies. As Foucault argues, the confessional has been replaced by police stations, psychiatrists' and medical doctors' offices, and hospitals as loci of confession. Axthelm points out that the enclosed space is a necessary ingredient for making literary confessions. Finally, Ellmann portrays incarceration as one point of the triangular relationship that she posits as existing between expression, self-starvation, and imprisonment: the practices of forced enclosure are conducive to the examination of the hungering self in writing.

The main narrative strand in *Life Size* takes place within the hospital. Josie views the hospital and those who treat her with derision, hostility, or ironic detachment. Repeatedly, she compares therapeutic practices to forms of rape. She plays with the word "therapist," pointing out that nothing separates it from "the rapist" other than a single space (*L-S* 144, 217). The psychiatrist whom she refers to with the derisive nickname "Dr. Frog" repeatedly questions her about her sexual feelings and history. Steadfastly, she refuses to answer him or cooperate with his "probing" methods in any way. Likewise, she envisions the psychology student, who measures her with electrodes, and the endocrinologist, who takes samples of her blood, as invasive, penetrating vampires (*L-S* 144). She resents the staff's attempts to make her visible and translucent and fights to maintain autonomy over her body and mind.[17]

When, towards the end of the novel, she refuses to be filmed as part of a body awareness exercise, she points out that this exercise is futile. She attests that she can never be made to see herself objectively, for she will always be comparing herself to the (thin) actresses she has seen on television. Furthermore, she resents the imperfections of those who treat her. She nicknames them according to what she perceives as their negative physical attributes and abhors their, in her eyes, visible lack of self-control. Josie cannot imagine how a—to her mind—fat psychiatrist, overweight art therapist, and a nutritionist with sausage calves may teach her about healthy eating habits:

> It seems ironic that those trying to regulate my diet are themselves in need of a little self-control: this doctor, for instance, has quite a belly erupting over his belt. I focus on that and try to imagine him naked, with this mound of pale flab jiggling as he moves. I wonder if he's married—of course he would be, to some lumpy middle-aged lady: I envision their doughy coupling, his tired dick piling into her wobbly thighs. The image makes me giggle. (*L-S* 36)

Only Dr. Frog's inefficacy, overweight (as she, the emaciated anorectic, perceives it), and his interest in her non-existent sexual life impress Josie.[18] The carceral system she has constructed for herself—her anorexia—is far more powerful and compelling than anything the doctor disposes over. Josie's development into an anorectic thus illustrates Foucault's thesis that methods of surveillance and control have gradually been transferred from institutions to the subject. Josie's scrutiny of herself resembles a self-inflicted version of the

[17] "There's no privacy here, none at all: I'm the Visible Woman, with all my veins and nerves and guts on display. What goes in, what comes out, even what stays inside me is everybody else's business. To them, I'm merely an intestinal tube on legs" (*L-S* 173).

[18] This attitude of derision extends to Josie's other caretakers as well, except in time to Suzanne: Josie imagines the notes that a social worker takes about a meeting between her and the doctor, nurse, and nutritionist as follows: "Patient seems inexplicably resentful of flabby, decaying strangers gathered to prescribe her diet" (*L-S* 71).

Panopticon. Of her anorexia during her college years, she confesses "Yes, I was involved in politics—and economics, too—but not the way he [Dr. Frog] meant it. I lived under an absolute dictatorship, with myself as both subject and tyrant" (*L-S* 154). In this dictatorship not only food intake is regulated but also consumption of all kinds: nothing can be purchased until something else has been thrown away, no drink of water may be taken after ballet until Josie has returned home. While the narrator's ironic parodies of diagnostic profiles and staff manuals show that she views hospitalization as anything but therapeutic, the course of her treatment there provides the basic story line, which begins shortly after Josie's admittance and ends before her discharge. Following Ellmann's argument that incarceration leads to loquacity, one could say that for Josie to leave the confines of the hospital and the restrictions of her anorexia, she has to testify about the nature of her illness and self in full.

Aesthetic Qualities

According to Rosenthal it is the use of "affective language" that marks the difference between successful confessional poetry and mere revelation of personal details. As a confessional novel *Life-Size* is artistically convincing. Firstly, the two central narrative strands are interwoven masterfully and represent a metaphoric counterbalance to one another. In the framework story Josie enters the hospital feeling physically and emotionally weightless and empty of desire other than the wish to be thin. Radically alone, she is close to death, and her perceptions have a mostly hallucinatory quality. In the background narrative Josie loses weight and contact with the outside world until she is driven into a self-destructive, dreamlike state caused by her starvation.

In the foreground narrative she gradually begins to eat and "cohabit" with the healthier and heavier body (*L-S* 228). She also gains a sense of connection to another person, Suzanne. Initially only able to eat in Suzanne's presence,

Josie voices the realistic fear at her last interview with her psychiatrist that she will relapse into anorexic habits once she leaves the hospital. The "support" she most needs would come from her continuing to see Suzanne, whose steady presence in her life has been more therapeutic than any of Dr. Frog's strained investigations into her psyche (*L-S* 226-227). Once having totally rejected women's flesh and all forms of closeness, Josie now recognizes that she wants to hold onto Suzanne's warm and reassuring body. The novel's open end suggests that Josie may be able to accept the human burden of dying "slowly" by leading a normal life rather than dying rapidly as an anorectic.[19]

The narrator interweaves the narrative strands by incorporating words and associations from one story in the other. For instance, Josie's binge, after a night spent with a medical student during college, culminates in her consuming chocolate doughnuts. She comments on this episode and picks up the strand of the main story as follows:

> Something savory: I was sick from sugar. But on the way out, afraid to stop even for a few minutes, I bought another doughnut—Choc D'Lite—and, abandoning shame, ate it as I walked, smearing chocolate on my face and hands like shit.
>
> 'We're not *going* to give you a laxative, and that's all there is to it.'
>
> 'But I'm in agony. I haven't been to the bathroom for days.' (*L-S* 172)

"Shit" and "laxative" are, of course, the connecting images, one resulting from the ingestion of the other. This passage again illustrates Josie's tendency to mix food and body-related imagery. As in the poem "Surrounded" chocolate is associated with feces—perhaps because of the speaker's shame that she is

---

[19] The following interchange occurs between Josie and Suzanne at the end of the novel: "Then it strikes me that perhaps the larger question is equally simple. After a while, I try out this idea. 'Well, maybe I only have two options.'

'Oh yeah? What are those?'

'Well, the same as anyone else. Live or die.'

'Oh for heaven's sake—'

'And even if it's, you know, I still have a choice: Quickly or slowly' (*L-S* 229).

consuming this type of "bad" fattening food. Eating chocolate is as shameful as wallowing in, or consuming, one's own fecal matter.

Usually, the narrator uses physical images to bridge the two narrative strands: e.g. a scene in which Josie's hand starts to bleed after she has injured herself with a broken glass in the hospital is followed by a description of how she bled after she lost her virginity; a flashback to all the vegetables she could eat during family dinners at home—those which took the longest to eat—and those she could not, for instance salad and potatoes—because they were saturated with fat or "evil" respectively—proceeds a scene from the hospital in which Josie feels unable to eat the potato she has been served, because it is "alive" (*L-S* 126). Such narrative shifts illustrate the narrow range of the protagonist's mind; her thoughts travel from images of food to bodily waste and back again. This concentration on anthropomorphic images of food and bodily waste demonstrates the tendency common to many eating-disordered women to project personality traits onto inanimate objects, particularly food.

While revealing a number of possible interrelated causes of Josie's anorexia, the novel never becomes heavy-handedly didactic. The triangulation in Josie's family of origin, including her mother's obesity, emotional dissatisfaction, and repressed violence towards her daughter, her father's emotional disengagement and latent incestuous urges; Josie's inability to engage emotionally or sexually with others without punishing her body with starvation or engorgement afterwards; and societal pressure on all women to try to be perfect by being thin—all of these factors contribute to Josie's difficulties with her body and food.

The novel succeeds in making the anorectic's mindset comprehensible. This has much to do with the first-person narrator's being an intelligent and articulate observer. Repeatedly, Josie refers to herself as an artist of the self, whose materials are "air and bone and will" (*L-S* 129). By appreciating the auto-eroticism involved in Josie's anorexia—the glorying in the "perfections" of the self she has constructed—the reader may begin to understand how it is that she has sacrificed everything else in her life to the pursuit of thinness:

> Only I know what kind of shape this body is in, only I can appreciate its various perfections. What lover, in his urgent rush to ram himself into me, could properly appreciate what I have created here—the lean skid of the flank, the poignant ridging of the rib cage, the tiny bones of the feet? (*L-S* 43)

Josie combines the roles of Pygmalion and Galatea in her own person. Pygmalion, a sculptor from Cyprus, fell in love with the sculpture he had made out of perfect white marble of an exquisitely beautiful woman. Desperate, he offered sacrifice to the goddess of beauty and love Aphrodite during a festival in her honor in the hope that she might make the sculpture come to life. Aphrodite granted Pygmalion's wish, and when he returned home from the festival and kissed the sculpture's lips, he felt them turn warm beneath his touch. Josie takes an artist's pride in having created a perfect object—one that displays the maker's discipline and mastery of the materials. And she loves this image in itself, particularly its sculptural articulated qualities, and feels more for it than she could for anyone or anything else. Finally, Josie is Galatea as well: she embodies the perfectly formed sculpture.[20]

Josie's pride and sensual enjoyment of her skeletal form bespeaks her idealized image of herself as a hunger artist. That her self-image also has a negative side is revealed in her visions of herself dancing or swallowing splinters of glass. Both of these visions are heightened versions of a pivotal moment in Josie's history. After a protracted binge, she takes a shower and is

---

[20] Similarly, Elisabeth Bronfen describes how some women writers such as Anne Sexton and Sylvia Plath simultaneously adopt and subvert the traditional poetic likening of beautiful femininity and death when they write about their own and each other's deaths. In these poems the speakers take on both the positions of subject and object of the image just as Josie envisions herself in the above passage as both the artist and the artistic object. Elisabeth Bronfen, *Over Her Dead Body: Death, Femininity and the Aesthetic* (Manchester, Manchester UP, 1992) 401-403.

horrified by what she perceives to be the enormous bloated girth of her body. As an antidote, she decides to take some diet pills or laxatives (the reader does not learn which, but knows she abuses both), and, accidentally, drops a glass on the floor of her shower. To clean up the glass she puts on her winter boots to protect her feet and, for lack of a dustpan, starts to clean up the glass with a teaspoon. In a semi-hallucinatory state, she forgets what she is doing, dances on the glass shards until they are crushed into tiny splinters, and then proceeds to eat them with a spoon, imagining that they are sugar or ice crystals (*L-S* 218). As a result of this episode, Josie concludes that she cannot continue to live alone. Her roommate Jane later calls Josie's parents to insist that Josie needs help.

An exaggerated, verbally-heightened version of this scene is repeatedly referred to by Josie. In the second chapter Josie envisions herself eating ground glass with the doctor's approval. She pictures herself as a kind of Ophelia, floating on water, with blood running out of her mouth: "I smile slightly: my lips turn vivid red from the inside out, my skin chalk-pale (with my dark hair, I'm Snow White, I'm an image floating up from a Pre-Raphaelite lake)" (*L-S* 21). Even when she pictures her death, an aesthetic quality prevails. Recalling her history in a series of photographs, she describes her pre-pubescent self "as a nymph, my toe shoes very shiny, my mouth blood-dark)" (*L-S* 51). Such images recall Sylvia Plath's last poems in which dying women are stylized as perfect, mythic, or even, like Lady Lazarus, invincible. For instance, in the first lines of "Edge" (1963)[21] the speaker declares:

> The woman is perfected.
> Her dead
>
> Body wears the smile of accomplishment
> The illusion of a Greek necessity

---

[21] Sylvia Plath, "Edge," *The Collected Poems,* ed. Ted Hughes (New York: Harper & Row, 1981) 272. For further discussion of the idealization of death by an eating-disordered narrator and her adoption of Plath's imagery, see the description of Hornbacher's *Wasted* below.

As in the passage cited above in which Josie envisions herself as the lover of her own skeletal form, the speaker of "Edge" describes the dead form of the woman as having finally achieved a state of perfection.

The memory of herself as a ballerina is amplified on in Josie's ecstatic vision of herself as a leaping dancer and then retold in a darker fashion some hundred pages later in the narrative:

> My toe shoes are very shiny, my mouth blood-dark. Attired as a nymph, I pick my way delicately over the shattered glass—no, they're only snowflakes, ice crystals (but beware, they can travel to the heart and lodge there). The aroma of rosin intoxicates me; the lights are blindingly hot and white; beyond them, a velvet murmur. With a flourish, I unfurl a long, pale leg; my arm swims through space to hold me up. I could stay there forever, my being poised upon a single point, but the music tells me it's time to come down, to gather for the final leap. This time I know I can do it. The audience seems to sense something, too; the darkness draws in its breath. I coil, I spring, and it happens: I'm strong and spare enough to soar, to keep soaring, my arched front foot slicing space like the head of an arrow. Up, up, buoyed by the air, buffeted through the flies, past the startled stagehands, and out into the infinite night, while the audience, amazed and then afraid, waits in vain for me to reappear. (*L-S* 33-34)

The imagery in this scene is martial. Josie "unfurls" her leg like a flag, she "coils" and "springs" like a leopard during the hunt, she "soars" and slices "space like the head of an arrow"—all of which images suggest a battle or onslaught. The Amazon-like creature whom Josie imagines herself to be reminds the reader of the speaker of "Becoming a Woman" who describes her efforts to hunt out and destroy invasive calories. In both the fantasies of herself as a soaring dancer and a Pre-Raphaelite beauty, floating dead on a lake, the lightness of Josie's idealized vision of her body is emphasized. In both cases, gravity is defeated, and the body soars or floats above the masses.

Scenes in which the narrator pictures herself as an invincible dancer or as a beautiful dying Snow White such as the ones cited above are problematic from a culturally critical point of view. The aestheticism of these passages may seduce the impressionable reader, who has been just as conditioned by the images of beautiful, thin young women as Josie has been, into emulating Josie's unhealthy behavior and thinking patterns. Yet this quality marks successful confessional writing: intimate and painful details are rendered compelling.

Compare the pride and sense of accomplishment expressed in the above passage about Josie as a leaping dancer with the following retelling of the same scene. This retelling occurs after Josie has been forced to gain weight in the hospital, and she no longer feels a Pygmalion-like adoration for her creation, her perfect body, nor a general's pride in having conquered the enemy. The ballerina has been transformed into a harlequin or clown:

> My toe shoes are very shiny, my mouth blood-dark. Masked like a harlequin, I pick my way over broken glass. The aroma of rosin sickens me; the lights are blindingly hot and white; beyond them, a hostile buzz. I try to unfurl a leg, but something is wrong, I can't balance, my arms flap like fins. I want to run offstage, but the music commands me to stay, to give the audience what it paid for. I know I can't make it, but, grinning desperately, I go through the motions, trying to hold out until the end. I almost do, but as I recoil for the final leap, an ankle folds under me and I stumble instead, landing on hands and knees, gravity's pied fool. (*L-S* 180)

In both passages the public element of anorexia is stressed: an audience and musicians—who rub the bows of their stringed instruments with rosin—observe the ballerina and harlequin's heroic efforts to make themselves disappear. We remember that Kafka's hunger artist died of starvation when the audience lost interest in observing how long he could fast. In the second passage the audience is no longer adoring but hostile, and the speaker is no longer capable of flourish. Metaphors concerning weight and weightlessness are played with in the transition from the first telling of the scene to the second one. Whereas in the first version of this scene the ballerina has complete control over her body and is able to leap over her observers as though she were lighter than air, the harlequin in the second version is clumsy. Instead of leaping, she falls heavily to the floor in a debased position. On a metaphorical level this retelling of the scene exhibits how Josie perceives her weight gain to be a form of weakness and fallibility. The recovering Josie experiences herself as horribly transformed. Her vision of herself as deformed and physically deficient expresses her crushing sense of shame.

The final chapter of *Life-Size* contains none of these fantasies of exaggerated public performance by the narrator. Shortly before her discharge Josie considers whether she shall be able to continue eating once she is outside of the hospital and whether she shall be able to bear living within her heavier body, a body that no longer offers her a sense of security when she measures and mirrors it:

> For reassurance, I grasp my thighs and run my hands upward, probing for hipbones, but all I feel is flesh. Sitting up anxiously, I look down at my thighs, huge now, spread out to double their dimensions, with a Y-shaped fold where my belly meets them—or, more accurately, rests on them. (*L-S* 228)

These feelings of sadness and heaviness contrast with the sense of weightless invincibility she had at the opening of the novel when her brain was "taking in colors, sounds, with a fine, vibrating intensity" (*L-S* 7). The narrative voice has moved from the hyperbolic to the realistic. This stylistic change mirrors Josie's move away from the absolutism of her anorexic mindset to a more ordinary manner of perceiving the world. Reshaped, she no longer envisions herself as a bloody-mouthed ballerina who leaps into weightlessness or falls on her face. This shift suggests that part of the anorectic's process of healing consists of no longer dramatizing experience. Gone is the rich imagery of Pre-Raphaelite ladies and leaping dancers. In the final chapter of *Life-Size* we find Josie watching television and feeling depressed. To put it colloquially, she has become just like the rest of us, no longer enchanted by her grandiose—and in part compelling—sense of her own invincibility.

In the movement to greater insight into the self that Axthelm describes as the defining moment in the confessional novel, Josie recognizes that she is in grave danger of returning to her anorexic behaviors. She asks, "Can I learn to be so present? Can I learn to be so full?" (*L-S* 228). This painful knowledge of her limitations contrasts with the alternating sense of invincibility or monstrousness that marked her previous sense of self. Telling the worst—the details of how she came to swallow glass at the end of chapter seventeen—seems to have been the necessary precedent for Josie's becoming healthier and less exaggerated in her way of perceiving things. Purgation occurs through the narration of the most sensationalistic and dramatic of personal bodily events. After this narrative climax a calm ensues, and the novel comes to a conclusion. The narrative process itself is not made explicit. The narrator does not dwell on how the telling of her painful history contributes to her recovery. Rather, events are dramatized, and the reader sees how the disparate and conflicting images that the narrator has had of herself are resolved into a more unified sense of self.

3.3) Comparing *Life-Size* to Margaret Atwood's *Lady Oracle*: Confessional and Anti-Confessional Treatments of Disordered Eating

As a way of opening *Life-Size* up further I want to compare it briefly to another novel that also explores the effect of an eating disorder on its protagonist's life. The text is *Lady Oracle* (1976), written by the critically acclaimed Canadian author Margaret Atwood and published 16 years before *Life-Size* appeared. *Lady Oracle* shares many thematic and metaphorical similarities with *Life-Size.*

Like *Life-Size, Lady Oracle* deals with the protagonist's problems with an eating disorder and her interrelated sense of identity. Joan Foster was a binge eater during her childhood and early adulthood and used food as a way of enraging her weight- and appearance-conscious mother. Her obesity served as a continual reproach to her mother. Strikingly, both Shute's and Atwood's narrators employ the same imagery of rising dough to describe their own flesh in conjunction to that of their respective mothers. Joan writes about her adolescent obesity: "I swelled visibly, relentlessly, before her very eyes, I rose like dough, my body advanced inch by inch towards her across the dining-room table, in this at least I was undefeated" (*LO* 70). When Josie contemplates her own weight gain, she writes: "Dense and polluted, this immense mass of flesh swells like dough as I lie here; raising my hand to the light, I see only my mother's fat paw" (*L-S* 30). This likening of the unaesthetic body to food is familiar from the poem "The Angel That Feeds Me."[22]

As an adult Joan manages to lose one hundred pounds and tries to destroy all evidence of her past as a fat woman. However, she is repeatedly visited by visions of herself as a fat lady in the circus, who, while dressed in a tutu, either sits in the freak show knitting, or performs physically impossible or embarrassing feats before a huge audience. These visions recall a humiliating scene from her childhood in which she was forced to perform in a mothball costume rather than a tutu at a ballet recital, because her mother thought she would look too ludicrously fat in the latter. In three of her fantasies Joan imagines the Fat Lady in an elevated position, as tight-rope walking across the expanse of the Canadian nation, as floating above Olympic figure skaters, as rising like an enormous ghost from beneath Joan's rented apartment in Terremoto, Italy (*LO* 102-103, 273-274, 320-321). She does not resemble the slender flying arrow in Josie's image of herself as a leaping dancer but is described in comedic, absurd terms:

> She was even fatter than I had imagined her, fatter than the crude picture of her painted on the hoarding, much fatter than me. She was wearing pink tights with spangles, a short fluffy pink skirt, satin ballet slippers and, on her head, a sparkling tiara. She carried a diminutive pink umbrella. (*LO* 102)

[22] See chapter I, section 1.3) above.

The costumes in Josie's and Joan's fantasies of themselves are virtually identical; they are that of the ballerina—a symbol of desirable femininity in both American and the Canadian cultural settings. Whereas Josie's idealized ballerina is emaciated and flies above the heads of her viewers, Joan's monstrous ballerina is obese and defies her audience's expectations when she is elevated above them. Joan's visions of herself as the fat woman, who tightrope walks or floats above the heads of ice skaters, play upon conventional notions of weight and lightness. Like a balloon floating above the ground the Fat Lady is in a vulnerable position; she may fall down—from the tightrope—or be shot down like a balloon. She is perceived as a monstrosity, as something that must be removed from public view: "Really it was an outrage. 'They've gone for the harpoon gun,' I heard the commentator say" (*LO* 274).

Both Joan's and Josie's visions of themselves as ballerinas demonstrate their awareness that their bodies are public property. The protagonists assume that everyone is ready to applaud or boo their public performances. As Joan reflects about a Freak Show that she wanted to visit as a girl: "The man with the megaphone sounded the same for freaks and dancing girls alike: They were both spectacular, something that had to be seen to be believed" (*LO* 90). To have a female body—whether emaciated or enormously fat—is to be a performer in the public circus.

Despite the differences in their ages and their nationalities, both Joan and Josie were raised in cultures that dictate conformity to a narrowly-defined norm of female appearance.[23] In part this is attested to in their descriptions of their girlhood fascination with their Barbie dolls' physical perfections. In dating rituals both women also experienced how vital slenderness and good looks are for feminine success. Josie fears being considered a "dog" by the adolescent

---

[23] Joan gets married in her early twenties in 1964, and Josie begins going to college during Bobby Sands hunger strike in 1981. Hence it becomes clear that Joan grew up in the forties and fifties in Toronto, Canada, and Josie during the sixties and seventies in the United States.

boys in her school; Joan's best hope of a part in the high school dating drama is that of playing confidante to her thin friends.

In one of her sub-identities Joan writes esoteric poetry. In this context she is compared by journalists to a Pre-Raphaelite figure;[24] and Joan makes repeated references to Tennyson's "The Lady of Shalott," in which the lady dies by drowning. Josie's vision of herself floating with bloodied mouth on top of the Pre-Raphaelite lake is reminiscent of Joan's romantic girlhood desire to "have someone, anyone, say that I had a lovely face, even if I had to turn into a corpse in a barge-bottom first" (*LO* 105). A romanticized vision of womanhood as beautiful, long-haired, slender, and sorrowful commands Joan's as well as Josie's imagination. The image of the beautiful Pre-Raphaelite woman has such a power over the collective imaginations of girls in Western culture that it seems literally worth dying for.

In another curious similarity between the two novels Joan and Josie both dance upon broken glass. In Joan's case this happens inadvertently at the end of the novel when, while fantasizing about waltzing with her idealized lover, she steps on shards of broken glass. As she points out she thus re-enacts the plot of *The Red Shoes* literally: the cuts from the glass shards make her feet turn red. In the 1938 movie a beautiful ballet dancer must choose between her career and the love of her handsome husband. The dancer resolves the conflict by committing suicide.[25] Since *The Red Shoes* was released some forty years before the events in *Life-Size* occur, it is unlikely that this melodramatic movie played a part in Josie's imagination.

This marks an important difference between the two protagonists. The texts and images that inform Joan's ideals of feminine behavior are romantic

---

[24] "[...] hair in the female was regarded as more important than either talent or the lack of it. *Joan Foster, celebrated author of* Lady Oracle, *looking like a lush Rossetti portrait, radiating intensity, hypnotized the audience with her unearthly* [...] (The Toronto Star)" (*LO*, 14).

ones: *The Red Shoes*, "The Lady of Shalott," the Costume Gothics she writes. In these narratives the central tension is between men and women, and the suffering the woman must endure before she wins love or dies. Joan tries to live out her compelling interest in the romances she fantasizes about. Josie, however, has grown up during the age of *Seventeen* magazine after the appearance of Twiggy. Arguably, romantic, neo-Gothic clichés about the behavior of men and women persist, but the importance of the thin body to a woman's positive sense of her own identity has grown steadily more important. Josie's cultural references are not to Moira Shearer's dilemma or Joan Crawford's tragic face with all the associations of unfulfilled romantic love they imply, but to the idealized body she has seen incessantly depicted and described. "*Be Some Body*" (*L-S* 64, 66) is the credo of faith she grew up with and which shaped ten years of her eating-disordered life.

Striking as the thematic similarities between the novels are, I suspect they are incidental. Atwood's and Shute's use of imagery overlap, but their explorations of a woman's relationship to her identity and her weight are radically different in their purpose and style. Furthermore, the author of *Life-Size* refers to various fictional texts that were instrumental to her writing Josie's story in the Acknowledgments and does not mention *Lady Oracle* (*L-S* 231).

Atwood is not interested in giving us a realistic portrait of an eating-disorder sufferer's point of view. Rather, she uses the protagonist's weight concerns and fluctuations as one part of the puzzle she puts together concerning personal and textual identity. If anything, *Lady Oracle* is an anti-confessional novel, because no unified vision of the first-person narrator is provided or striven for. Joan's vacillations, her assorted identities as a fat adolescent duenna to more attractive girlfriends, a Polish Count's mistress, the bright but inept wife of a Canadian revolutionary, the secret author of Costume Gothics, the esoteric

---

[25] See *LO* 82 for Joan's girlhood attachment to the movie and 334-335 for her absurd re-enactment of it as an adult.

poetess, the sexually exuberant lover of the Royal Porcupine, and the runaway—who tries to shed her physical identity by cutting off her long trade-mark red hair and dying it brown, just as she once shed a hundred pounds—are never resolved. Similarly, the various types of texts in the novel, the Gothic Romance, the realistic narrative, the poetry, the intertextual references to Tennyson, etc., and the fantasies about the Fat Lady are never unified. While it is explained why Costume Gothics are so compelling to many women, the genre itself is subverted when the identities of the villainous Felicia and the angelic Charlotte are merged during their search through the maze.[26] The disparate and conflicting nature of the texts and Joan's roles in them is part of the point—identity is fluid and not fixed.

Women's troubled and myriad relations to their bodies, to clothes, and to their general appearances have always been of interest to Atwood. In her debut novel *The Edible Woman* (1969), Marian McAlprin's unhappiness with her engagement and the conventional feminine role it implies—including the end of her career, her becoming a dissatisfied housewife and mother like her friend Clara, and the trophy wife her fiancé Peter desires—are marked by her increasing inability to eat. None of the anorectic's obsession with weight loss or thinness accompanies this, but rather a sense that the body has taken on an absurd will of its own. When Marian at last breaks off her engagement, she bakes an image of herself in effigy as a gaudily decorated cake, which she offers to Peter to eat. When he refuses, she eats the cake herself and is finally able to nourish herself again by symbolically consuming the image of a self she could not truly own.

In *Life Before Man* (1979) the middle-aged Elizabeth worries about her overweight figure and envies the fact that her young and slender rival Lesje can wear jeans. In the short story "Hair Jewellery" from *Dancing girls* (1982), the speaker views her frequent wardrobe changes as synonymous with changes in

[26] See *LO* 332-333 and 341-342 for parallel versions of the third Lady Redmond's fate.

her identity.[27] In *Cat's Eye* (1988) the protagonist Elaine Ripley is dismayed by the sight of the "broad expanse" of her bottom sighted in the changing room mirror and thinks "It's amazing how much bigger you always look from the back."[28] Tony, Charis, and Roz of *The Robber Bride* (1993) are obsessed by the transformations of their rival Zenia's body—how she manages to be thinner and to have larger breasts with every new appearance in their lives.

But Atwood makes no single programmatic statement about women's relationships to their bodies in these works. Plainly, Atwood is critical of a culture that identifies women with their bodies and uses the female body to buy and sell everything from automobiles to perfumes.[29] On the other hand she displays canniness regarding simplistic notions of how to change these cultural patterns; men are not simply to be blamed for women's uneasiness with their bodies or for eating disorders. This is demonstrated in the playful dialog "There Was Once" from *Bones & Murder* (1994) in which a male speaker tries to tell a fairy tale and is constantly interrupted by a female speaker who criticizes his lack of political correctness:

---

[27] "That's my technique, I resurrect myself through clothes, In fact it's impossible for me to remember what I did, what happened to me, unless I can remember what I was wearing, and every time I discard a sweater or a dress I am discarding a part of my life. I shed identities like a snake, leaving them pale and shrivelled behind me, a trail of them, and if I want any memories at all I have to collect, one by one, those cotton and wool fragments, piece them together, achieving at last a patchwork self, not defence anyway against the cold." Margaret Atwood, "Hair Jewellery," *Dancing Girls* (1977; London: O.W. Toad, Ltd., 1982) 102.

[28] Margaret Atwood, *Cat's Eye* (1988; New York: Bantam Doubleday, 1989) 46.

[29] "It [the female body] sells cars, beer, shaving lotion, cigarettes, hard liquor; it sells diet plans and diamonds, and desire in tiny crystal bottles. Is this the face that launched a thousand products? You bet it is, but don't get any funny big ideas, honey, that smile is a dime a dozen.

It does not merely sell, it is sold. Money flows into this country or that country, flies in, practically crawls in, suitful after suitful, lured by all those hairless preteen legs. Listen, you want to reduce the national debt, don't you? Aren't you patriotic? That's the spirit. That's my

- Stop right there. I think we can cut the *beautiful*, don't you? Women these days have to deal with too many intimidating physical role models as it is, what with those bimbos in the ads. Can't you make her, well, more average?
- There was once a girl who was a little overweight and whose front teeth stuck out, who—
- I don't think it's nice to make fun of people's appearances. Plus, you're encouraging anorexia.
- I wasn't making fun! I was just describing—[30]

Atwood portrays a male speaker who is unable to say anything acceptable about the fairy tale heroine's appearance. Traditional ways of describing women (and men) are obsolete and are judged as being politically incorrect and malicious towards women in their intent.

Men's lack of comprehension of women's complex feelings about their bodies is explored further in the "Spring Song of the Frogs" from *Bluebird's Egg* (1983). The well-intentioned Will is dismayed by the weight loss and bizarre eating behaviors of the women who surround him. His lunch date reacts to the bread he offers her as though he were threatening her with poison. His teenage niece, once a vital, strong, and energetic girl, lies in the hospital where she is being treated for anorexia like a limp, white sheet. His former lover eats only half of the meal he has prepared and—as he witnesses—forces herself to vomit up what she did consume. Will longs for the generous proportions of the *Playboy* models of his youth and cannot understand the obsession with thinness.

Although the body of the protagonist and her distorted sense of self stand at the thematic center of *Lady Oracle*, the novel is anti-confessional in tone. The testimony of intimate bodily details does not transpire in a purgative fashion. How Joan was teased about her body as a girl, how she came to despise her own fatness, and fears her fat self as an adult are all told with humor and

---

girl." From Margaret Atwood, "The Female Body," *Bones & Murder* (London: Virago, 1994) 81.

[30] Margaret Atwood, "There Was Once," *Bones & Murder* 23-24.

distance. Joan describes her moment of shocked self-recognition when she realizes how fat she is:

> There, staring me in the face, was my thigh. It was enormous, it was gross, it was like a diseased limb, the kind you see in pictures of jungle natives; it spread on forever, like a prairie photographed from a plane, the flesh not green but bluish-white, with veins meandering across it like rivers. It was the size of three ordinary thighs. I thought, That is really my thigh, It really is, and then I thought, This can't possibly go on. (*LO* 121)

Mikhail Bahktin's description of the grotesque images of the body in literature and art is applicable here. Exaggerated and hyperbolic language is used to mark the grotesqueries of the scene. The "limits between the body and the world are erased."[31] Hence the thigh in question becomes a prairie viewed from above. The veins covering it resemble rivers. The repetition of the word "It" to describe the thigh with ever more fantastic images underlies its absurd, monstrous qualities. It is not a thigh, an integrated part of the body, but a monstrous growth, "a diseased limb" with a life of its own; this life is presumably its potential for limitless expansion. The humor begins with the notion of a thigh staring the speaker in the face. The limits of credibility are already stretched, and the idiomatic expression is heard literally: a thigh—an enormous one—and a face stare at each other.

The grotesque humor of this scene contrasts starkly with the painful seriousness with which the anorectic Josie regards her thighs (cited above). No sense of better-understood self is striven for through the uncovering of the naked bodily self but rather comic effect. Whereas *Life-Size* gives its reader the impression that the anorectic may begin to have a unified sense of her mind and body when she recovers, *Lady Oracle* suggests that there are multiple bodies lurking within every form. As Joan says of her life as an adulteress:

---

[31] Mikhail Bahktin, *Rabelais and His World*, trans. Helene Iswolsky (Cambridge: M.I.T. Press, 1968) 310.

> That was the beginning of my double life. But hadn't my life always been double? There was always that shadowy twin, thin when I was fat, fat when I was thin, myself in silver negative, with dark teeth and shining white pupils glowing in the black sunlight of that other world. [...] But not twin even, for I was more than double, I was triple, multiple, and now I could see that there was more than one life to come, there were many. (*LO* 246)

In Atwood's post-modern novel a unified sense of textual, bodily and, psychological identity is not to be won by testifying about the truth of the body. Bodies, texts, and identities remain disparate and contradictory; they may even multiply themselves when they are spoken about.

IV Stephanie Grant's *The Passion of Alice* An Ironic Take on Coerced Confession in an Eating Disorder Clinic

Plots, settings, and protagonists of *Life-Size* (1992) and *The Passion of Alice* (1995) resemble each other greatly. Both novels offer first-person accounts of being hospitalized for life-threatening anorexia. And both novels' narrators come from highly educated, upper-middle-class Anglo-Saxon backgrounds from the American Northeast. Josie and Alice personify the typical 'golden girl' anorectics whom Bruch portrays in her *Golden Cage* other than that they are adults at the time of the narratives. Set in the 1980s the novels explore the cultural background of eating disorders and critically comment on how American culture encourages young women to articulate problems in food and body abuse. Hospitals provide the settings for both novels. In remembered scenes the narrators reveal the history of their families, their first diets, and their evolution into anorexia.

Yet the differences between the two novels is what makes a comparison between them interesting. Unlike *Life-Size*, *The Passion of Alice* wholly lacks Gothic elements. Alice retains a distanced and highly rational voice throughout much of the novel that bears her name; her perceptions of herself and her body never take on the hallucinatory, hyperbolic quality. Nor does Alice view her body in an exaggerated fashion as being either monstrous or idealized. Instead, she scrutinizes her figure in a harsh, seemingly objective light and measures it constantly and pseudo-scientifically against the bodies of the women around her. Memories of Alice's life prior to her hospitalization are presented with more conventional narrative means than in *Life-Size*. Alice recalls her past in a series of isolated reminiscences. Visiting the hospital's swimming pool with her mother, she remembers the underwater infant swimming course she and her mother once attended. After describing her first two weeks in the eating-disorders unit of Seaview in Parts I and II, the narrator begins Part III with a brief family history that centers on her parents' divorce. A scene in which Alice masturbates precedes a chapter in which she describes how she and her best friend Roland first had sexual intercourse in high school. Finally, *The Passion of Alice* differs from *Life-Size* in that it offers an anti-confessional account of anorexia and hospitalization.

4.1) *The Passion of Alice*'s Critique of American Culture

The Passion of Alice lays the blame for the narrator's anorexia largely on America's obsession with an idealized version of feminine appearance. This obsession manifests itself in the improbable standards of physical perfection embodied by Barbie dolls. Alice's negative comparisons of her body with her mother's also comments on America's beauty standard. Despite the fact that Alice's mother is unhappy, her 'perfect' body renders her a vehicle for infinite romantic and heroic possibilities—in her daughter's eyes—whereas Alice's own highly imperfect body destines her to be a failure. Finally, the narrator examines how women's position of dependency within American culture makes them more likely to manifest their problems in covert forms of self-torture such as eating disorders and mutilation rather than in more overt demonstrations of unhappiness.

As for Josie, Barbies were a part of Alice's cultural training as a girl. Alice owned three kinds of Barbies and played with them regularly. During an excursion to a mall, Alice chooses a Barbie doll as a gift for her fellow patient, the binge-eater Louise because she correctly assumes that Louise probably never played with one. Louise's childhood obesity excluded her from those rituals that inculcate Western girls with feminine behaviors and ideals. As Alice reflects, "Why practice at what you can never be, not in the fullest sense of what it means to be a girl. Which starts with being recognizable in your body" (*PoA* 149). Thus Alice offers the reader a definition of girlhood that brings American culture's fascination with beauty into clear focus. To be a girl is to be a body and to aim to have one's body resemble Barbie's idealized form. (Of course, Barbie's body is not truly recognizable as that of a woman: With the waist of a young child, the hips of an adolescent boy, and the breasts of a silicon-enhanced porn star, she is a composite picture of a culturally-propagated, unattainable model).

Alice re-enacts some of the rituals of girlhood when she undresses the Barbie she has brought into the dressing room: "This was something we did every day as girls: compromise our dolls" (*PoA* 153). Touching Barbie's changeless, anatomically-impossible plastic body is "oddly reassuring" (*PoA* 153). The icon of femininity remains without alteration. The passage suggests that the practice of undressing Barbie and caressing her oddly exaggerated adult female body is a process by which girls learn to covet a type of feminine appearance that they will try to emulate.

Indeed, an idealization of the perfect female form informs Alice's picture of herself and causes her to feel inadequate as an adolescent. Alice explains how she came to understand that she would never conform or "measure up" to the beauty ideal and how this realization led her to become anorexic. Unlike Josie, who cites women's magazines and diet books as her source of knowledge about how she should look, Alice finds a model of physical perfection in her mother. In seventh grade she begins to recognize that she will never be beautiful. Whereas her mother has a "body for possibility" (*PoA* 57), made to be the subject of every narrative about winning and success, Alice's body remains imperfect, with too-wide hips, mismatched breasts, and a short waist.

When Alice learns that the American work ethic will not function in regard to her physical appearance, in other words, no matter how hard she diets she will remain average looking, she resigns herself to never looking like her mother. While her high school contemporaries first perform the typical Western rite of passage for girls by going on diet after diet—"Stillmann, Scarsdale, high-protein, low-protein, steak-lovers, grapefruit, etc." (*PoA* 56)—Alice recognizes the immutability of her imperfect body. This sense of imperfection becomes her constant mental companion: diving off the starting blocks in swim meets, her sense of other swimmers' physical superiority tells her she will lose the race (*PoA* 57); bent upon losing her virginity to her best friend, a glance in the mirror and an inventory of her "[h]ips impossibly wide, flabby stomach, lopsided breasts, narrow shoulders" are enough to make her lose desire altogether (*PoA* 135). So deeply ingrained in Alice's mind is the cultural script for how erotic partners should appear that, failing to comply with them, she cannot picture herself as the object of Roland's desire and feels incapable of desiring him.

Anorexia, then, at first represents a defense against wanting at all. Alice reasons that by cultivating a lack of desire for food, she shall become indifferent to the wish to be beautiful. Resigning herself to her physical mediocrity helps little, however, since she remains conscious of her lack. As she recalls:

> I was in high school when I realized I would never be beautiful; before I had realized *I wasn't*, but in high school it dawned that *I'd never be*. I pretended faith, then intellect, were the things I truly valued. Nothing so superficial as appearance. I looked down my nose at girls who fussed. But with time came the suffocating recognition of what I'd lost. (*PoA* 58)

This sense of loss remains undiminished throughout the narrative. Near the end of the novel Alice's mother expresses her lack of comprehension of why Alice is starving herself to death, with the comment that she has "so much going for" her including good looks. To this, Alice replies angrily:

> I have never had looks, and don't you suggest I have. The last thing I want at my memorial is people commenting on what a pretty girl I was. And you know as well as I do that personality is a consolation prize, the fruit of an

> unpretty life. All I've ever been is smart, and apparently, not smart enough. Or I wouldn't be in this position. (*PoA* 227)

Alice equates prettiness of body with having a good life. No amount of intelligence can compensate for the lack of beauty, the quotation suggests.

Alice's awareness of her physical mediocrity is most acute when she regards her mother. (Ironically, beauty has not guaranteed Syd happiness; her husband, Alice's father, leaves her for a succession of women all less pretty than herself.) When Alice imagines what it was like when her mother took baby-swimming lessons with her as a child, she pictures how the other mothers must have envied Syd her faultless body: "I bet they coveted her clinched waist and flat stomach that made no reference to childbirth" (*PoA* 52). As for most women in American culture Syd's appearance is crucial to her sense of self-worth, and provides an unattainable standard for her daughter. While explaining the minutia of dealing with menstrual blood to her daughter, Syd refers to her flat belly and curved waist with the proud comment, "'Not bad for an old lady?'" (*PoA* 65).

The influence of the beauty myth is not just apparent in Alice's problematic relation to her own looks. Physical perfection, even in men, repels her as it reminds her of her own lack. The stunningly good looks of a visiting dentist, who teaches the eating-disordered patients how to care for their teeth, is cause for Alice to want "to trip him" (*PoA* 60)—to see him humiliated in front of the group of women to whom he has spoken condescendingly. She is acutely aware of the "imperfection" (*PoA* 69) of other women's bodies and measures her own thinness against that of Amy and Gwen. The fact that she is the thinnest among them fills her with pride. That the counselors in the unit, all recovered sufferers of eating disorders, are not thin irritates Alice enormously (*PoA* 90). During the first part of the novel Alice is particularly disdainful of Louise's morbid obesity. Secretly giving Louise those foods from her meals that she herself is loath to eat, Alice reflects, "Most people believed that anorexics only hate fat on their own bodies. Most people were wrong" (*PoA* 29). Repeatedly, she notes and categorizes Louise's various physical imperfections. Her distaste for Louise's volume is reflected in the following passages:

> I'd never understood how fat people got their strange physiques, why the weight didn't distribute itself evenly, why it usually collected in one or more distorted body part. Louise was diamond-shaped, with a great big ring of fat at her hips, her layered flesh tapering toward her head and feet. (*PoA* 23)

> [Louise] had a bad fat person's hairdo: blunt cut, but at an angle so that it was shortest at the nape of her neck and longest by her face, leaving the ropes of fat at her neck exposed. It was meant to frame her blotchy face, give it shape somehow, but that was impossible. Louise's face was endless, a face within a face within a face. (*PoA* 27-28)

It is a mark of the great mental distance Alice covers during the course of her hospitalization that she no longer views Louise's body with disgust at the end of the narrative. At this point, it enrages Alice to observe how a young nurse's aide regards Louise's obesity with disgust and obvious dislike.

During the course of her hospitalization Alice also reflects on why women may be more likely to be afflicted by eating disorders and men by alcohol and drug addictions. The women in Alice's eating disorders unit regularly take part in an Alcoholics Anonymous meeting with the men and women from the alcohol and drug rehabilitation center at the hospital. At one meeting they hear how a man named Joey describes or "shares" how he lost his wife, job, and freedom due to his addiction to cocaine. As Alice notes, the lower the usually-male addict has sunken, the more things he lost, the more he has been degraded, and the more he tells about his degradation and loss, the more he is admired by the others in this atmosphere of therapeutic confession. In terms of what they have "to lose," the situation differs quite radically for eating-disordered women:

> We had not lost jobs or wives or houses. For the most part we did not have things to lose; we were part of what most other people lost. Fat or

> emaciated, average-looking but obsessed, garbage pickers and pukers, we lived in houses that we did not pay for, houses with convection ovens and Cuisinarts, juicers and microwaves. None of us shared at the big mixed meeting. [...]
>
> Listening to the others, we felt ashamed caring as much as we did about food. We felt frivolous. (*PoA* 46)

Although for the most part better educated than their male counterparts, the women are not in positions in which they could have or lose possessions, jobs, spouses, or stature. Alone, they lose or gain weight. The "girls," as Alice calls them, do not make or fail to make mortgage payments on homes. Rather, they were requisite components of the upper-middle-class homes before they became hospitalized just like the convection ovens, juicers, and other expensive appliances listed above. Alice's observation underscores the hypothesis that eating disorders are cultural ills. The middle-class college-educated women in the eating disorder unit certainly have the wherewithal necessary to hold property. Yet their obsessive behavior regarding their appearances and food reinforces patriarchal relations. Their psychological disorders, which they express through the abuse of food and their bodies, render them weak and limits them to positions of dependency.

Women's cultural dependency is further illustrated by gender relations in the clinic, particularly by Maeve's interactions with Dr. Paul Sampson, the admitting doctor at Seaview. His flirtatious manner towards women, his fat hands, and his opinion that being single makes a woman more likely to have psychological difficulties with her mother (*PoA* 70)—all this irritates her. Alice's intuition that Dr. Paul is malevolent is proven true when he blackmails Maeve into having sex with him. Maeve initially believes that she can strategically avoid Dr. Paul's machinations. Having accepted cocaine from him at a bar where she and Alice have gone "illegally," she confidently informs Alice that she need not worry about Maeve's having to repay the "gift" with sexual favors: "'[...] for as long as men have been giving women cocaine so that women will fuck them, women have been doing their cocaine and not fucking them'" (*PoA* 190). Yet ultimately she does have to agree to sex with Dr. Paul in order to buy his secrecy. He literally holds all the keys of power to the clinic: he owns and distributes illegal drugs, may punish patients and ex-patients, and coerces a woman who despises him into having sex with him.

Alice comments on women's state of relative dependence in American culture in other contexts; she notes that "Self-control, self-effacement, [and] self-denial" are behaviors for which girls are usually rewarded and praised (*PoA* 61). When Alice learns after Gwen's death that her friend not only suffered from anorexia but also from a hair-pulling disorder which she kept secret, it comes as little surprise to her that this phenomenon occurs almost exclusively among women. Obsessive-compulsive behaviors like self-mutilation, or "cutting," and hair-pulling appear—as Alice sees it—to be women's domain, whereas, for instance, cocaine abuse with its more immediate public consequences such as losing houses, wives, and jobs remains a male prerogative for the greater part. On a metaphoric level the sites of female self-abuse are relegated to the home, to the kitchen, the bathroom, and the bedroom and remains largely invisible. By contrast, men's addictions and their consequences are played out more often in public spaces like bars and job sites.[1]

Yet the narrator of *The Passion of Alice* seems reluctant to view gender inequality as the sole cause of "female" disorders. She is far too committed to regarding her own anorexia as a form of religious self-knowledge and self-empowerment. This becomes clear when Alice describes the three prevailing "schools of thought" (*PoA* 25) regarding eating disorders at Seaview. Advocates of the addiction model perceive food as a substance over which the addict must admit his or her powerless to control; treatment then copies the twelve-step program of Alcoholics Anonymous. Neo-Freudians regard eating

[1] Of course, such an analysis is simplistic. Alcoholism may remain a hidden addiction that is played out in the private sphere by both men and women.

disorders as symptoms of a deeper psychological pathology: when the underlying trauma or illness is addressed the eating disorder will be cured. Finally, one woman psychiatrist at Seaview is a proponent of a feminist theory of eating disorders; she argues that when women started to claim more public space and a greater share of the economic pie in the 1970s they were simultaneously required to make themselves smaller physically. Alice regards this theory with caustic alarm as a justification for being fat:

> The big girls loved it [the feminist theory] because the treatment line was to stop dieting, stop trying to change your shape. We were all as we were meant to be, a variety of sizes, not a single and singular ideal. But most of us wouldn't touch it. I could almost see the collective thought forming: there go the feminists again, rationalizing unsightliness. (*PoA* 26)

The last sentence reflects an attitude common to many young women: Being feminist is acceptable if not desirable, being overweight is not.[2] Alice draws an analogy between her own form of feminism and Catholicism; she picks up and discards those ideas and beliefs that suit her personally. Although a feminist, she regards fat women like Louise with horrified disgust. While the narrator carefully observes men and women's different behaviors with regard to drug and food abuse and implies that women's lack of economic clout enforces their "frivolous" obsessions with food, she does not want to make any political statements about the genesis of or possible cure for eating disorders. Her commitment to maintaining her anorexia is far too great for her to advocate any feminist theory that might encourage her, or others, to gain weight.

[2] Esther D. Rothblum describes a seminar in women's studies in which all of the students had more radical views than their instructor, with the important exception of women's weight. The students were unwilling to see any correlation between feminism and attitudes towards female fat, "'I'll Die for the Revolution but Don't Ask me Not to Diet': Feminism and the Continuing Stigmatization of Obesity," *Feminist Perspectives on Eating Disorders*, Patricia Fallon, Melanie A. Katzman, Susan C. Wooley eds. (New York, London: The Guilford Press, 1994) 53.

Changes in Tone to Reflect Alterations in Consciousness

Initially, Alice gives a sarcastic portrait of the clinic, her caregivers, and her fellow patients. Much of her sarcasm rests on her conviction that she is not ill, should not be in a clinic, and has nothing in common with the people there. In contrast to Josie in *Life-Size*, Alice has been hospitalized entirely against her own will, namely after she suffered from a heart attack—a common cause of death among anorectics. Out of immediate medical danger she has been transferred from the medical unit of Seaview to the eating disorder one. There she becomes an unwilling observer of types of eating-disordered women and the clinical staff people who have the task of curing them. In a sense, Alice happens into the eating disorder clinic as Alice of Lewis Carroll's *Alice's Adventures in Wonderland* (1865) unwittingly falls down the rabbit hole into a strange world of overgrown, anthropomorphic animals and talking playing cards. Whereas her literary predecessor regards her strange environment with wonder and timid respect, the anorexic Alice regards those around her from a perspective of intellectual and moral superiority.

The narrator's dark humor and distance to her subject allows her to give a lively portrait of the characters in her eating disorder unit.[3] Alice gives a kind of Thackerayan attention to scenic details and the individual qualities of secondary characters. Psychological portraits are offered of Alice's eating-disordered co-patients Maeve, Gwen, and Louise, as well as of Roland, Alice's best friend and former lover, who introduced her to Catholicism, and even of Alice's parents. A great deal of the narration occurs in dialog. Particularly the repartee between Maeve and Alice is amusing and lively. To Alice's question of why she doesn't use the toilet to throw up into like other bulimics, Maeve

[3] Here, the novel also differs significantly from *Life-Size,* in which the narrator was far too absorbed in her own obsessions to take much note of the persons around her.

replies: "'I got tired of putting my face where other people shit [...]. It was giving me low self-esteem'" (*PoA* 88).

The narrator's picture of the eating-disordered community members and their ways of behaving provides social commentary. By keeping her own sensations and feelings at arm's length, she scrutinizes the characters of those around her. In the following passage Alice moves from experiencing herself as a part of the group in the first-person plural "We entered" to being a neutral observer of the scene, which she then describes using the third-person form. Finally, she returns to a first-person perspective with the "I'd brought" in order to describe her position within the scene:

> We entered the lecture hall—somewhat misnamed—it was a regular meeting room like the others only twice the size—still smelling of Old Spice. But no one was there to receive our splendor. We began setting up chairs. The other units came ten minutes later, escorted by their counselors. We heard them before we saw them: their shuffling weight against the staircase, the unrestrained male voices. All the girls ran to a spot to sit or stand. Janine and two of the other bulimics waited by the entrance to greet the men, a garish welcome wagon. They had teased their hair and wore the same brick red lipstick; there must have been only one tube. The color was so dark that their lips stood away from their faces. When they talked, the lips moved like little erratic birds. The sluttiest one wore a fat, sixties-style belt that cinched her waist tight enough to pinken her face. Gwen and Amy fussed at the empty food cart in the back of the room, arranging the napkins in an elaborate fan. Queen Victoria sat in one of the middle rows with Louise, who was trying to hide two front strands of hair, which she'd singed with a curling iron. I'd brought a book and was pretending to read. (*PoA* 44)

In a single paragraph the narrator offers pithy caricatures of the three major types of eating-disordered women and their personalities. Bulimics are extroverted and flirtatious; anorectics are hyperactive in their efforts not to eat but rather to fuss with foodstuffs; compulsive overeaters try to hide themselves from the critical eyes of others. And Alice observes all this in a tone of flat gallows humor from behind her book. Particularly the bulimics with their exaggerated feminine paraphernalia, including garish make-up, teased hair, and trussed up waists, appear as grotesque and exotic creatures. Alice's lively descriptive style contributes to her narrative distance. Reflections on the narrator's emotions are kept to a minimum. Rather, she describes events as she sees them. Sentences are short; active verbs are favored over passive ones; often verbs are omitted as a way of giving sentences *pointe.*

Initially, Alice presents the clinic and her caregivers in as highly critical a manner as she does her fellow patients. Dr. Paul is portrayed as a power-hungry manipulator whose own sexual appetites are every bit as out of control as the appetites for food of the patients he treats. Alice describes the therapist Gert as an overweight—a crime in Alice's eyes—and humorless proponent of simplistic therapeutic techniques. Her life is an uninspiring example of what a woman may accomplish in recovery: she has become a counselor for the eating-disordered in order to keep her own head "out of the toilet" (*PoA* 93). In Alice's eyes the central rule of the clinic appears to be to control the environment and movements of the patients completely. This includes keeping windows dark and drapes closed, as though to block out any influences from the outside world. As Alice comments on this practice: "Control, even by degrees, was pleasurable. They enjoyed keeping us in a dim light" (*PoA* 24).

At first Alice spends much of her mental energy on trying to beat the system of which she has been made a part. She wishes to be put in a single room but knows that asking for this privilege directly will surely backfire and that "acting [too] bad" will "prolong [her] stay" (*PoA* 62). Further refusing to play by the rules, she does not eat all of the food that is allotted to her but feeds it to the obese Louise instead.

Through her father's law practice she is able to learn about Seaview's legal and economic history without the hospital's administrators or staff knowing so. She discovers that Seaview began catering to the needs of substance abusers in the 1970s and the eating-disordered in 1980. These population groups—and their families and employers—were in a better position to pay for treatment than the mentally ill patients the hospital had treated in the post-war period. In a sense Alice reverses the roles of patient and doctor by studying Seaview's problematic "case history." Her ironic presentation of the hospital's legal and financial history, like her detached summary of the competing philosophies of how to treat eating disorders at Seaview, reinforces the reader's sense of her objectivity. By retaining her own voice and critical distance, she keeps her identity out of the reach of her caregivers' hands even if she cannot avoid her body's having to submit to their regulations.

Alice's attitude changes after Maeve's admission to the clinic. Maeve's larger-than-life quality fascinates Alice and shakes up her system of thinking. Most striking to Alice at first is Maeve's size: she is six feet tall and unapologetic in her brash sexuality. As Alice describes her first impression of Maeve: "She wore high-waisted black leather pants and a soft lavender sweater with a giant plunge cut out of the front. As if she were going someplace" (*PoA* 84). Maeve's extroverted style extends to her openness about her bulimia; she vomits in front of Alice immediately after meeting her and is unashamed to recite the details of her purges. She is also overtly hostile towards therapy.

During her first group therapy session she responds to Gert's request that she share something private by saying that she farts when she has orgasms (*PoA* 90). Making a parody out of the distinction between private and public information, Maeve utters something conventionally considered private and shocking that has no bearing on the problems Gert wants to address. Maeve then manages to upset Gert's equanimity so much that she breaks down during the session and admits the embarrassing truth that she is a therapist solely because it keeps her from continuing to be actively bulimic.

Much like the dynamic card-dealing McMurphy in Ken Kesey's *One Flew Over the Cuckoo's Nest* (1962), Maeve acts as a catalyst figure in *The*

Passion of Alice: she challenges both the authority of her caregivers and the narrator's sense of complacency. As McMurphy's presence in the psychiatric ward seems to awaken Chief Bromden out of his wordless stupor and, after years of willed silence, he begins to speak, so Maeve's verbal and physical challenges to Alice enact changes in her attitudes towards herself. Maeve encourages Alice to admire her own breasts as well as Maeve's and challenges her to end her "[s]exual anorexia" (*PoA* 166). Furthermore, she suggests that Alice's anorexia is a form of egomania rather than anything more transcendental (*PoA* 180).

As in *One Flew Over the Cuckoo's Nest* an excursion outside of the institution works as a vehicle in *The Passion of Alice* for the principle characters and inmates to be drawn together emotionally. In the former text the inmates of Big Nurse's ward go on a drunken fishing expedition, which has been organized by McMurphy and his prostitute girlfriend. In the latter text Maeve, Gwen, Louise, and Alice embark on a shopping trip that has been organized by the clinic and which only becomes eventful due to their subversive actions. Alice's steals presents for the others; then they all try on wedding and bridesmaid dresses together, pretending that Alice is mortally ill and about to get married. This leads to a moment of solidarity in which the women's identities as hospital patients are forgotten: "I couldn't believe how nice it was. The four of us admiring each other. Imagining normal lives" (*PoA* 167). Union in play is followed by a solidarity in sorrow after Gwen collapses while looking at herself in the wedding boutique mirror and it is discovered that she has severe osteoporosis—another common ailment of severe anorectics.

After Gwen's collapse Alice's resistance to treatment wears down and she begins to experience time in the clinic differently. In Parts 1 and 2 of the novel the days of hospitalization are counted by the narrator, who is on the constant alert to figuring out a way to be released from the eating disorder unit. When Maeve is introduced to the clinic in Part 3 Alice stops measuring time so closely; the hospital setting has clearly become more inherently interesting to her. After Gwen collapses at the end of Part 4, Alice ceases to count out her days of incarceration at all. Louise, Maeve, and she all start to "get better:" Alice clears her plate for the first time, Louise stops hiding and consuming food secretly, Maeve stops vomiting nearly altogether. All have been worn down by the "vigilance" (*PoA* 171) of the hospital staff. At this point the women have to "look[] for ways of measuring time. The days had a sameness" (*PoA* 175). This experience of time from within the institution is similar to that described by Hans Castorp in Thomas Mann's *The Magic Mountain* (1924). As less and less occurs for the patient and what does occur is repetitive, time appears to elapse rapidly and monotonously.

Although Alice continues to detest the clinic, she becomes emotionally involved with the other patients there in the second part of the novel. Her narcissism gives way to a genuine concern for others.[4] She no longer caricatures people and their bodies, and her changing views of Maeve's and Louise's figures reflect this. As the narration progresses Alice comes to desire Maeve's imprecise, voluptuous body more and more and she no longer views Louise's obesity with detestation. Whereas at the beginning of the novel she regards Seaview's old priest as pitiful because she assumes that he has been demoted to the sad duty of performing Mass at the hospital, she recognizes in the last scene of the novel that he genuinely wishes to be there and is filled with a sense of religious duty.

Rather than focusing on the Orwellian atmosphere of the clinic and its inmates, Alice dwells more and more on her own feelings. In a heated exchange with Maeve, Alice cries for the first time at Seaview. Alice comes to see that anorexia is a way of combating a sense of emptiness rather than a form of

[4] Both Maeve and Alice's mother call Alice's self-starvation narcissistic, Maeve when she tells Alice: "'You anorexics. You're so famous to yourselves'" (*PoA* 180), Alice's mother when she suggests that Alice's emaciation is a form of "being in the mirror" (*PoA* 228).

superiority.[5] Not only does Alice realize that she loves Maeve and that she is lesbian, but also that desire is a messy business that one cannot ignore and control at will. Through the recognition of her longings Alice's form of strict Gnostic Catholicism, as she terms it, is challenged as well. Her belief that the "divine" (*PoA* 3) can only be sought in individual insight and the cultivation of a lack of desire is undermined by her experience of her very real need for others.

4.2) The Anorexic Mindset and the Experience of Passion

Unlike the counselors and doctors of Seaview, Alice does not regard anorexia as an illness. Rather anorexia represents a religious quest and a form of self-knowledge to her. Pursuing the "clarification" of the essential self is Alice's method of understanding the limits of the world: "Just to know where I begin and end seems, in this day and age, a remarkable spiritual achievement" (*PoA* 2). Contrary to the staff, who regard recovery as literal "Resurrection" (*PoA* 2), as a return to acting like the person one was before one became eating-disordered, Alice understands revival more figuratively. She shows no interest in "curing" her anorexia and promises herself that she will return to her "faith in deprivation" (*PoA* 172) as soon as she can get released from the hospital. Just as she enjoys submitting herself to the rules of Catholicism, so she enjoys the rituals of calorie counting: "Five hundred a day to maintain, four hundred to lose" (*PoA* 17).

---

[5] Near the end of the novel, when Alice is dying from the effects of self-starvation, she gives her friend Roland this explanation of eating disorders in her mind: "So I almost told him right there about the emptiness that the overeaters tried to fill with impossible amounts of food, again and again; the emptiness that the bulimics tried to disgorge, as if it had been caught, a chicken bone or a fragile green fish's gill in their quivering throats; the emptiness which we anorexics, in our superior knowledge and practice, tried to constrict, tried to compress by strangulation and deprivation, tried to irradiate with nothing, with time, with consistent daily loss, that trapdoor of emptiness which I tried instinctively to make collapse into itself years before I knew of Louise's black holes, years before I could picture in my mind's eye that enormous whooosh of nothing sucking nothing into smithereens, into a number of infintesimally small value, into zero volume, zero density. Gone" (*PoA* 242-243).

Her distorted sense of herself does not become clear to her until the end of the novel. Instead, her attitude toward anorexia is one of arrogance. She feels misunderstood by both the other patients and the staff who try to treat her. A recognition of the physical dangers that her anorexia entails appears to be fully lacking from Alice's consciousness; that she nearly died from a heart attack seems irrelevant.

Early in the narrative Alice describes Christ as an "anorexic" (*PoA* 37), noting the number of ribs that show in the representation of him in the hospital's church. She explains to a nurse that "passion" means "suffering" in Latin: According to Alice Christ's passion lay in his suffering awareness that he would die at the hands of the same people who celebrated his arrival in Jerusalem on Palm Sunday. To Alice it is not Christ's resurrection that marks the miracle of Easter but his willful abnegation of his own needs in life: "The miracle was in his complete denial of self" (*PoA* 38). Implicit in this exegesis of the Christ story is a self-aggrandizing comparison between Christ and herself. She regards her suffering in anorexia as a kind of passion story, as a chosen form of self-denial, which will perhaps like Christ's passion end in death: "If I had to say my anorexia was about any single thing, I would have said it was about living without desire. Without longing of any kind" (*PoA* 58).

Forgotten in this comparison is that according to Christian belief Jesus' act of self-denial was committed out of love for human beings and not as an individual exercise in self-renunciation. Alice's exploration of self-denial in anorexia is hardly motivated by a love for others. Rather, Alice initially becomes anorexic as a way of accepting her average looks; the lack of desire for beauty that she cultivates is extended to an indifference to food and other needs. As the quotation about the gestation of Alice's anorexia suggests, no amount of faith can ever compensate for "the suffocating recognition of what I had lost" (*PoA* 58), read good looks. Alice's continued bitterness about her looks and her critical analysis of other people's physical flaws demonstrate that her self-denial has more to do with her inability to accept herself than with the religious knowledge she stylizes it to be.

Part of Alice's "self-knowledge" concerns her sober awareness of the exact limits of her body. In this she differs greatly from the protagonist of *Life-Size* in that she does not view herself or her body in exaggerated or hyperbolic terms. Not as a leaping ballet dancer or as a horribly fat monster, she sees herself as an "average anorexic," whose body should offer as few "surprises" as possible (*PoA* 58). Yet like Josie and other eating-disordered narrators, Alice attributes an enormous importance to bodies in general. Since she understands the awareness of the limits of her own body as a source of self-knowledge, it follows that she observes other people's bodies as a method of knowing them. Dr. Paul Sampson's fleshy hands become a symbol of his greed and lack of feeling. How he touches all attractive women with his hands, including Alice's mother and Maeve, is a synedoche for his larger spiritual "fatness" and greed, his boundless desire to possess what does not belong to him.

Alice is acutely interested in how the clinic divides women into different groups and body types. As she herself comments, "Anorexics are observers, measurers" (*PoA* 69). Measuring others, she notes that anorectics are grouped together for exercise and art therapy as are bulimics, exercise bulimics and compulsive eaters; bulimics, she notes, serve as visual bridges between the emaciated women and their obese counterparts. The outline she is told to fill in of her own body in art therapy interests her only in that it allows her to debate whether her body type is ectomorph or mesomorph. She notes at the beginning of the novel that she is "almost certainly the thinnest woman" (*PoA* 22) in the unit. Later, when she looks in the mirror at the mall, she finds it reassuring that she is still thinner than Maeve, Louise, and Gwen.

Like other eating-disordered narrators Alice has an enormous interest in mirrors. Looking at her reflection has two meanings for her. It represents a way for her to measure herself and express her enormous interest in her person. At the beginning of her stay in the hospital Alice spends a morning examining her body in the mirror. This activity is described by Alice as "being in the mirror" (*PoA* 55). She adopts this expression from her mother who used to yell at her to "'[g]et out of the mirror.'" Near the end of the novel Syd angrily responds to Alice's attempt to starve herself to death with the following words: "'Look, Alice, just because you hate the way you look doesn't mean you're not a narcissist. You're still in the mirror all day. You're still looking'" (*PoA* 228). Indeed, Alice's journey through the wonderland of the eating disorder clinic is also a trip through the looking-glass into her obsession with her looks. Since Alice perceives knowledge of the limits of her body to be knowledge of the world, the mirror is an obvious place for her to search for who she is.

By staring at other women's figures and looking for their imperfections, Alice may further confirm her own identity. The bodies of the exercise bulimics command Alice's attention when she sees them under the shower. Their lack of linearity fascinates her, and she finds that they resemble "malformed toys" (*PoA* 65). Only the bodies of the drug and alcohol addicted women in the hospital hold no interest for Alice; their "furtive, unintentional" (*PoA* 45) skinniness appears to be without larger meaning. Unlike the eating-disordered women who express a variety of things with their bodies—the desire for perfection, an urge to be seen or to disappear from sight, a sense of emptiness—substance-abusing women happen into their body shapes accidentally. Their lack of flesh is a byproduct of their addiction rather than an integral element of their identities as it is for bulimics, anorectics, and compulsive eaters.

Of particular interest to Alice is Maeve's body. From the moment of their first meeting to their lovemaking and Alice's fantasies of how they will be reunited, Maeve's voluptuous body repels and attracts Alice simultaneously. On first seeing all six feet of Maeve's form, dressed in revealing clothes, and noting its effect on the short balding Dr. Paul, Alice thinks "She was the kind of woman I instinctively avoid" (*PoA* 84). Accompanying her to the mixed

Twelve-Step meeting, Alice notes with disgust how the roll of Maeve's belly clearly shows through her tight miniskirt. Alice does not hide her observations and tells Maeve repeatedly that she needs to lose weight. Even after observing Maeve's body for a number of weeks, Alice is surprised again by a total view of her surplus of flesh and lack of bodily precision when they shower together.

Yet it is also this highly imprecise body that increasingly awakens Alice's general interest in Maeve's person, specifically her sexual desire. She becomes fascinated by the way Maeve dresses, moves, speaks, and even plays pool. In bed with Maeve, Alice thinks, "Her breasts were too big and too floppy to be the breasts in magazines. [...] Her fleshy stomach glistened" (*PoA* 211). But for the first time in her life Alice feels real desire "so enormous, so pressing, vital and intact" (*PoA* 212). In all three of Alice's fantasies of how Maeve will return to the hospital to spur on or halt Alice's death by starvation—depending on whether Maeve wants to remain with Alice or not—she pictures Maeve as fatter than she was when she left the hospital. In each of these scenarios Alice comments derogatorily on Maeve's weight gain but also wants desperately to have sex with her. Although her weight gain renders Maeve all the more imperfect and imprecise in Alice's eyes, this physical enlargement seems an integral part of Alice's enhanced craving for her. Having been on the constant alert for physical imperfections, she finds that it is just this deficiency and lack of precision that she loves in Maeve.

Her desire for Maeve shows Alice that her rejection of food, sex, and emotional closeness was an artificial way of distancing herself from desire and pain. At the close of the novel she turns back to the congregation at Gwen's memorial service and re-enters the human community despite her knowledge that she will not see Maeve again. Rather than seeking her limits in isolation, starvation, and the espousal of needlessness, Alice decides to be a part of the noisy group of individuals whom she recognizes that she needs and cares for.

Whether she will be able to remain a part of this community, in which limits and self-knowledge are such uncertain quantities, remains open:

> What seemed remarkable, finally, when I thought of it, was not that I loved women, but that I loved a woman so imprecise. Maeve in all her chaos. This was what I would have said to her if she had been there at the chapel entrance when I reached it. That I loved her imperfection. But she wasn't there. What else could I do? I turned back to the few stragglers left inside. (*PoA* 258)

The novel's title, then, is a play on words: Alice's passion is at first a religious quest, a cultivation of self-deprivation as a method of renouncing desire of all kind; during the course of the novel her passion turns into a very tangible desire for Maeve. This passion and its implications, recognition of her need for others, may lead her to reject anorexia as a path to enlightened understanding.

4.3) Institutionalized Confession: Secrets of the Eating Disordered

Ellmann, Foucault, and Hepworth and Turner all suggest that enclosed spaces provide the settings for the making of literary and actual confessions. In the case of *The Passion of Alice* the protagonist's incarceration makes her aware of how confessional practices function in the hospital environment: testimonies of secret information are coerced out of patients in the interest of healing them. Although Alice's experience of herself and others changes radically during the course of the novel, she remains throughout a critical observer of the culture that expects a return to health for the public testimony of private bodily experience.

In the novel's Prologue the hospital staff's equation of confession with emotional betterment is compared with the narrator's belief in the power of insight as a key to personal development. For Alice there is no one dark secret whose unearthing will explain and heal her anorexia. She regards her anorexia as a positive form of choice. Whereas the therapists assume that their patients require an interpreter to translate the language of their inner pain and make sense of their secrets, Alice assumes that only she alone may make sense of her experience. The novel opens as follows:

> We wait for epiphanies. Grouped in circles, seated on folding metal chairs, or cross-legged on foam mats on the floor, we wait for moments of insight and self-clarification. They come regularly. Not unlike how salvation in evangelical churches must come. First a strained silence. Then a flutter, a flap of ugly words rushing in the room like wind, a halting confession. Then contagion. [...]
>
> The therapists are like tuning forks for epiphanies. In individual [therapy], they hammer *and then, and then,* and *how did that make you feel?* But in group therapy, they demonstrate their true genius, quietly inciting multiple confessions from a single wormy word. Shame. Fault. Responsibility. Father. Brother. Mother. The truth is, everyone blames somebody. Everyone pretends that being here is not, somehow her doing. (*PoA* 1)

Note the succession of auditory images in the quotation above: "a flutter, a flap of ugly words," "tuning forks," "hammer," "word." Epiphanies traditionally concern the physical or spiritual manifestations of the divine, particularly of Christ.[6] As in Christ's appearance to the three kings, epiphanies occur in moments of revelation, often in silence. In James Joyce and Virgina Woolf's fiction epiphanies are the "showing forth" of things and the unconscious mind; they may not be commanded to happen. As James Joyce calls them through the voice of Stephen Hero, epiphanies are "the most delicate and evanescent of moments"; such "sudden spiritual manifestation[s]"[7] cannot be gained by force. They cannot be "hammered" out with Evangelical fervor in group therapy but may only be experienced in moments of individual insight.

---

[6] "Ephiphany" comes from the Greek "to manifest," from the roots "to, unto" and "to show." In its primary meaning the word refers to the festival commemorating Christ's appearance to the persons of the Magi; in its secondary meaning the word denotes an appearance or manifestation of the divine. *The Oxford English Dictionary*, Volume III (Oxford: Clarendon Press, 1961) 293.

[7] James Joyce, *Stephen Hero* (London: Jonathan Cape, 1944) 216.

In these opening paragraphs Alice plays with the meanings of "epiphany": she presents the reader with the counselors'—in her eyes—perverted understanding of the word, which in turn informs their treatment of patients. For the counselors epiphanies must be coerced out of the dark unconscious of their patients. For them epiphanies occur in therapeutic settings and may most effectively be produced in series. The meaning of epiphany as a showing of itself of the divinity, by its nature a singular event, is lost altogether. With this introduction the narrator highlights the difference between her own individual and highly theoretical concept of revelation and that of the cheapened form of disclosure encouraged in the hospital.

The first paragraph of the quotation highlights the culture of confession that prevails in many therapeutic situations today. It is assumed that the unearthing of a hidden quantity—incest, lack of love, pain—is the key to self-knowledge and healing. As in fundamentalist church services an atmosphere is created in which self-revelation is expected and self-generating and is rewarded. The first reluctant confession leads to the next, until an outpouring of personal details occurs in a sort of Dionysian purgation of whatever has been kept private and hidden until the present. And blame is fixed. As the last two sentences of the quotation demonstrate, the model of therapeutic confession is that *the* family member or *the* wounding event will be disclosed that caused the eating disorder to occur in the first place.

Alice's sense of having greater knowledge than those who try to treat her informs all her actions. With a sense of superiority bordering on disgust, she notes how the culture of therapeutic confession is adopted by the patients in the eating disorder unit of Seaview. One of her first sarcastic observations in the clinic involves Janine, the well-behaved recovering bulimarexic[8] who has been given the assignment of helping Alice to become accustomed to Seaview.

---

[8] A bulimarexic is an anorectic who induces vomiting or abuses laxatives as a way of maintaining her very low weight.

Janine, a "goody-two-shoes" who is soon to be released, talks about the details of the ways she formally abused food in a confessional tone and describes the great variety of diets she once went on. Alice remarks in response to this surplus of unasked-for information, "I realized everyone would be eager to tell the thing she did with food. Like the way girls talked about masturbation in college" (*PoA* 17). She also regards the tearful outpourings of other eating-disordered patients in group therapy with distaste.

One way the hospital and the counselors enforce their control over the patients is to dictate a standard of confessional practice. When patients respond in the correct way by admitting their inner pain, they are rewarded with privileges and eventually with freedom. The communicational code of confession, surrender, and absolution is common to both Overeaters Anonymous and Alcoholics Anonymous meetings. To be released from Seaview she will have to "surrender[] all of what was mine—maybe especially—the way I spoke" (*PoA* 48). She provides a sketch of the required form of soul-baring when she describes a counselor's gratified response to an emotional outburst of personal information from Louise:

> Louise wailed about the trials of being the nongifted daughter of a onetime child prodigy who'd scored "borderline genius" on the Mensa test. She made disgusting snuffly noises until Gwen handed her a tissue.
>
> Non sequiturs were prized at Seaview, especially ones that revealed some personal trauma. Ask a patient how she did in high school; if she answers that her brother tried to drown her in the bathtub when she was three, you know it's straight from the UC—the unconscious. Sometimes, before our meetings, we did what they called guided visualizations in order to call up the UC. Apparently, the unconscious was either a room at the end of a long corridor or a private grotto that only you knew about. (*PoA* 28)

Just as the unconscious is visualized as a dark secret place, so the rooms where the patients have therapy and meditate are kept dark with closed drapes. Only the counselors are expected to be able to throw light into the dark secret self or open the windows wide. When the patients adopt the counselors' preferred language of emotional excess, disclosure, and surrender, then they supposedly graduate into a state in which they can treat themselves therapeutically by "opening" themselves.

The clinical atmosphere that Alice describes illustrates Foucault's theory of confession. He argues that calculating and describing the body and confessing its secrets has become the focus of many sciences and the leitmotif of modern literature as well.[9] Seaview practices a method of eliciting individual "truths" from its patients. At first the therapist is required to interpret the information emitted from the unconscious and to absolve the person who discloses hitherto unspoken information from her pain. Through practicing confession with others, the patient, here Louise, will presumably learn to extract confessional truths from her own unconscious. Becoming her own interpreter or therapist will then heal her.

Alice's impatience with the simplistic thinking and codified language that dominates the clinic expresses itself in a variety of ways. She refuses to adopt the sharing confidential tone expected of her. She also refuses to behave in the condoned, properly self-examining, contrite manner: At a going-away ceremony for Janine all the patients are required to give their departing fellow patient some highly meaningful symbolic gift. Alice, who dislikes Janine intensely finally settles on wishing her the gift of "grace." This is a malicious comment on Janine's having broken the chair she was sitting on during her parting ritual and on her having gained weight while she was in the clinic. Moreover, Alice consciously adopts "therapy-speak" in order to achieve her own ends: To deflect the counselor Gert's attention away from a salacious conversation that Maeve, Louise, Gwen and she are having, Alice pretends that they are discussing whether it is superior to "have one's true feelings" or "to act as if" one is healthy (*PoA* 104).

---

9 Michel Foucault, *The History of Sexuality* 59.

The resistance to the culture of confession that Alice demonstrates is expressed even more vehemently by Maeve. Maeve embodies a philosophy of showing all and telling nothing. She dresses in a provocative and flashy manner that makes no reference to any physical problems or sense of contrition she might have in response to her bulimia. Eager to disclose sensational information about herself, Maeve takes on a kind of celebrity status within the clinic, making everything about her into a source of publicity-motored interest. Alice observes how Maeve manipulates private information about herself and others: "With Maeve, reticence was always a prelude to display" (*PoA* 178). Yet Maeve never reveals her profession or lack thereof or any details of her family history. Instead, she presents the world with various versions of herself and consciously tries to subvert attempts to excavate her psyche made by the treatment team. Alternately, she employs humor to deploy those who would delve into her depths or simply lies. On a symbolic level Maeve is a study in contradictions. Her extreme visibility contrasts sharply with her psychological opacity. Maeve explains her unwillingness to comply with therapy as follows:

> What I object to in all this therapy crap is the idea that saying it out loud is somehow going to make the horrible details of your life less horrible. That all this fucking sharing brings catharsis. And that, for example, if you know my father left my mother when I was two and a half and fucked every woman he could get his hands on in our hometown for years after and my older brothers locked him in a closet once to keep him from banging on me and he broke one of their arms when he got out, you will be able, first of all, to understand why I do what I do and, second of all, you will be able to explain it to me. As if I couldn't. (*PoA* 208)

Later the text suggests that this revelation was made up on the spur of the moment. Alice learns that Maeve previously told Louise that she had been a single child who had never known her father.

While rejecting the hospital's notion that "sharing" will bring health, Alice, nevertheless, witnesses revelations about herself and others. Arguably, these epiphanic moments are not brought about through testimony but are experienced. When Alice cannot run to or break into Dr. Paul's car to save Maeve from being sexually exploited by him, she realizes for the first time that her anorexia has made her small and weak rather than cosmically large and vigorous:

> For the first time in my life I wanted to be huge. Absolutely huge. As big as one of the Dumpsters, as big as three Seans stacked on top of each other. I wanted to be big enough to pick up the car and hurl it across the parking lot. I wanted to sit on Paul and crush him with my weight. I wanted to hear his chest explode. [...] There was no strength anywhere in my body. How had I let that happen? How come I had never pictured needing to be strong? If not for me, at least for someone else? (*PoA* 200)

This experience of frailty is repeated when Alice cannot continue a telephone call with Maeve because her heart gives out, and again, when she cannot physically reach Maeve at Gwen's funeral service.

Similarly, the bodily secrets of others reveal their inner truths. After Maeve has been coerced into having sex with Dr. Paul, she vomits in the parking lot when getting out of his car. For the first time Alice sees that Maeve wears dentures, that her "beautiful model teeth so free of bulimic moss" (*PoA* 201) are fake. Until then, Alice had thought that Maeve had somehow managed to defy one of the physical inevitabilities of long-term bulimia, having damaged teeth enamel due to the constant presence of stomach acid in the mouth. Maeve, who has appeared to contradict every stereotype of bulimia—she is gorgeous, physically intact and unapologetic—is actually profoundly physically and, one suspects, psychically wounded.

Similarly, Gwen who always appeared "model-pretty, a Ralph Lauren dream of wholesomeness" (*PoA* 58), who never spoke loudly, came from an independently wealthy family, was, like Maeve, in a deep sense physically damaged. Alice understands then why Gwen's perfect French braid always seemed to be coming undone and why she was reluctant to have anyone else touch her hair: the model of ladylike perfection had bald patches all over her scalp.

Alice's epiphany at the end of the novel also differs greatly from the ones she describes as occurring in group therapy. For Alice revelation occurs in silence: Catching a glimpse of Maeve in the doorway at the end of the memorial service, Alice commands herself to move towards her before she disappears again into the outside world. Yet self-starvation has rendered Alice far too feeble to pass ahead of all the other memorial visitors who are eager to leave the Chapel as well:

> For the second time, my anorexia failed me. My progress was absurdly slow. Half the congregation—Gwen's family and friends—reached the door ahead of me, their nonchalance more powerful, more profluent than my most intense desire. (*PoA* 257-258)

Alice believes that she will never see Maeve again. Just as she had been unable to rescue Maeve from Dr. Paul's sexual manipulations, so is she now physically unable to enact a reunion between Maeve and her. The power of Alice's determination is not strong enough to transcend the reality of her physical weakness. Determination cannot move the bodies of the people between Maeve and her; it cannot make Alice's skeletal form move fast. Just as she has come to see that anorexia has not made her as free of want and full of knowledge of the self as she wished it to, she now experiences that her powers of will cannot overcome physical reality.

Anorexia has represented the cultivation of the lack of desire for Alice—a divine knowledge won through abnegation. Yet in wanting Maeve, Alice discovers that she cannot command herself not to desire as she has so commanded herself not to eat. The decision to desire—on a metaphorical level to experience and to sate hunger—has been made long before when Alice "first tried to impress" Maeve (*PoA* 258). This decision lay outside of Alice's conscious will.

The novel illustrates how revelation occurs through natural experience in the individual's thoughts rather than through the public, pre-scripted disclosure of secrets in the so-called therapeutic setting. This focus bespeaks Alice's anorexic obsession with physical appearances. Accidental revelations of bodily secrets reveal truths of the self, for instance that Alice, who has tried to convince herself that anorexia makes her invincible, is actually quite weak.

In an echo of John Fowles's *The French Lieutenant's Woman* (1969), the narrator of *The Passion of Alice* offers three possible conclusions to Alice and Maeve's love affair. Similarly, Fowles provides three variations of the culmination of Charles Smithson and Sarah Woodruff's difficult romance. In the first ending Sarah and Charles never become lovers. In the second ending, perhaps the most conventionally Victorian one, the lovers are happily reunited, and Charles discovers that he and Sarah have a daughter. And in the third and final ending Sarah makes it clear to Charles that she cannot be his wife or lover but perhaps his friend, an option that he is unwilling or unable to accept. Like Charles in the earlier novel, Alice obsessively imagines a meeting with her former lover. As in Charles's case, Alice's passion was consummated only one time, and this physical intimacy proceeded her lover's deserting her. Like Sarah, Maeve has disappeared from her admirer's life without a trace. Alice's whole existence appears to depend on whether her enigmatic lover will reject her or not at their reunion. In the former case Alice imagines that Maeve's rejection of her will constitute a death sentence: she will continue to starve herself and will die rapidly. If Maeve chooses to reunite with her, however, Alice imagines that she will leave the hospital and be cured of her illness immediately. Like Sarah in *The French Lieutenant's Woman*, Maeve becomes the key to the protagonist's sense of her own identity and the decisive figure in her future. Again Maeve resembles Sarah in how she presents alternative versions of herself and her history and refuses to be pinned down to any one identity. Maeve also resembles Sarah in being an opaque conglomerate of contradictory behaviors. Hence Alice's future, as contingent upon Maeve's decision to continue the relationship, is not clear. Just as *The French Lieutenant's Woman* suggests several possible visions of its protagonist's future life, *The Passion of Alice* leaves the reader to imagine what Alice's life may be.

Significantly, all of the reunion scenarios that Alice imagines occur just before Gwen's memorial service. Since Gwen's unexpected death precipitated Maeve's leaving the hospital, Alice assumes that a formal event to mark this death will bring Maeve back to Seaview. As mentioned above, in all three scenarios Maeve has gained a significant amount of weight. This may be a symbolic counterbalance to the twenty pounds that Alice loses after Maeve abandons her. In the first scenario Maeve sneaks into the hospital disguised as a nurse and takes Alice away with her illegally. This is, as in Fowles's novel, the most conventional end to the love story—a Victorian happy end with the twist of the lovers being eating-disordered lesbians who abscond from the hospital in a sort of *Thelma and Louise*-inspired getaway. In the second scenario Maeve appears in the clothes she originally came to the hospital in, looking much the same but heavier, and tells Alice there is no hope for their love and that she should attend Gwen's memorial service. After Maeve leaves Alice collapses onto the floor, apparently preparing herself for death. In the third and final scenario Maeve also tells Alice that she cannot love her but that Alice will go on to love other women. The presentation of these three scenarios gives the novel an open-ended post-modern quality similar to that of Fowles's work. Yet the narrator goes one step farther when she suggests—"that in some alternate universe all three of my scenarios were taking place simultaneously. All three plus this one, the real one, me climbing by myself out of bed" (*PoA* 251). Alice decides to stop waiting for fate in the form of Maeve to determine whether she shall live or die. She takes the initiative to visit the memorial service in her weakened state and to try to see Maeve again there. With this turn the narrator manages to present a fourth alternative ending to the novel within the scope of a realistic chronological narration.

While the hospital setting provides the narrative frame for *The Passion of Alice*, illness is only one of the many themes the novel explores. Another theme is the "coming-out" story, a variation of "coming-of-age" novels. Although the novel primarily concerns the protagonist's painful recognition of the fact that anorexia is a form of sickness rather than a path to transcendence and health, the novel also explores the meaning of sexual and religious passion. Hence it would be difficult to assign *The Passion of Alice* to any one genre, and this is one of the novel's strengths. Just as Alice's anorexia has a number of meanings for her and no one cause, the recognition of her sexual orientation does not occur in any simplistic generalized way. Her growing interest in and love for Maeve demonstrates more to her than that she is lesbian.

Unlike the narrators of *Life-Size* and *Wasted*, Alice does not perceive her identity in terms of her being an eating-disordered woman. In this she differs from the typical confessional narrators of literary accounts of eating disorders. In no way does she believe that her anorexia requires treatment. Rather, she initially sees herself first as an unwilling hospital inmate and later as a lover and friend. Only within the context of her having learnt to care for others does she come to see that anorexia has made her too frail to accomplish important tasks—to save Maeve from Dr. Paul and to make contact with her again after she has left the hospital.

Insight and healing are won through experience in *The Passion of Alice* rather than through personal testimony. Thus the novel provides a commentary on the culture of confession by presenting an alternative model of how personal development may occur. That *The Passion of Alice* does so with humor makes its exploration of eating disorders, hospitalization, and therapeutic confession a pleasure to read.

V Marya Hornbacher's *Wasted: A Memoir of Anorexia and Bulimia* The Apotheosis of Confession

Of the three texts handled in depth in this study, Marya Hornbacher's memoirs of the eleven years she spent as a bulimic and anorectic is certainly the most disturbing and complex one. Written by a highly articulate, sensitive, and profoundly self-absorbed narrator, *Wasted: A Memoir of Anorexia and Bulimia* (1998) represents an intimate portrait of everything that can go wrong in a middle-class, late twentieth-century American girlhood.[1] The text also tells its reader much about confessionalism as a popular mode of literary expression in America today. Significantly, this memoir of physical and psychological horror were written by a twenty-three year old. The operating assumption is that a whole life can be narrated after just two decades, when these two decades include as many physically horrendous experiences as Hornbacher's do.[2]

Hornbacher describes in great, if not excessive, detail and a myriad of styles how her emotional isolation and anxiety about her appearance, weight, and personality began in early childhood and were never assuaged. Her childhood sense of profound alienation gave way to precocious, unhealthy forms of acting out her unhappiness. Her first bout of bulimia occurred at nine years of age. As a young teen she experimented with casual, unprotected sex with multiple partners, and abused alcohol and drugs. After several years of flirting with anorexia while she was becoming more and more seriously bulimic, she

---

1 *Wasted* has been used as a primary text in courses on problems in American girls' development, for instance, in Prof. Lisa Machoian's "Risk and Resilience in Girls' Development," Harvard Graduate School of Education 2001-2002. Unpublished class syllabus.

2 In this chapter I alternate between using "narrator," "the author," and "Hornbacher." In each case I refer to the narrating persona who appears to tell the story in *Wasted.* I am reluctant to make any summative statements about the relationship between the narrating "I" in *Wasted* and the real person Marya Hornbacher. The mercurial quality of the narrative voice suggests that the narrator is a complex construct.

left home to attend boarding school at 15 and subsequently attempted to stop eating altogether. Several years of anorexia later (interspersed with occasional bouts of bulimia), she had reduced her weight by over seventy pounds from a high of 135 pounds to a low of 52 pounds (*W* 2) and was told that she had a week to live. In the Afterward Hornbacher informs her readers that her trip through the eating disorder chamber of horrors did not end with her final hospitalization. Her period of recovery, if one may call it that, from anorexia was accompanied by self-mutilation, depression, and at least one suicide attempt. The reader is left with the sense that Hornbacher is by no means fully recovered. Despite her critical comments about weight obsession in American culture, she still romanticizes the image of her emaciated body and is involved in a desperate struggle not to become actively anorexic again.[3]

A hybrid text, *Wasted* is a literary autobiography that is interspersed with quotations from handbooks on eating disorders and epigraphs and citations from fictional texts, including the poetry of Sylvia Plath, Anne Sexton, Theodore Roethke, Adrienne Rich, Robert Frost, D.H. Lawrence, Emily Dickinson and the prose of James Agee. Quotations from these sources illustrate the themes of Hornbacher's tale of sickness, including darkness, falling, and wreckage.

Significantly, the memoir begins with a statement from Nietzsche's *Thus Spoke Zarathustra* (1892), an exploration of irrationality and darkness and a reversal of the traditional philosophical association of light and reason. In the quotation from Nietzsche, bodily experience is given precedence over that of the

---

[3] Indeed, this view is verified by a subsequent interview of the author in which she speaks of her ongoing struggle with anorexia. "Every time I relapse, it has a different face, it sort of shows up with new clothes on and you don't recognize it, and of course it kicks you in the ass, and you're like, 'What happened, man?' so like this time around, one of the things that happened was I got really cocky. I was like, 'Hey, I'm well. I've been well for a couple of years now. I think I'll go on a diet.' So, after I went on a diet, like some alcoholic becoming a social drinker—ha ha ha ha ha!—that didn't work out so well. My diet turned into compulsive exercising, which lead to a bulimia relapse, which lead to the current state it's in, which is more anorexia than I've seen since 1993." "A Never-Ending Battle with Anorexia," 2 July 1998 <http://www.amazon.com/exec/obidos/subst/...hornbacher-interview/002-0204924-2702259>.

soul in a direct challenge to the Platonic idealization of rationality.[4] Indeed, Hornbacher's memoirs demonstrate how she consistently and exclusively regards her body as the defining principal for her entire identity. Hornbacher highlights her description of her metamorphosis from a bulimic to a purging anorectic by quoting a letter written by the fasting medieval Saint Margaret of Cortona to her confessor in the thirteenth century. Here St. Margaret describes not only the pleasures of starvation but also her desire "to die a thousand times a day, were it possible" (W 126). Her sentiment resembles Hornbacher's infatuation with death and her desire to starve herself.

Throughout the text, Hornbacher quotes from *Alice's Adventures in Wonderland* (1865). Most frequently, she identifies herself with Alice, likening Alice's interactions with the disagreeable Caterpillar, for example, to her own interactions with her first psychiatrist. The epigraph to the Afterward from Adrienne Rich's "Diving into the Wreck" provides a poetic comment on Hornbacher's effort to describe the immutable remnants of her own damaged self with words. Finally, diagnostic material concerning Hornbacher, including notes taken by her various care takers, medical records, and a series of diagnoses tracking her escalating eating disorder and other psychological and medical problems are interspersed throughout the text. The variety of textual types included in the memoirs and their sometimes jarring juxtaposition with each other contribute to Wasted's pastiche quality. Quotations from poetry, prose, text books, and a letter interrupt the relation of the story of Hornbacher's evolving eating disorder, and these textual interruptions are never discussed. Rather, the excerpts appear to stand for themselves as a disjointed commentary of the narrator's experience.

Stylistic variations underscore the hybridity of the text. The narrator shifts between the uses of the first-person singular, plural and the second-person forms

---

[4] "The awakened and knowing say: body I am entirely, and nothing else; and soul is only a word for something about the body," as quoted in *Wasted* 1.

of address. Perhaps, the fluidity between the "I," "we," and "you" represents a stylistic metaphor for the author's mercurial sense of her own identity. Events are described in rough chronological order as Hornbacher traces her evolution from a food- and weight-obsessed child to a bulimic and then to an anorectic. Yet the narration of the past is interspersed with interludes describing the author's current state of health and mind and her attitude towards her subject. Time is experienced as erratic and non-linear. In the following passage, for instance, Hornbacher's developing breasts have just been explained to her by a doctor as normal signs of puberty.

> It was a sunny day and the seat belt hurt my chest. I kept shifting around. Dear God I'm sorry for everything. Counting the driveways, the cars, my breaths, counting, counting, counting the even, steady throbs in my head.
>
> I am aware that puberty is not an occurrence that's particularly *uncommon*, but I was (a) not prepared, and (b) not interested. (*W* 40)

The shift from a first-person retrospective narration of events to an interior monologue is demarcated by a switch from past tense verbs to present tense ones, rather than by a lexical clue such as "I thought" or the use of inverted commas. Another shifting of gears occurs in the break between the paragraphs. The narrator, who has been relating events first-hand, as though she were actually experiencing them in her thoughts, is replaced by a commentator, who reflects on what has just occurred from a contemporary perspective.

Such shifts have a jarring effect. The reader never has the leisure to adopt one narrative perspective for long but is forced to move rapidly from one view of events to another. Just as the excerpts and epigraphs provide an intertextual commentary of the narrated events, the contemporary narrator provides the reader with an opinionated account of why she did what she did when she did it. Whether the narrator who experiences events or the one who comments on them afterwards has the final word never becomes clear. The cumulative effect is one of instability, the formal instability of the text matching the narrator's sense of her own fragile and fragmented self.

The narrator's tone varies greatly as well. Mostly her writing has a racy, fast-paced 'zine quality when she mixes polysyllabic words or theoretical concepts with casual grammar and wordplays, as in: "I'm sick of despair. It's so magazine-model-looking-apathetic-and-underfed-and-stoned-and-exactly-the-same-as-all-the-other-wan-sickly-models" (*W* 278). Here she refers to the much touted concept of "heroin chic," which described the look that models and their copyists aspired to at the beginning of the nineties. Integrating a formal quality of literature from the seventeenth and eighteenth century into her "sexy" contemporary prose, she capitalizes nouns of significance:

> You either decide you will take the trite business of life and give yourself the option of doing something really cool, or you decide you will opt for the Grand Epic of eating disorders and dedicate your life to being *seriously* trivial. (*W* 284)

Here orthographical conventions from prior centuries meet with colloquial turn-of-the-moment phrases: "Grand Epic" collides with the soon-to-be-dated "really cool."

As will be described in further detail later descriptions of protracted binges have a Gothic quality: The sense the author has of being possessed by the need to fill and empty herself with food is mirrored in atmospheric descriptions of supermarkets, disoriented drives in the dark, and endless trips to the toilet. The narration then takes on a rushed quality, exemplified by the use of active verbs and short sentences. By contrast, a leisurely quality pervades descriptions of Hornbacher's step-mother's home in California or her arts boarding school Interlochan. In these passages the narrator seems interested in setting the scene. In the beginning of chapter 5, for example, the flora and fauna around the California house are described at length; next, the "sagging deck" (*W* 160) in front of the house is mentioned; then moving indoors, the layout of the house receives mention, before the narrator moves into what is for her the most important room of the house, the kitchen. Here the pace of the narration slows down even further: Nearly a whole paragraph is devoted to listing the foods on the counter, another one to describing the contents of the refrigerator. In such descriptive passages the memoirs resemble a novel.

However, when the narrator criticizes the culture that encouraged her to be profoundly troubled by food and her body, her voice more resembles that of an essayist. At other times descriptions degenerate into clichés as when she writes of her time in California that: "Life was good, and I was giddy with freedom" (*W* 167). Elsewhere, the author breaks up the flow of her narration by making asides to the reader about how tired she is of telling her story of sickness. In such moments the text has a distinctly post-modern tone—a self-conscious, skeptical quality—that counterbalances passages where the author earnestly proclaims that her memoirs should keep others from experiencing pain like hers.

Adding to the post-modern effect is the narrator's attention to the problem of language itself: When she writes that the words "hunger," "cold," "flesh," and "bone" have entirely different meanings for her than for the reader (*W* 275), she acknowledges the breakdown of communication practices. The individual—here the ill individual—may no longer assume that the assumptions about self, experience, and language that inform her utterances will also inform those of her listener.[5] Still at other times the author appears to dissemble. For instance, after

[5] Linguistic and philosophic insights that undermine a straightforward relationship between reality and signification offer one explanation for the breakdown of language. Since Ferdinand de Saussure demonstrated in his 1916 lectures on linguistics that the linguistic symbols we use to describe things are only arbitrarily related to the things themselves, the whole relation between language and "reality" has become problematic. The philosopher and deconstructionist Jacques Derrida's notion of *différance* (from his 1968 lecture of the same name) further undermined the one-to-one relation between signification and reality: Derrida understands the sign (or signifier) to represent the absence of the concept it represents (the signified) and the thing in itself that the signified refers to (the referent). Rather than referring to real things with language, we demonstrate their absences and the delayed quality of our capacity to understand signification.

she has related how her enormous ambition to succeed academically and artistically contributed to her eating disorders as a young teenager, she describes herself at fourteen as being nothing more than "a fuck-up with good tits, useful for sex and laughs" (*W* 87). The narrator's awareness of her youthful ambitiousness and her professed belief that she was nothing other than a party girl seem dichotomous. One wonders if she is misleading herself or her reader. One suspects that the narrator's inability to integrate conflicting characteristics and behaviors into a unified sense of self contributed to her psychological instability and the etiology of her eating disorders. Furthermore, Hornbacher's penchant for exaggeration and unwillingness to settle on any one narrative perspective lend her prose an uneven and experimental quality and render *Wasted* a highly variable and ambiguous text.

Hornbacher does much to imply that the reader must regard the truth value of her narration as questionable. In the tradition of the murderer in Edgar Allan Poe's short story "The Tell-Tale Heart" (1843), she alternatively asserts her extreme acuity and sensitivity on the one hand and the fallibility of her perceptions—due to illness—on the other:

> I felt like I was going out of my mind. My head was never quiet. Quiet is an in-between point, implying a balance between noise and silence, between the strange blackouts I began to have—pure silence, not sleeplike but deathlike—and the hellish shrieking jumble of my own thoughts and the voices of the world. (*W* 69)[6]

Hornbacher's suggestion that her perceptions are distorted may awaken a sense of sympathy on her reader's part. Her admitted weakness awakens pity. Her espousal of her mental instability may also invite the reader to lend her memoirs particular credence. After all, the person who admits to mental illness must be telling the truth about him or herself.

---

[6] E.A. Poe, "The Tell-Tale Heart," *The Short Fiction of Edgar Allan Poe,* ed. Stuart and Susan Levine (Indianapolis: Bobbs-Merill Company, 1976) 259-260.

The reader may object to my not explicitly treating *Wasted* as an autobiographical and hence non-fictional text in contradistinction to the more overtly fictional *Life-Size* and *The Passion of Alice*. As the boundaries between literary genres become fuzzy and Madonna's videos and Walt Whitman's "Leaves of Grass" may both be termed autobiographical texts, distinguishing autobiography proper from autobiographical fictions becomes an increasingly academic pursuit.[7] Due to its hybrid nature and the variety of narrative selves and situations explored in the text, *Wasted* displays a high level of fictionality and literariness. A great deal of fiction-making occurs as the narrator implicitly compares her experience to crises described in works by literary giants. Surely, Hornbacher—or the narrator or the implied author—makes as many conscious choices about the form and content of her story of illness as the authors of *Life-Size* and *The Passion of Alice* do.

In describing *Wasted* I wish to draw attention to its confessional qualities, how the narrator's narcissistic interest in herself is reflected on the textual level. As in other confessional narratives, mirroring and measuring the body are enormously important. Bodily experience is viewed as paramount and defining, and identity is sought in a plethora of somatic detail. What one weighs determines who one is; the evolution from being a bulimic to being an anorectic to being a person with an eating disorder not otherwise defined is, for Hornbacher, the process of determining her identity. Like *Life-Size*, *Wasted* explores a woman's romance with her dying self. Thus *Wasted* recalls Sylvia Plath's *Ariel* poems.

In the second part of this chapter I explore *Wasted* as a scathing cultural critique of American culture and, dichotomously, as a handbook for how to

[7] On this subject see, for instance, Hans Bak and Hans Krabbendam's "Introduction" to *Writing Lives* (Amsterdam: VU UP, 1998): "[...] traditional dividing lines of form and genre (biography, autobiography, fiction) have become increasingly blurred and untenable: 'writing lives'—of the self *or* of others—has become a hybrid and porous genre, yielding a rich

become eating-disordered. *Wasted* is both these things. On the one hand the author clearly sees how the equation of wealth, success, and desirability with thinness nearly killed her and impedes the development of many young American women. Yet she also narrates the story of her increasing emaciation in glowing terms: "success" in seducing men, studying intensely, and working as a journalist and editor went hand in hand with weight loss. Hornbacher's disorder sometimes takes on a celebrity status, which the commercial success of the book has done little to belie.

In the final section of this chapter I discuss two descriptions of bulimic episodes in order to determine their place within the context of other writings on eating disorders and to question why literary descriptions of bulimia remain scarce.

5.1) *Wasted* as the Apotheosis of Confessional Writing

More than any other extended text treated here *Wasted* is a confessional one. These memoirs are a nearly three-hundred page relation of sickness and bodily detail. Bodily minutia, including the quality and quantity of vomit produced in purges, the escalation from one binge a day to two, three, and four, the drug abuse, and the promiscuous sex lend this text a distinctly grotesque quality. Seemingly, anything that can hurt the body and keep it at the center of the author's and the reader's attention including laxatives, ipecac, and razor blades is experimented with by Hornbacher and told about. Furthermore, the physical deterioration wrought on the author's body by the multiple forms of her self-abuse is closely documented: We learn, for instance, how the anorectic's sense of cold is never alleviated even after she recovers, how Hornbacher was forced to put tissue paper in her shoes to cushion her fleshless feet when she was at her most emaciated, how self-mutilation has ruined the veins in her arms, how she

---

fluidity of forms. The self, however mediated, adopts a kaleidoscopic multiplicity of (dis)guises and strategies of self-representation" (1).

has become infertile and prematurely aged, how her heart is weakened and beats irregularly. As in grotesque literature, physical details are exaggerated and shown in disconcerting graphic detail in contrast to the more atmospheric quality of gloom and fear that characterizes Gothic literature.[8]

One wonders how a child that considers itself fat at four and ranks the bodies of women in its mother's gym class in relation to their perceived fatness and thinness can become any more disturbed than it already is. This child ricochets between bulimic excess and self-abnegating starvation during junior high school and high school, becomes pregnant twice, is repeatedly hospitalized, and finally very, very nearly dies. Just when it appears things cannot get worse another even more horrible event occurs—the narrator coughs up or defecates blood or collapses onto the ground.

Appropriately, the metaphor of falling is used throughout the memoirs: the narrator passes out in boarding school due to a lack of nourishment, falls down a flight of stairs to end her second pregnancy, collapses in Washington twice, once after visiting her closest friend and once again in the subway, before she exhaustedly gives in to being hospitalized. These real falls are reflected on the meta-fictional level in epigraphs: D.H. Lawrence's poem "Bavarian Gentians," which describes the speaker's descent into Persephone's underworld, is excerpted (*W* 160) as is Alice in Wonderland's fall into the rabbit hole (*W* 36). Thus Hornbacher's memoirs resemble a kind of Dantesque descent into the

---

[8] One is reminded of the Flannery O'Connor's short story "Good Country People" (1955) in which the arrogant intellectual Hulga believes that she may corrupt a simple-minded Bible salesman by seducing and disillusioning him of his religious beliefs. He, in turn, deceives her by stealing her false leg—described in great detail—when she is physically compromised and unmasks himself as an opportunist who has liquor, a set of obscene playing cards, and other stolen prostheses in his suitcase rather than Bibles. For a historical examination of the grotesque in American literature that attempts to reconcile Mikhail Bahktin and Wolfgang Kayser's understanding of the phenomenon, see Dieter Meindl, *American Fiction and the Metaphysics of the Grotesque* (Columbia and London: Missouri UP, 1996). Again, I would argue that *Wasted* is neither simply grotesque nor Gothic in tone. As with the shifts in narrative perspective, the erratic relation of time, and the pastiche of textual types, the tone of the memoirs varies from grotesque to Gothic to journalistic to pseudo-scientific.

lower circles of Hell. While her pain is vividly told, it is also nearly endless. The reader may experience a sense of fatigue and exhaustion regarding this litany of intensely-felt horrible physical experiences.

In respect to *Wasted*'s exhaustive detail, one might return to Ellmann's thesis regarding incarceration, starvation, and loquacity: whether the author be an imprisoned IRA member or the beleaguered Clarissa in Richardson's novel of the same name, individuals, Ellmann says, protest their lack of freedom by starving their bodies and filling the world with words. Correspondingly, Hornbacher's prison is of her own making. As she starves her body down to a mere skeleton, she requires more and more words to tell the world and her reader about the process, the proliferation of words balancing out, as it were, the disappearance of the flesh. The first part of the memoir's title "Wasted" highlights this process. Not only does Hornbacher's body waste away, but her life is wasted due to her fixation with starving herself. The voluminous form of the memoirs symbolically contradicts the diminishment of life and flesh they record.

Hornbacher articulates her own tendency to imprison herself and discipline her body and behavior repeatedly.[9] As a small child she slaps her face because she perceives it to be fat and ugly. On the evolution of her punishing attitude towards her body she writes:

> Somehow, I learned before I could articulate it that the body—my body—was dangerous. The body was dark and possibly dank, and maybe dirty. And silent, the body was silent, not to be spoken of. I did not trust it. It seemed treacherous. I watched it with a wary eye.
>
> I will learn, later, that this is called "objectification consciousness." There will be copious research on the habit of women with eating disorders perceiving themselves through other eyes, as if there were some Great

[9] The text again illustrates Foucault's work on disciplinary practices. Hornbacher's extremely punishing self-consciousness regarding her body and food behaviors is exemplary of the transition he describes from centralized, institutionally-based disciplinary systems to self-imposed ones.

> Observer looking over their shoulder. Looking, in particular, at their bodies and finding, more and more often as they get older, countless flaws. (*W* 14)

The Great Observer, who is Hornbacher herself, develops a system of punishments and rewards for her bodily behaviors that is increasingly severe. In this she resembles Josie from *Life-Size*, whose patterns of consumption become increasingly restrictive as her anorexia worsens. For example, Josie determines that to buy anything at all she must get rid of something else. Similarly, Hornbacher devises ever more strict methods for consuming food. While still living at home she decides that she will not eat anything the next day if she judges her reflected image to be fat and she finds this strict system reassuring: "The punishment seemed just, seemed as if it might make things better, more organized, the calming twist of hunger in the chest might remind me that things were all right" (*W* 73-74). In boarding school Hornbacher's disciplinary measures regarding her eating habits become even more extreme: She decides at one point to eat only once a week. And shortly before her final health crisis in Washington she consumes just one yogurt and one bagel per day. Elaborate rules determine the length of time required to consume these, relatively speaking, miniscule amounts of food.

Hornbacher's memoirs again demonstrate the validity of Foucault's hypothesis that confessional practices have come to characterize therapeutic and literary practices. Through willing or coerced confession, individuals may be healed and some essential truth about their identities will be revealed. By this logic, the more details that are offered, the more authentic the narration will be. Confessing pain publicly, in print, appears to confirm Hornbacher's post- or still-eating-disordered identity. The bloodier and sexier the details are, the better the confession.

As for other confessional narrators, the narcissistic focus on bodily detail is reflected in innumerable references to the protagonist's interactions with mirrors.[10] Firstly, Hornbacher attests that she never emerged from the "mirror phase" of development (*W* 15).[11] Secondly, in an adaptation of Lewis Carroll's imagery from *Through the Looking-Glass* (1871), the mirror represents the entry point to the realm of sickness and madness—the point of intersection between the normal world and the "shimmery, fun house mirror-covered hell" (*W* 7).[12] Hornbacher describes herself as having first fallen "into the mirror" (*W* 14) when she was just four years old, when she—copying her actor parents and their co-workers' actions—made herself up garishly and felt a sense of "dissociation" (*W* 15) as she studied her reflected image in her mother's bathroom mirror. As for the seven-and-a-half-year-old Alice in *Through the Looking-Glass*, the experience of going through the mirror represents a reversal (as in the mirrored poem "Jabberwocky") of the youthful protagonist's hitherto known world. For Hornbacher, a highly narcissistic and insecure individual, mirrors appear to be everywhere. They both define her understanding of past experience—"I remember my entire life as a progression of mirrors" (*W* 14)—and represent the diffuse boundary between health and a return to actively-destructive food obsessions. In the Afterward she describes how her marriage means that she may not "seep slowly back into the mirror" (*W* 278). Furthermore, Hornbacher muses that once one has experienced as serious and as extended a period of

---

[10] There are more than thirty descriptions of mirrors and mirroring in *Wasted*..

[11] Typically, Hornbacher does not say explicitly what she means by "mirror phase" but simply coins the term to describe her own development. Two major theories about the "mirror phase" are those of Jacques Lacan and D. W. Winnicott. Lacan's "mirror phase" describes a child's first attempt to grasp a sense of self when it sees its reflection in the mirror. The child's initial sense of having a self occurs when it observes its not-self in the mirror. Based in part on Lacan's work, D. W. Winnicott envisions the mirror stage as the period when a baby reassures itself of its own existence by regarding its image in the mirror that its mother's face provides. According to Winnicott, if a child does not receive enough confirmation of its own existence in the face of its mother (or primary care-taker), the child will develop narcissistic tendencies and spend the greater part of its psychic life looking for confirmation in others. D.W. Winnicott, "Mirror-role of Mother and Family in Child Development," *Playing and Reality* (1971; New York: Routledge, 1991) 111-118.

[12] Given Hornbacher's eating problems as an infant and her parents' eating preoccupations, it is questionable whether she was ever not in the looking-glass world of body distortion and food obsession.

being severely eating-disordered as she has done, one never fully emerges from the looking-glass world of reversed and distorted images:

> You never come all the way out of the mirror; you stand, for the rest of your life, with one foot in this world and one in another, where everything is upside down and backward and sad. (*W* 285)

Significantly, the second-person "you" is used in this passage to describe the narrator's perceptions. This form of address may mark the narrator's tendency to divorce herself from her own experiences.[13] However, one might argue that the use of "you" rather than "one" to describe a generalized experience is typical of informal American language usage today.[14] The vernacular quality of "you" also lends Hornbacher's memoirs an immediacy—a sense that they are being told to rather than written to the reader.

Finally, mirrors are the sites where the most important rituals of Hornbacher's life are performed. There she confirms and measures herself in ever-constant body checks.[15] These body checks, in which the bones are felt and counted and the presence or absence of flesh is confirmed, are familiar from the poems "Conform" and "Dedication to Hunger" as well as the novels *Life-Size* and *The Passion of Alice*. Common to all of the minute physical self-

---

[13] "As I indicated earlier, it is also not uncommon for individuals with eating disorders to experience episodes of dissociation or multiple personality disorder. In these disturbances, the person feels most disenfranchised from her own body—walled off in another state of awareness altogether or taken over by an alter personality, often of a different age and gender. One's bodily self thus becomes totally abrogated and denied." Kathryn J. Zerbe, *The Body Betrayed* 156-157.

[14] Note Hornbacher's frequent usage of "you" rather than "one" in the interview of her by amazon.com, quoted above in footnote 3 of this chapter.

[15] The following are just a sample of the many body checks in front of the mirror that Hornbacher describes herself as performing: Shortly before her hospitalization at 52 pounds she visits a friend from boarding school and eats an infinitesimal amount: "Having eaten less than the total of one normal-size muffin, I began crying standing up to look in the mirror, checking my bones, feeling for signs of softness, my brain veering back and forth from pig-pig-pig-fat-pig to stop-it-you're-okay-it's-okay-okay-okay" (*W* 259); about her current state of mind and health, Hornbacher writes: "The loose ends are the Bad Days [...]. They are the constant trips to the mirror, the anxious fingers reading the body like Braille, as if an arrangement of bones might give words and sense to my life" (*W* 276).

examinations recounted in these texts is the exaggerated sense of pleasure and pride in her "achievement" that the eating-disordered woman experiences based on whether she feels sufficiently emaciated or the horror she suffers from if she finds herself to be too fleshy. Judgements are polarized, and perceptions have a black-and-white quality. Even when she can objectively see that her extreme emaciation has made her ugly (*W* 254), Hornbacher cannot concentrate on her work—her other obsession—without making frequent trips to the mirror to perform body checks in which she "satisfie[s]" herself that her "body had stayed within its spatial confines and had not encroached" (*W* 252-253).

During Hornbacher's almost exclusively negative sessions of measuring her body and checking for fat in front of the mirror, she focuses her considerable self-hatred on her bottom. Even at nine years of age, Hornbacher perceived this body part to be huge and hugely unacceptable. Throughout the coming years, she repeats variations of the following derisive comments on her "butt" as though they were mantras, "butt too round, juts out, major gross, ohmigod, the butt, the horrible butt" (*W* 44). This ritual repeats itself whatever other horrors Hornbacher experiences. After defecating blood in the aftermath of a weekend-long binge and purge session at her parents' house, she responds with fear and by "check[ing] the size of [her] ass in the mirror. Fat. I was sure I'd put on weight over the weekend" (*W* 223). Similarly, after Hornbacher has miscarried her first pregnancy at 14 years of age, she stares at the aborted embryo in the toilet and the blood on her thighs and then relates how she became "distracted. I turned to one side and scrutinized at my butt. Fat ass, I thought. Pig." (*W* 75). Any potential horror at or fear of this experience is overshadowed by the compulsion to measure her worth in relation to the size of her bottom.

True to Rosenthal and Axthelm's accounts of confessional literature, Hornbacher's memoirs are written from the perspective of a diseased or sickened I. To quote from Rosenthal's description of confessional poetry again, "The terrors, pains, early miseries, regrets, vexation, and lassitudes that Wordsworth suffered are now the main proofs of one's existence."[16] Certainly, Hornbacher's psychic and physical suffering is the defining element of her narrative and the key to her sense of her identity. Indeed, a large part of the memoirs concerns her determination of what kind of illness/disorder she has and what this illness means. For Hornbacher as for Robert Lowell, as Rosenthal describes him, the interior state represents a prism through which all experience is viewed and distorted.[17] Hence Hornbacher's description of her transformation from a bulimic to a purging anorectic (one who vomits) to a woman with eating disorders not otherwise specified[18] is accompanied by an exploration of what these various states symbolize for the author personally and society in general.

Hornbacher writes of her life as a constant fight against her desire to eat and partake of life sensually.[19] Although her self-image changes from fat brat to sexy girl to obsessed artist to laid-back bohemian to working woman in a business suit (to name only a few of her permutations), a consistent element remains her desire to be thin and her vacillations between excessive and abstinent consumption, between bulimia and anorexia. Each new identity is accompanied by a new set of bizarre eating behaviors. From the first, however, bingeing and purging has an erotic as well as a horrific, quality for her. Describing her early binges in grade school, she writes:

---

[16] M.L. Rosenthal and Sally M. Gall, *The Modern Poetic Sequence*, 393.

[17] "[...] Lowell carried to an extreme our sense that the private life embodies the national life. For him this premise was an expanded dimension of his not always welcome empathy, which had a cannibalistic edge and imposed the feeling that everyone else, and the country, and history as a whole were somehow identical with Lowell and explainable in his private terms" (Rosenthal and Gall 394).

[18] This diagnostic term is used most frequently to describe the binge-eating syndrome or for other eating disorders that do not fit within the clinically accepted categories of anorexia and bulimia. For a description of eating disorder types and their criteria, see chapter I.

[19] "In fact, my whole life has been this, moving in and out of the day-to-day world, both fascinated by and afraid of its sheer voluptuousness. The parallels in my approach to food and my body are striking: bulimia, feasting on food and then throwing it back; anorexia, refusing food and feasting on hunger itself" (*W* 18).

> I remember the toast, the butter I spread on it, the crunch of toast against teeth and the caress of butter on tongue. I remember devouring piece after piece, my raging, insatiable hunger, the absolute absence of fullness. I remember cheerfully heading off for my bath. Night, I said. Locking the bathroom door, turning the water on, leaning over the toilet, throwing up in a heave of delight. (*W* 43)

"The caress of butter on tongue" has a tactile sensuality. "Devouring," "raging" and "insatiable" are all words commonly coined in descriptions of sexual desire. Feeding the body food as it is described here resembles the fulfilling of sexual longing; the "heave of delight" brought on by vomiting then resembles the fulfillment of physical desire in orgasm. Simultaneously, "devouring," and "raging" are used to describe the consumption of food by wild animals. Their use in the description of a binge bespeaks Hornbacher's tendency to associate her appetite for food with desirousness and animality. As she later explicitly states, bulimia represents the inescapability of the body and its needs to Hornbacher as well as the inescapability of emotions (*W* 93).

Yet a desirous, emotionally expressive female is precisely the opposite of what the adolescent Hornbacher aspires to become. At 15 she wishes not only to leave her home in Minnesota to go to a boarding school for talented arts students in Michigan but also to leave her loud bulimic self behind:

> I had had enough of bulimia. It seemed so crass, so gauche, so unlike the person I wanted to become: a woman, dark and mysterious, regal. Like my mother. I wanted to turn heads not with lecherous leers of bemusement but with awe. I wanted to become untouchable, cruel, glittery, sleek and haughty as a cat. (*W* 90)

Bulimia comes to stand for everything Hornbacher dislikes in herself, most particularly desirousness and a lack of self control. Describing her feelings during a binge, she again dissociates her experience from herself and projects them onto the reader:

> You know you're out of control. The first time you ever eat without stopping [...]. And then the horrible, nauseating realization that you are, in fact, as uncontrollable, as needy, as greedy, as you've always secretly suspected. (*W* 224)

Moreover, bulimia is associated in the author's mind with her fatness—as she perceives it—her sexual promiscuity, and her obstreperousness. One of the reasons she later decides to "give up" sex is that it always makes her feel hungry and hence may trigger off a bulimic episode. The period before she became anorexic is characterized by her verbally antagonistic relationship to boys at junior high school, her plethora of casual sex partners, and the variety of her drug abuse. During this time an overweight co-worker from McDonald's makes a comment on Hornbacher's being cute and chubby like herself, and Hornbacher hears this comment not only as a sentence on her for being overweight, which she objectively-speaking is not, but also for being too loud and expressive. As Hornbacher more and more comes to equate her selfhood with the outline and weight of her body, her bulimic and, in her mind, fat self becomes increasingly intolerable to her:

> Up to that point, the bulimia had had a life of its own. It was purely an emotional response to the world—under pressure, binge and purge; sad and lonely, binge and purge; feeling hungry, binge and purge—and actually had little to do, believe it or not, with a desire to lose weight. I'd always wanted to be thinner, sure, but I wanted to eat as well. The year I got to boarding school, I actually began to hate my body with such incredible force that my love of food was forced underground, my masochistic side surfaced, and anorexia became my goal. (*W* 108)

Anorexia and the thinness that attends it come to represent the promised land in the narrator's mind. When she is thin, she believes she will inspire respect and fear in others rather than lust. Her passions, she imagines, will be "pure" (*W* 107). To be perceived as bulimic by herself after a binge or by others becomes the worst form of punishment. When another boarding school student describes

Hornbacher's spitting out of the popcorn she had just chewed as bulimic, she is infuriated. When the head doctor of the Methodist Hospital Eating Disorders Institute says in an extraordinary bout of insensitivity that as a bulimic Hornbacher is not terribly ill since "it's not like [she's] a sixty-pound anorectic or anything" (*W* 178) she calls his bluff: seven months later she will be readmitted to the hospital as an anorectic after she has lost 20 pounds. Several years later she even ups the doctor's ante by reducing her weight to a mere 52 pounds. Whereas bulimia is a cause of shame for the narrator, anorexia becomes the motivating force of her life.

Indeed, Hornbacher becomes—or always was—infatuated by the image of herself as being sickly thin and anorexic. It is not just the "implication of Thin" (*W* 69) that inspires her pursuit of anorexia, but the attraction that an identity as being sick, obsessed and self-destructive holds. Just as the narrator retrospectively criticizes America's worship of thinness in females and enumerates the negative consequences of this worship, she also comments on the cultural identification of illness with intensity and artistry quite objectively. About her fellow students at the arts high school Interlochen she reflects from her current standpoint:

> A few too many of us fell for the old romantic story of the mad artist, the genius made idiot savant by the swells and falls of music, language, color on canvas, ceaselessly, manically, playing inside his head. (*W 104)*

Yet as a young girl she was highly susceptible to the attraction of the association of illness with creative intensity. At Interlochen she embarks on a career as an artistically driven anorectic and goes "on a mission to be another sort of person [than a bulimic], a person whose passions were ascetic rather than hedonistic" (*W* 107). Increasingly, she aspires to a life of self-destruction and stylizes illness in her mind as a kind of auto-erotic mental and physical exercise. Hornbacher comes to embrace pain as an art form in itself. She takes pleasure in starving, in running 25 miles a day, in abusing her body with cigarettes and cocaine. Punishing self-control becomes so automatic that she vomits up the orange juice she is given after fainting in boarding school, while nearly unconscious (*W* 129).

Similarly, Hornbacher feels threatened in her identity as a successful anorectic during those times when she cannot confirm it by gazing into the mirror. When she learns that she must share her dorm room in college with a new roommate after months of living alone, she has a sense of being gravely endangered and asks herself: "How was I supposed to go back and forth, from mirror to desk to mirror to desk, all day, all night, as I'd been doing for months? Shit. Shit. Shit. Shit" (*W* 265).

Moreover, the act of willful self-renunciation in illness and starvation is solely meaningful when it can be recorded in some way and recognized by others. In the Eating Disorders Institute her weight and that of the other eating-disordered women is recorded in kilos rather than pounds. Without this knowledge Hornbacher feels disoriented. Like Kafka's *Hungerkünstler* who simply dies of starvation when circus goers cease to admire his heroic self-denial, Hornbacher needs to be recognized for her feats of self-abnegation; she wants "to have the sick admiration that comes to those of us who destroy ourselves particularly well" (*W* 124). And she asks rhetorically, "What are you worth if no one's looking?" (*W* 125). Without anorexia and the superhuman self-control associated with it, Hornbacher is, by implication, not worth anything. This is only one of the multitude of reasons that she finds it so difficult to renounce eating disorders completely.

In her romance with her sick and dying self, Hornbacher resembles—like *Life-Size*'s Josie—the narrator of Sylvia Plath's *Ariel* poems. Significantly, Hornbacher quotes from Plath's "Lady Lazarus" (1962) twice. In the epigraph to chapter four, in which she describes being hospitalized for the first time, she quotes the "Herr Doktor" line of Plath's poem and the following three stanzas to highlight her resistance to therapy:

> So, so Herr Doktor.
> So, Herr Enemy.
>
> I am your opus,
> I am your valuable,
> The pure gold baby.
>
> That melts to a shriek.
> I turn and burn.
> Do not think I underestimate your great concern.
>
> Ash, ash—
> You poke and stir.
> Flesh, bone, there is nothing there—[20]

As for the speaker of "Lady Lazarus," those who treat Hornbacher, such as Dr. J, are regarded by her as "Herr Enemy" as the hated other.[21] Their efforts to make her into their work or "opus," to objectify her, and to "poke and stir" in her psyche are without effect, since the essence of her person is beyond their grasp. Hornbacher's life may be seen as a kind of on-going disappearance act, in which she works to turn herself into thin air while those around her struggle to grasp on to what is left of her spiritually and physically.

Indeed, Hornbacher's eating disorders are only considerably worsened by her three stays in the Eating Disorders Institute. There she can indulge in her obsession with food and her body without any outside distractions; there she learns new techniques from other hospitalized women for punishing her flesh. Hornbacher borrows the title for chapter eight from the fifteenth stanza of

---

[20] In Hornbacher's epigraph, demarcations between the stanzas of the original poem are not shown, and a period is added after "nothing there" rather than a hyphen (*W* 145). The above quotation is from Plath 246.

[21] It is notable that in *Life-Size*, *The Passion of Alice* and *Wasted*, the primary psychiatrist—Dr. Frog, Dr. Paul, and Dr. J respectively—is regarded with loathing and derision by the female protagonist.

"Lady Lazarus": "Dying Is an Art, Like Everything Else" and entirely quotes this stanza and the following one in the epigraph:

> Dying
> Is an art, like everything else.
> I do it exceptionally well.
>
> I do it so it feels like hell.
> I do it so it feels real.
> I guess you could say I've a call.[22]

Here Plath's Lady Lazarus writes ironically about her ability to destroy herself, describing it as something she does "exceptionally well" as though she were speaking of entertaining guests. Her "call" to dying appears to be a brilliant performance of which others wish to partake in their desire to analyze her and to witness her resurrections from the dead. Her "Comeback in broad day"[23] recalls the biblical Lazarus's miraculous return from several days in the grave after Christ calls to him to come out.[24] For the narrator of "Lady Lazarus" these brilliant charges into death "feel like hell" and are not conceived of as repeat performances.[25]

---

[22] In this epigraph, Hornbacher's citation is true to the original (*W* 244); Plath 245.

[23] Plath 246.

[24] Lazarus's burial in the cave-like grave recalls in turn Plath's own suicidal attempt at self-emulation. This suicide attempt is treated fictionally in *The Bell Jar* (1963) where Esther Greenwood takes at least 50 sleeping pills and attempts to bury herself in a cellar room behind a wood pile in her family home.

[25] In advertising blurbs, *Wasted* is compared to *The Bell Jar*. Narrative similarities between the texts include a sensitive young woman's relating the history of her illness and the indeterminate endings. Esther muses at the end of the novel that she cannot be sure if the bell jar will not descend again, Hornbacher reports that eating disorders are never really cured. Another likeness between the two texts is their renditions of the protagonist's standing high over the place she lives at night and expressing her sense of depression and disorientation. As Esther sheds her fragile sense of identity by dumping out her wardrobe over the streets of New York during the last night of her apprenticeship at a woman's magazine, so Hornbacher feels the lightness of her existence during her nighttime wanderings in California: "Sometimes I stood on the railing above the little town with its scattered lights, above the steep drop, wondering if the wind would come up and lift my feet and throw me into the swimming for that hung over the valley" (*W* 172-173).

Significantly chapter eight describes the apotheosis of Hornbacher's anorexia and her romance with her intense workaholic dying self. It is also the last act of the disappearance act she describes in her memoirs. She goes from weighing an extraordinarily low 85 to just 52 pounds while working as journalist and editor and attending college full-time. Part of her equation of anorexia with a romanticized image of death seems to be her sense of being in a kind of Promethean struggle with her own limits. To overcome these limits, to eat nothing at all, to die is the ultimate test of herself and hence hugely attractive: "I had an insatiable curiosity about the limits of my self. Combined with my self-hatred, that curiosity was dangerous" (*W* 206). For Hornbacher identity is inextricably fused with the desire to make herself ill: her "only means of self-regulation was self-destruction" (*W* 192).

The idealization of her own death was a preoccupation that Hornbacher had long before she embarked upon her final suicidal drive to become weightless. At boarding school Hornbacher accompanies her transition from bulimia to anorexia by writing stories about women who grow so thin and silent that they eventually disappear (*W* 114). While staying with her step-mother in California and resuming her anorexic habits after her first hospitalization, Hornbacher writes insomniac poems about a dying woman. The image she describes in these poems of a beautiful, tragic woman in a boat resembles the gorgeous dying heroine that has inspired other eating-disordered women in literature as well:

> I write about her silence, her face turned away, her still and patient biding of time, a war bride waiting for her dead husband to return. About her pushing her rowboat away from shore, oarless, floating toward invisibility. (*W* 172)

The poetic conflation of water, death and a beautiful tragic women is reminiscent of Atwood's ironic stylization of herself as "The Lady of Shalott" in *Lady Oracle* and Josie's idealization of herself as a Pre-Raphaelite Ophelia or a dying ballerina in *Life-Size*. Hornbacher, like Plath in a serious tone and Atwood in a comic one, appropriates the image of the dying female familiar from the work of Shakespeare, Edgar Allan Poe, Henry James and other authors. One thinks of Shakespeare's Cordelia and Ophelia, Poe's "Annabel Lee" (1849), and James's Milly from *The Wings of the Dove* (1909) to name only a few examples of the coupling of dying or dead women with images of grace and beauty.

Even in the early phase of her anorexia, Hornbacher began to covet death and imagined this state with a sense of heightened eroticism:

> Death is at your shoulder, death is your shadow, your scent, your waking and dreaming companion [...]. The sickness occupies your every thought, breaths like a lover at your ear; the sickness stands at your shoulder in the mirror, absorbs with your body each inch of skin and flesh, and you let it work you over, touch you with rough hands that thrill.
>
> Nothing will ever be so close to you again. You will never find a lover so careful, so attentive, so unconditionally present and concerned only with you. (*W* 125)[26]

Death and illness hold an attraction comparable to that of a passionate lover. The focus of the lover's desire on the beloved is likened to the way in which death permeates the sick person's body and mind. This image of death as an impassioned lover has an element of narcissism. Concerned with Hornbacher's person and body and no one else's, the personification of death provides her with further validation. This imagery reminds one of pictorial images in which a skeletal Death is depicted as passionately embracing a naked young woman, for instance in Edvard Munch's "Death and the Maiden" (1894).

In this passage Hornbacher lumps thinness, anorexia, and death together in one positive association field, just as she throws bulimia, fat, and emotional

---

[26] For a discussion of the idealization of the dying female as creative muse, see Elisabeth Bronfen's *Over Her Dead Body,* particularly the conclusion in which she discusses women authors' appropriation and inversion of this imagery: "In this discussion I did not distinguish women from men writers, because both wrote within the cultural context that uses femininity (as image, enigma, aporia) to represent alterity. Inevitably women write, in Mitchell's terms

excess together in her thinking. Alternately, death in the form of self-starvation appears as male or female lovers in Hornbacher's mind. In the above quotation the eating disorder takes on the form of an attractive seducer, a bit akin to the Angel in the poem "The Angel That Feeds Me," who is by turns gentle and seductive and violent and forceful.[27] This ambivalence is palpable in "rough hands that thrill"; "rough" would imply that death's hands have the potential to hurt the soft skin of the woman they touch; "thrill" implies that the potential violence of these hands is channeled into producing sensations of pleasure. The villainous lover's double-character, familiar from figures ranging from Richardson's Lovelace in *Clarissa* to Heathcliff in Emily Brontë's *Wuthering Heights* (1847) to the heroes of Victoria Holt's popular novels, rests in his mutability. The heroine may never be sure (until the end of the narration) whether the villain wants to marry or rape and kill her.

Hornbacher also sometimes portrays her eating disorder as a slender *doppelgängerin* who wants to murder her. In the Introduction to her memoirs, she writes that the "bad guy in this tale" is herself: "My double image, the evil skinny chick who hisses, *Don't eat. I'm not going to let you eat. I'll let you go as soon as you're thin, I swear I will*" (*W* 10). This "skinny chick" is present up to the end of the memoirs when Hornbacher describes her present self in the dissociated second-person as "bicker[ing] with the bitch in your head who keeps telling you you're fat and weak [...]. Bear in mind she's trying to kill you" (*W* 286). In contrast to this passage, she describes her attraction to thinness and anorexia as being like the desire to have a beautiful woman walk on one's arm.

On the one hand Hornbacher idealizes the image of the beautiful, emaciated dying woman. On the other hand she, already skeletal, embodies this image. Rather than objectifying the beautiful dying female or stylizing her as a muse, she, like woman writers before her, also describes the dying woman from

---

from a masculine position, even if they do so to point out and denounce the way women's position arises from, through and with death" (405).

a subject position, from the inside. At the same time the attraction of how this woman appears to others remains a paramount concern. This ambivalence regarding the dying woman is comparable to Hornbacher's sense of her relationship to her own body: she both has a body (objectifies it) and is a body (experiences it subjectively).[28]

Even after Hornbacher has become cured of her eating disorders to the degree that she is no longer actively anorexic or bulimic, she admits that the romance with illness continues. She finds her relative health and its lack of remarkableness to be a "pitiful" state. In this description of her current state of mind the author once again uses the second person pronoun to describe those emotions closest to her:

> [...] you do not qualify as an eating-disordered person. And you feel bad about this. You feel as if you really *ought* to count, you ought to still merit worry, still have the poser to summon a flurry of nurses, their disdain ill hidden, your skeletal smirk. (*W* 180)

No longer emaciated or deathly ill, the former anorectic feels insufficient. The identity of being an intense, sick and, most importantly, an emaciated young woman is difficult to abandon. Hornbacher's romance with illness never really ends.

Another confessional quality of *Wasted* is its explicitly public message. Both in Hepworth's and Turner's sociological study of actual confessional practices and Axthelm's descriptions of modern confessional novels, the public consequences of confessions are emphasized. Axthelm describes how the

---

[27] See chapter I, section 1.3) above.

[28] I believe that it would be simplistic to analyze this appropriation of traditionally male-dominated imagery as a feminist act. The practical implications of a propagation of the idealized dying female are ugly. Just as Hornbacher bought into the myth of the transforming qualities of thinness and supposed that if she were thin she would also become wealthy, blonde, tall, and regal, an embrace of the romance of dying led her to try to die and remains a dangerous attraction in her post-memoir life. Her conceiving of the story of her life as a heroic pursuit of death may well serve to glamorize the pain she wants to hinder other women from having.

confessional author needs a mirror figure or double to tell his shameful or difficult tale to. Hepworth and Turner point out that no confession is a confession without a confessor, someone to whom the testimony may be directed publicly. Only then, in a culture of individual responsibility, can private guilt or shame be used to underscore the public system of rewards and punishments.[29] Contrary to the narrators of *Life-Size* and *The Passion of Alice,* Hornbacher announces the intended purpose of her book and addresses the subject of confession. She purports to be highly conscious of the effect reading her book may have on the reader. As quoted above, she writes that she has written her memoirs with the explicit purpose of "keep[ing] people from going where I went":

> I would not wish the bitter aftermath—that stage we can never foresee when we're sick, the damaged body, the constant temptation, the realizations of how we have failed to become ourselves, how afraid we were and are, and how we must start over from scratch, no matter how great that fear—on anyone. I don't think people realize, when they're just getting started on an eating disorder or even when they're in the grip of one, that it is not something that you just "get over." (*W* 7)

Repeatedly, the author warns against the danger of the reader's romanticizing her experience, of her thinking that because Hornbacher managed to survive a weight loss of over seventy pounds and has gone on to tell about it that the reader is justified in pursuing an eating disorder as well. Most often these passages are written as direct addresses to the reader. Unlike the many text passages in which Hornbacher distances herself from her own horrific experiences by writing in the "you" form and the narrative takes on a surrealistic dreamlike aspect, these remarks to her reading public have a great immediacy.

---

[29] Hepworth and Turner, *Confession: Studies in Deviance and Religion*: "The interior freedom of conscience as the arena of confession thus requires the public supports of authority and social control. It is this ambiguous overlap between individual conscience and public constraint which constitutes the confession as a social institution and which marks its central sociological interest as a cultural practice" (176).

Again and again Hornbacher emphasizes the fact that there is no happy ending to her story of illness: no doctor, sudden revelation, or romance caused her to see the error of her old unhealthy ways. Hence, unlike the confessional heroes Axthelm describes, Hornbacher does not consciously experience the release from pain and shame that confessional purgation may brings. Quite the opposite. Hornbacher writes that composing her memoirs was a painful, non-therapeutic chore: "You know, sometimes I get sick of writing this" (*W* 179); and:

> I have not enjoyed writing this book. Making public what I have kept private from those closest to me, and often enough from myself, all my life, is not exactly my ideal of a good time. This project was not, as so many people have suggested, "therapeutic" for me—I pay my therapist a lot of money for that. (*W* 275)

And in a passage quite reminiscent of the opening of Salinger's *The Catcher in the Rye* (1945, 1946), she writes that she has no intention of having her memoirs resemble an outpouring of family history to a therapist:

> I'm not here to spill my guts and tell you about how awful it's been, that my daddy was mean and my mother was mean and some kid called me Fatso in the third grade, because none of the above is true. (*W* 4)[30]

These passages suggest that the last thing Hornbacher believes in is that by telling the story of her illness she may become well.

However, the narrator repeatedly describes herself as a master of lying. Child of actors, she becomes an actor in order to keep the reality of her eating disorders hidden. Her fictions include a complex fabric of subterfuge invented for her parents, friends, and therapists demonstrating her health and her desire to

[30] Compare this passage to the opening of J. D. Salinger's debut novel: "If you really want to hear about it, the first thing you'll probably want to know is where I was born, and what my lousy childhood was like, and how my parents were occupied and all before they had me, and all that David Copperfield kind of crap, but I don't feel like going into it, if you want to know

become healthy. The most graven of these lies concerns the story of sexual abuse she invents near the end of her eight-month stay in Lowe House, a mental institution for children. Hornbacher appropriates another patient's genuine fear of inappropriate sexual behavior in her fabrication of a story about how she was sexually abused in her father's theater as a child (*W* 212). This lie keeps the Lowe House staff from pursuing the real multiple causes of Hornbacher's various psychological and physical problems. Perhaps this subterfuge simply exemplifies the narrator's narcissism: when attention lags from her own person onto another patient's more pressing issue, she invents a reason for the spotlight to return to her.[31]

Since the narrator of these memoirs describes herself as a master of disguises and admits to her continuing attraction to illness, the reader cannot know if, and when, the narrator is sincere. When her tone becomes flippant, as in "But what's a girl to do" (*W* 57) about her friends' inability to help her with her bulimia, the reader may ask, how much of this outpouring of personal detail represents staged confession. Is the taking off of layers of psychological truth a kind of exhibitionist striptease, in which the "real" (or the fictional construction of the real) Marya Hornbacher remains completely hidden?

5. 2) Cultural Criticism or How-To Guide for Bulimia

Wasted represents an analysis and a condemnation of the culture that encourages eating disorders in women. Indeed, the memoirs have an explicit didactic purpose—to educate women to the pain of eating disorders and to indict American society for encouraging these disorders. Like the narrator Josie in *Life-Size* and Alice in *The Passion of Alice*, Hornbacher is quite conscious and

---

the truth." *The Catcher in the Rye* (1945/1946; London: Penguin Books, 1994) 1. Here and in other passages Hornbacher's voice recalls Salinger's self-ironic vernacular style.

[31] For a complete list of Hornbacher's psychological "firebomb[s] to the right" to protect her eating disorders, see *Wasted* 212-213.

explicit about the cultural factors that contributed to her becoming ill. She is careful to say that it is not all her parents' fault that she had problems with food. She is also careful to distance herself from popular theories about eating disorders, which she regards as overly simplistic or one-sided. Her eating disorder, she believes, was not just the symptom of her family's emotional triangulation (M.S. Palazzoli and Hilde Bruch). Nor, was it an expression of her unwillingness to become a sexually adult woman (Freud and followers), although her early puberty[32] contributed to her lack of ease with her body. The author rejects such explanations and speaks instead of a combination of factors, including her emotional intensity and sense of insecurity, and her family history, which within the context of America's thinness-obsessed culture gave rise to her severely disordered eating habits. The cult of thinness takes the greatest share of the blame:

> [...] I do believe that the cultural environment is an equal if no greater, culprit in the sheer *popularity* of eating disorders. There were numerous methods of self-destruction available to me, countless outlets that could have channeled my drive, perfectionism, ambition, and an excess of general intensity, millions of ways in which I could have responded to a culture that I found highly problematic. I did not choose those ways. I chose an eating disorder. I cannot help but think that, had I lived in a culture where "thinness" was not regarded as a strange state of grace, I might have sought out another means of attaining that grace, perhaps one that would not have so seriously damaged my body, and so radically distorted my sense of who I am. (*W* 6-7)

The process of acculturation in which Hornbacher became obsessed by her weight began early. Indeed, the author asserts that she cannot remember any time in which she was normal about her food and weight. As in the case of Ellen West,[33] Hornbacher's problematic relationship with food began as a baby: She

---

[32] Her menarche ensued when she was just ten years of age.

[33] Hornbacher shares a number of similarities with the anorectic West, subject of the existential psychologist's Ludwig Binswanger's case study from 1944 and poems by Adrienne Rich and Frank Bidart (See chapter I, 1.1). Like West, Hornbacher suffered from an

was allergic to cow's milk and had a number of food allergies. As a four-year-old she complains to her parents that she is "fat" (*W* 16). Another memory from her early childhood is of bragging to her friend Gina at five that she's "gonna be as thin as my mom when I grow up" (*W* 11).

Like other eating-disordered women, Hornbacher is obsessed by her mother's body and weight and sees this body as a measuring stick of her own relative worth. Josie from *Life-Size* envisions her mother as the fat monster she will become if she ever let her desire to eat overwhelm her self-flagellating efforts. For Alice the decisive moment in her struggle to assert her own identity comes with her realization that even if she loses an infinite amount of weight, she will never have a "great body" like her mother. Surely, Hornbacher learns her obsessive interest in measuring the size of her bottom from her mother, who also was or is bulimic, and whom she remembers as interspersing her meals with trips to the mirror to "stare at her butt" (*W* 23).[34] To outdo her mother in thinness becomes part of Hornbacher's life plan and, indeed, she experiences a moment of triumph when she realizes that she, as a severe anorectic, has actually become thinner than her mother (*W* 240).

Hornbacher's mother's (and grandmother's) obsessions with becoming or remaining thin match predominant mores in American society. As a girl of

---

intolerance to milk as a baby, and was an intense, passionate, and artistically-driven child. Other similarities include laxative abuse, weight fluctuations, and the writing of poetry. Binswanger 237-364.

[34] Both sides of Hornbacher's family seem to have troubled relations to food. Hornbacher's father eats compulsively and competes with his daughter when she is already eating-disordered to see who can perform the more strenuous night time exercises. Hornbacher's mother, in a complete failure to see the gravity of her daughter's illness, comments on her daughter's post-hospitalization 100-pound-frame with the dry words: "I wouldn't call you thin" (*W* 100). Hornbacher's grandparents match their children in their dangerously distorted perceptions of how much is the right amount to eat and weigh. Hornbacher's paternal grandmother likes to stuff her granddaughter with food and complain about her daughter-in-law's excessive thinness (*W* 24). By contrast, her maternal grandmother is constantly taking food away from Hornbacher and her other granddaughters as well to "help" them from becoming fat. This distaste for "fat" is shared by Hornbacher's maternal grandfather and his wife, her step-grandmother, who only order appetizers for their granddaughter when she

six, Hornbacher comes to associate thinness with greatness. In a dramatic moment she writes down her life plan and buries it in the yard. She wants "only": "To get thin. To be great. To get out" (*W* 35). At eight she is already comparing her body negatively to those of girls around her. She wants to, like them, wear slim-legged jeans rather than regularly-sized ones. The books she reads as a girl feature blonde-haired, perfect looking girls who wear size 6 clothes. Rather than having a real Barbie doll, whose body girls learn to aspire to copy, Hornbacher has these "literary" models of perfection (*W* 46). Like Josie in *Life-Size*, she diligently studies the magazines directed at teens and pre-teen girls that are intended to sell body self-hatred and products. In magazines such as *Seventeen* she reads about new diet techniques and studies the pictures of models who—she finds—are without flaws. She enters a competition with herself and the girls around her to attain the "Perfect Body" (*W* 47), that hidden irresistible entity that once attained will make all of one's dreams and aspirations come true.

The myth of the perfect body—reputed to be hidden within everyone—is coupled with the American faith in hard work and discipline. This sentiment is familiar from *Life-Size* and *The Passion of Alice* as well: if one tries hard enough one can embody the American ideal of female success and be gorgeous, tall, and thin.[35] Hornbacher is quite specific about what this myth entails:

> I fell for the great American dream, female version, hook, line, and sinker. I, as many young women do, honest-to-god believed that once I Just Lost a Few Pounds, somehow I would suddenly be a New You, I would have Ken-doll men chasing my thin legs down with bouquets of flowers on the street, I would become rich and famous and glamorous and lose my

---

comes to visit them as an eleven-year old because they don't think she needs any more food than that.

[35] Commenting on her drive to embody this ideal, Hornbacher writes: "In America, you can have anything if you just work for it, dammit, and I was bloody well ready to work" (*W* 92). Compare this passage with *Life-Size's* Josie's desire to "measure up" to the images she sees in women's magazines, and to Alice's (from *The Passion of Alice*) attempt to attain her mother's "perfect body" through dieting.

> freckles and become blond and five foot ten. I would wear cool quasi-intellectual glasses and a man's oxford shirt in a sunny New York flat and sip coffee and say Mmmm and fold my paper neatly and He would come up behind me and look at me with an adoring gaze. I would swing sexily into my red coupe, and the wind would blow through my hair as I drove into some great big city, stepping off the elevator and striding (with a feminine but authoritative step) into my office where everyone would be impressed with my every feminine but authoritative word. In the evenings I would go home and make magical gourmet meals and eat three bites, and He would look at me in the candlelight and I would be a superwoman 1980s goddess, yes indeed. As soon as I left my hometown and lost a few pounds. (*W* 91-92)

Some important ingredients in this American success story are that the players are WASP (blond and five foot ten), wealthy (New York flat, red coupe), urban, successful; traditional gender roles are not challenged in the least. Although the idealized woman is "ador[ed]" by the Ken-doll[36] man, her work does not keep her from looking great, moving in a womanly fashion ("a feminine but authoritative step"), making dinner and only "eat[ing] three bites" of it. What the woman actually does and how she has acquired her wealth and comparative power is insignificant in this description, since co-workers are "impressed with [her] every feminine but authoritative word." How she looks and that she is adored by a man and, hence, feminine and, above all, thin is central to this success story. The "yes indeed" near the end of the quotation functions like the repetitive phrase that punctuates a sermon or prayer. Furthermore, the American success story rests on the idea, sold to immigrants and natives alike, that the streets are paved with gold for those who are willing to work hard enough for that gold. "Anyone can become a millionare" and "you can be anyone you want to be" are favorite myths of self-actualization in American culture, which were cultivated in books like Horatio Alger's *Ragged Dick* series, about an impoverished boot jack's transformation into a young business man (1868-1870): these myths suggest that the realities of race and class, gender and ethnic

[36] Barbie's male counterpart, remarkable for his lack of genitalia.

groupings are irrelevant. With enough diligence anyone can be a Superman, a multimillionaire such as Donald Trump, or a Superwoman like the supermodel Cindy Crawford. For American women, and to a lesser degree for men, one of the central tenants of the myth of personal success is that if you lose weight you will automatically be happy, sexy, and economically secure.

The equation of success with the thin, perfect body informs Hornbacher's young life and much of women's lives within this culture. She notes that the workout-culture has much less to do with health than with the bitter competitive pursuit of thinness among women.[37] She is also aware of how difficult it is to demythologize thinness. As she points out, few women do eat normally in American culture. Dieting and talking about food and weight is a way in which women connect with each other, by complimenting each other on weight loss, sistering each other in weight loss efforts, and bragging about how little they eat.[38]

Occasionally, Hornbacher's tone takes on a somewhat misogynist edge when she comments on the eating habits of women around her: "To hear women tell it we're never hungry [...]. Food makes us itchy, food is too messy, all I really like to eat is celery" (*W* 118). In such passages she divorces herself from that whinny pack of women who have not like Hornbacher seen the error of their gender-related food behaviors.

---

[37] On dieting and working out, she writes: "On the surface you're doing this companionably, you're a friggin' unstoppable dieting army and you'll all go down together. On the underside, you're all competing with one another to be the thinnest, most controlled, least weak, and you have your own private crusade on which no one can join you, lest they be as fucked up as you" (*W* 110).

[38] "Women use their obsession with weight and food as a point of connection with one another, a commonality even between strangers. Instead of talking about *why* we use food and weight control as a means of handling emotional stress, we talk ad nauseam about the fact that we don't like our bodies. When you decide not to do that, you begin to notice how constant that talk is. I go to the gym, and women are standing around in their underwear bitching about their bellies, I go to a restaurant and listen to women cheerfully conversing about their latest diet, I go to a women's clothing store and the woman helping me, almost universally, will launch into a monologue about how these pants are very slimming, how

Nonetheless, she is aware of the larger pattern in which being perceived as a woman who is weighty or excessive is condemned and punished in American culture: It is considered unfeminine to want in any way, to be too emotional, to be too heavy, to be too loud, desirous, or physical.[39] Ultimately, the beauty myth with its attendant association of thinness and success is a tool with which society, women included, keeps women down and subservient. Hence Hornbacher considers her book's attack on the beauty myth to "amount to cultural heresy" (*W* 5) and her greatest desire other than to "keep others from going where she went" is "to write a prescription for culture, some sort of tranquilizer that will make it less maniacally compelled to climb the StairMaster right into nowhere" (*W* 283-284). In her optimistic moments Hornbacher sees her post-anorexic self as having transcended the snares of this cultural script:

> I had to learn strange and delicious lessons, lessons too few women learn: to love the thump of my steps, the implication of weight and presence and taking of space, to love my body's rebellious hungers, responses to touch, to understand myself as more than a brain attached to a bundle of bones. I have to ignore the cultural cacophony that singsongs all day long, Too much, too much, too much. (*W* 5)

This manifesto for body acceptance sounds quite positive. The adjective "delicious" implies that Hornbacher has learned to enjoy more than her desire for food. Learning to love her "body's rebellious hungers" suggests that she has also come to accept her sexual desires, and perhaps even her need to sleep.[40]

---

lucky I am to have the problem of never being able to find clothes that fit, 'Because you're *tiny*!' she'll squeal" (*W* 283).

[39] For a further exploration of this idea see Susan Bordo's "Anorexia Nervosa: Psychopathology as the Crystallization of Culture," *Feminism & Foucault* and *Unbearable Weight: Feminism, Western Culture and the Body* (Berkeley: California UP, 1993). Furthermore, Hornbacher sees being "too busy" as a doubly attractive state in American culture. Not only is this characteristic of thin individuals but also of those whose lives are so full of important things to do that they simply cannot find time to eat.

[40] Sleeping is something she does precious little of whenever she is busy starving herself, which is most of the time. See 171-172, 253 of *Wasted.*

Yet much textual evidence suggests that Hornbacher herself has not embraced the manifesto for body acceptance she subscribes to. In an Interlude describing the author's present life, Hornbacher recounts how the still-present desire to be deathly thin leads her to greet the re-emergence of her hipbones after a medically-induced weight loss like a long-lost lover (*W* 243). She is also explicit about how much she misses the gratifying aspects of purging and describes the ever-present desire to make herself vomit as an addiction: "I miss it. It hurts like a sonofabitch. It's disgusting, but it was my safeguard, my sure thing, my security, my life for all those years" (*W* 121). Thus there is no little ambivalence about this book's intentions. Hornbacher wishes to reform American culture but she is obviously in need of reformation herself. Given the author's own history of having aspired to become anorexic after she read a novel about an anorexic girl, it seems problematic at best to hope that her description of never having fully recovered from eating disorders will necessarily help other girls not to "go where she went."

As a bulimic nine-year-old Hornbacher reads the novel *The Best Little Girl in the World* (1978), a "rather romanticized account [...] of having an eating disorder" (*W* 43), in which a pretty teenage dancer is cured of her nearly-fatal anorexia by her compassionate psychologist. Significantly, Hornbacher is not frightened by the events in this novel but admires the heroine whom she sees as being enviably "withdrawn, reserved, cold, wholly absorbed in her own obsession, perfectly pure" (*W* 43). Hence, the novel intended to explain anorexia and help those affected by it find treatment actually contributed to Hornbacher's anorexia.[41]

Presumably *Wasted,* with its plethora of visceral detail, is intended to be anything but a romanticized account of eating disorders. Yet the author's

[41] This is argument enough for the "reading hypothesis" discussed by Habermas in his history of eating disorders, in which he suggests that models of illness which are read about—or, by analogy viewed on TV—may become models of behavior for those who read them. See section 1.5.3) above.

descriptions of her life during the most severe period of her anorexia, after she leaves Lowe House and works and studies first in Minnesota and then in Washington, D.C. are extraordinarily glamorizing. While her weight on the scale steadily decreases, the numbers of her conventional successes increase proportionally. Documenting her gradual starvation the last long chapter of the text is punctuated by numbers written out on the page:

> Seventy.
>
> I took off my belt and shoes.
>
> Sixty-seven. (*W* 267)

This effective narrative tool demonstrates how the author couples her identity with her weight. Furthermore, the written-out numbers have the quality of a countdown. The reader is reminded of the launching of a rocket; tension builds up gradually as the numbers proceeding the lift-off grow smaller and smaller. Perhaps a rocket launch is an appropriate image for an anorectic's idealized image of herself as she defies materiality by disappearing; one is reminded of *Life-Size*'s Josie's idealization of herself as a ballerina who springs above the head of her spectators into thin air. In fact, Hornbacher is describing the period before her final physical breakdown when she comes very close to death. However, this countdown to self-destruction holds many attractive qualities for her and, potentially, the reader.

During this time and up nearly until her final hospitalization, Hornbacher is batting a thousand. The reader learns that she is admitted with scholarships to the colleges she has applied to—although she never finished high school and was hospitalized three times—and that she has frequent successes with men. As a student in Minneapolis she sits in a café all night reading philosophical texts—in itself an image of idealized intensity—in order to keep herself from eating, and casually seduces men, making a sport of having them fall in love with her without her really trying.[42] Simultaneously, she enters more emotionally intense relationships with her co-worker Mark with whom she stays up all night talking about ideas and with Julian, with whom she has constantly corresponded since she lived in California, and whom she later marries. Since becoming more physically desirable motivates many women to begin the diets that eventually lead to their becoming eating-disordered, the picture Hornbacher presents of herself as the seemingly effortless seducer of men's bodies and hearts is certainly an ambivalent one.

Furthermore, Hornbacher describes how periods of starvation accompany phases of heightened creativity. While making the transition from bulimia to anorexia she writes countless short stories; while relapsing into anorexia in California she writes poetry; and after leaving Lowe House and resuming and intensifying her anorexic habits, she produces papers for college courses and articles for the newspapers she works for. In periods of self-starvation, Hornbacher appears to attain the Dionysian ideal with which she became familiar at her arts high school of living in a heightened stare of passion and creative productivity.

In Washington she adopts another American ideal, that of the terrifically busy workaholic. Emulating the harried life-style of Washingtonians as she perceives them, she "walks the walk" (*W* 249) and increases her already terrific pace of production. No longer sleeping at all, she subsists on nearly nothing other than coffee, holds down a full-time editor's job, several part-time journalism jobs, maintains a 4.0 grade average, and still manages to write poetry. These descriptions appear enormously self-aggrandizing. Already thirty pounds below her natural weight of 120 pounds, she describes herself during a

[42] "I did this, went about mentally seducing men just for kicks. The point was never the sex. I hadn't ever enjoyed sex much, and wouldn't for several years. The point was the game, and the game was not simply to get someone into bed. Men are embarrassingly easy to seduce. The game was to get them to fall in love with you first, or get them to think they were in love

visit to Washington in the following passage. Importantly, the candy and coke is the only food she has eaten since her "minimalist breakfast":

> I flipped on CNN, undressed in front of the mirror, admiring myself from all angles, standing up on the bed to get a good look at my legs, Thin. Very thin. I put on my robe and sat back against the head of the bed, smoking and drinking my Coke. Arranging my Skittles by color, eating them one by one, red ones last. I stared at myself in the mirror, glee and a sugar rush bubbling up in me thinking: Alone in a hotel room in Washington, D.C. Thus began my love affair with hotels, which has yet to end. The anonymity of it all, the just-another-woman-in-Washington, the solitude, the smoking in bed, the TV as late as I liked, the palpable proximity to speed and power, within spitting distance of the Real World. (*W* 235)

Hornbacher has come close to embodying the 1980s ideal of Superwoman femininity she aspired to as a young girl. Though she has not become 5' 10" and blonde, she does have all the other trappings of successful urban femininity: She is thin, close to political power, and attractive with her "Thin. Very thin" legs. The ability to stay in a hotel room alone also suggests affluence, another vital ingredient of the Superwoman's draw. Hornbacher fails to notice the disconnect, fails to recognize the discrepancy between her lambastations of society for promoting eating disorders in women by fetishizing the thin female body and her own idealization of her successful anorexic self.

The height of Hornbacher's romance with her driven anorexic self occurs during the 1992 presidential debates in Virginia, which she covers in her function as a reporter. She describes herself as being in a frenetic whirl of note-taking and interviews. Not incidentally, she is complimented on her work by an older old-style journalist. Her "big moment," however, occurs when she is able to beat out the other reporters in their efforts to question James Carville and Mary Matalin,[43] by virtue of her tiny size. As she describes the scene: "[...] I,

---

with you, think you were the most astonishing woman they'd ever met in their entire life, and if things went according to plan, fuck them up forever" (*W* 225).

[43] Carville and Matalin were political strategists for the 1992 presidential campaign, Carville for Clinton and Matalin for Bush.

being five feet tall and as wide as a twig, ducked under everyone's arms and stood with my tape recorder next to their faces and shouted questions over the din" (*W* 253).

In this case the assertive anorectic outdoes all the Big Boy and Big Girl reporters around her and gets her story for the express reason that she is "as wide as a twig." We might imagine the tabloid rendition of this story bearing the headline "Skinny Girl Reporter Beats Big Boys to the Punch!"[44] Even when close to physical collapse, she continues to ingest ideas rapidly. She becomes "obsessed," for instance, with the philosopher Hume's skepticism about the existence of the body (*W* 255-256).

In the collection of above images, the reader finds Hornbacher to be both physically and emotionally attractive to men, artistically productive and intense, and extremely—particularly for a Freshman college student—successful in her work. Hence, Hornbacher's warnings to her readers not to copy her behavior ring a hollow note. The anorexic ideal remains compelling to her even after recovery and informs her descriptions of her sick self.

Even more disturbing than the glamorization of illness and anorexia that Hornbacher's memoirs represent is the explicit information they give out on how to acquire and intensify eating disorders. This is another case in which the author's stated intentions directly conflict with her narrative actions: she wants to describe how awful eating disorders are, yet she unwittingly describes exactly how to get them. Hornbacher's experience suggests that the more contact one has with eating-disordered women, the more negative behaviors one may learn from them.[45] For instance, during her first hospitalization in 1990, Hornbacher

[44] Given the author's decided pleasure in relating the high point of her career as an anorexic workaholic, it comes as a bit of a surprise when she describes herself as looking ugly to herself for the first time on the following page of the memoirs: "I remember thinking in a rare moment of clarity, that I couldn't imagine who would be attracted to me, as ugly as I'd become" (*W* 254).

[45] Indeed, Gordon suggests that bulimia is an acquired behavior and that women are particularly keen to learn about new purging techniques. *Anorexia and Bulimia*, 112-114.

expresses disparagement about the women who use laxatives as a form of weight control and writes with characteristic disdain in the second-person form: "the whole idea of using them [laxatives] for weight loss will seem utterly stupid to you, because its not *real* weight you lose by shitting all day long" (*W* 147). Yet only a half a year later she is "eating whole boxes of Ex-Lax three times a day" (*W* 148).[46]

Among things the reader may learn, in the rough order of their placement within the narration, are that: one needs to use "markers" as a bulimic, that is, one needs to consume some kind of bright, unnatural-looking food like Doritos first during one's binge so that when one purges one may be sure that all of the consumed food has been vomited out, by virtue of the fact that the food comes out in order of last consumed first purged, and the markers show that one is finished; it is possible to vomit silently: "no hack, no gag, just bend over and mentally will the food back up" (*W* 97); starving can be pleasurable due to the amplified sense of sensory experience one has when the body is deprived of food (*W* 105); one can make such elaborate anorexic eating plans, for instance, to eat one hundred calories per day and eat so slowly that one it too busy to eat anything more; stashing away food may strengthen one's resolve not to eat because one knows one has food just in case; by drinking huge quantities of fluid, including water and black coffee, one can trick the body into believing it is full.[47] The impressionable reader may also learn that one can spit out food after chewing it to give one the sense of having eaten, that one needs to drink a lot of fluid to purge successfully, that one can use syrup of ipecac to induce vomiting. If this palette of self-destructive behavior does not suffice, self-mutilation remains, that is cutting oneself on the arms or hands in order to produce a comforting sense of physical release. Again, Hornbacher observed

[46] Ex-lax is a popular American laxative that comes in a chocolate flavor.
[47] This is common advice given on diets: drink, drink, drink, so as "to flush out the fat" or to trick the body into feeling full.

this practice while she was institutionalized. Whereas other patients and her parents could not understand the self-mutilator's actions, she could:

> I understood so well, in fact, that I would begin to do that very thing a few years down the road. After my eating disorder was "over," I would go in blind search for something with which to tear myself apart. I found a razor blade worked quite well. In Lowe House, what this girl was doing to herself made perfect sense to me. It seemed to me that only our means were different; our ends were very much the same. Carving away at the body to—symbolically and literally—carve up an imperfect soul. (*W* 206)

Is not the empathy with which Hornbacher describes her fellow patient's self-abuse precisely what some readers may experience when they read her memoirs? Here is a bright, sensitive, intense, and highly-articulate individual who shares the sense many young women have of not being pretty or thin enough.[48] While eating disordered, she experiences life with vividness and embodies cultural ideals of workaholism, Dionysian excess, and—till nearly the end—attractiveness.

Some readers may heed Hornbacher's explicit warnings: "There are people reading this who may think to themselves: What if I just tried it? What if I just lost a few more pounds? After all, *she's* still alive. Not quite" (*W* 129). Yet others may pay more attention to the images that contradict these warnings: two photos of Hornbacher on the hardback edition of the memoirs feature the author looking quite thin.

[48] "Although the disorder we have examined here is part of a general pattern of adolescent discomfort in the West, anorexia nervosa ultimately expresses the predicament of a very distinct group, one that suffers from the painful ambiguities of being young and female in an affluent society set adrift by social change. Intelligent, anxious for personal achievement, and determined to maintain control in a world where things as basic as food and sex are increasingly out of control, the contemporary anorectic unrelentingly pursues thinness—a secular form of perfection." Brumberg, *Fasting* 271.

5.3) The Demonization of Bulimia

In the introduction I posed the question of why there are so few extended literary accounts of bulimia. I have argued that this is in part due to the fact that no literary tradition of writing about bulimia exists as one does about women and self-starvation. I have also argued that characters who are bulimic or who compulsively overeat tend to be treated with derisive humor. Atwood's Joan Foster sums this up best when she muses that no one would have felt sorry for Desdemona if she had been fat.[49]

Wasted is of interest because it is the only extended literary text known to me that deals with the theme of bulimia explicitly. Bulimia is described nearly as frequently as anorexia in poems posted on the Internet. Yet other than in memoirs and novels specifically intended for youthful audiences, prose treatments of bingeing and purging are lacking.[50]

I want to examine the exploration of bulimia in these memoirs from several angles. As mentioned above, the quality of Hornbacher's writing sometimes reminds one of bulimic excessiveness when her prose veers into hyperbolic exaggeration. For instance, to describe her childhood nightmares she uses a series of connotatively-charged adjectives including "incoherent," "endless," and "desperate" to evoke an atmosphere of terror:

> The scream in the night, the sobbing as I fumbled my dark run across the endless house to the door of my parents' bedroom, the incoherent rambling about monsters that were stealing pennies from my penny jar, the desperate weeping: I won't know how many I *have* I howled. (*W* 20)

Sometimes the piling up of embarrassing personal information appears compulsive. When the narrator tells us that her brother's girlfriend had to ask Hornbacher's mother for new towels after Hornbacher's purge had caused the

---

[49] Atwood, *LO* 52.
[50] See the Introduction for a list of works.

house's sewage system to stop up and the bathroom to flood with vomit (*W* 223), one senses that this detail is told as a form of self-abasing expiation. The narrator appears compelled to tell the worst about herself, before she may stop. Similarly the bulimic shoves food into her mouth until her belly is so full that she has to induce vomiting. The compulsivity of the narration—a kind of textual bulimia—resembles the compulsivity of a binge.

However, Hornbacher's hyperbolic style does not necessarily extend to her descriptions of specific bulimic episodes. In such descriptions she is most prone to using the second-person address form or simple past tense verbs. The need to dissociate herself from her own experiences seems to speak out of this. In the following I compare two descriptions of bingeing and purging closely in order to determine how bulimia is treated in them and to see if they offer any clues as to why bulimia receives far less literary attention than anorexia does.

During the first scene I quote from, Hornbacher has already been released from her first hospitalization for bulimia. The seriousness of her eating disorder has not been recognized and, at her behest, she has gone to live with her father's first wife's family in California. She quickly resumes her eating-disordered habits, eating less and less, or bingeing and vomiting. In the following scene she has been unable to purge at home because too many people are visiting the house. Feeling impelled to purge, she visits a pharmacy in town, pretends to be the mother of small children (she is just 16) and lies to the pharmacist about needing the emetic syrup of ipecac in case any of her children swallows poison. Describing the effects of having taken a whole bottle of ipecac rather than the recommended spoonful, she writes:

> You don't even get the stall door shut. You vomit in insane, ripping heaves, blood spattering on the seat. You throw up a carrot stick, a bite of something, a pretzel, quarts of water, blood. When you're done, you pull the door shut and get down on your knees. Your hands will not do as they're told, you have to use both hands to get toilet paper, wipe off the seat, the walls, the floor. You sit on the floor, shaking for an hour. (*W* 171)

This passage has a fast-paced dynamism. Short sentences and present tense, for the most part, action verbs describe this vivid experience. The body so much exceeds the conscious control of the narrator that the experience of its violent vomiting is projected onto the you-subject of these sentences. Furthermore, this ipecac-induced purge leaves no room for self-reflection: the body alone dictates experience. Thus the bulimic experience is depersonalized from the narrator in two ways in this passage, through the use of the second-person pronouns to describe the narrator's first-hand experience and through the complete lack of reference to the narrator's conscious experience of the event.

The next scene is noteworthy because Hornbacher does not just use the second-person address form to describe her experience. At first the first-person narrator relates events retrospectively. In the middle of describing this extended binge, however, she switches to using present tense progressive verbs and brings the related events into sharper focus by telling them as though she were now experiencing them. After eating and vomiting out everything in her parents house besides the dog food and the old jar of lime marmalade she drives to the food store in order, as she justifies this action to herself, to replace the foods she has just eaten:

> No coat, no hat, no gloves. Freezing cold and short of breath, dizzy, I got out of the car and went into the store. The lights were blinding. I squinted and went from row to row with my basket, desperately trying to remember what I'd eaten. I had no memory of the event whatsoever except that I'd gone to the refrigerator for the millionth time, opened it, and realized with horror that it was empty [...]. Suddenly I am at the checkout counter with a basket full of food, I'm paying. I'm loading the bags into the car. I'm driving out of the parking lot.
>
> Less than a mile away from the house, I have no idea how to get home.
>
> I panic. All I can think about is my need to eat. Now. This minute. I need to eat, fast, I need to eat a lot of things very fast. My mouth needs to be full, I need to be chewing on something, something salty. I pull over to the side of the road, crawl into the backseat, and start digging through the bags, pulling out things I don't remember buying, finally landing on a bag of potato chips, getting back into the front seat, ripping open the bag,

> stuffing a handful in my mouth, pulling back onto the road, driving aimlessly around until I recognize a road and follow it home.
>
> In the house, I dump the bags on the kitchen table, the floor, the counter, and clear a space for myself. I keep eating. I mix up blueberry muffins and let them cook while I suck down everything in sight, run to the bathroom, desperately wanting to rid myself of the feeling of fullness, throw up, run back, frantic to get the fullness back. I stand there eating until all the food is gone. All of it. Gone.
>
> I look up from the empty bowl in front of me and catch sight of my bloated, hideous face reflected in the dark window over the sink.
>
> I lean down and throw up.
>
> Flip the garbage disposal switch, rinse out the sink. Turn off the kitchen sink, feel in the dark for the staircase's handrail. I make it most of the way down before I feel that weightlessness creeping through my body, the dark getting darker, before I feel myself start to pitch forward and take flight, soaring into a black hole. (*W* 221-222)

The mood is Gothic. The narrator is driven out of the house during the night just as the Gothic heroine leaves the sanctuary of her bedroom at the midnight hour in order to meet ghosts or demonic lovers. Think of Radcliffean heroines such as Emily from *The Mysteries of Udolpho* (1794), her terrified nighttime wanderings through the Castle of Udolpho and the Château-le-Blanc with their near rapes and sightings of blood-covered corpses and moving palls. Hornbacher's being underdressed in the Minnesota cold and her disoriented walk from "from row to row" of the supermarket is reminiscent of the Gothic heroine, who wanders around the castle or into the garden's labyrinth while wearing only her nightgown, a state that renders her physically and sexually vulnerable. Moreover, Hornbacher cannot remember what she has done, where she is, or where she is going just as disoriented, terrified Gothic heroine loses her grasp on reality. The use of the adverb "desperately" two times, the adjective "frantic" and the noun "horror" all contribute to the atmosphere of terror and oppression in the passage, as does the atmospheric description of "dark getting darker." Hornbacher falls down the stairs and loses consciousness at the end of her binge, just as the Gothic heroine collapses into unconsciousness at the end of her nightmarish rambling.[51]

Instead of meeting a ghost or a corpse or a dangerous man, Hornbacher is confronted with the image of herself mid-binge. She perceives her reflected face to be like a monster, "bloated, hideous." And she feels possessed by her desire to eat. She cannot remember having purchased the food she stuffs into her mouth; it is as though another person or inner demon completed these actions for her. This projection of her bulimic desires onto another entity is reinforced by her writing "My mouth needs to be full," rather than "I need to be full." Later in the text Hornbacher explicitly states her sense of being demonized by her bulimic yearnings: "Nothing in the world scares me as much as bulimia. [...] It feels very much as if you are possessed, as if you have no will of your own but are in constant battle with your body, and you are losing" (*W* 267). Since bulimia is experienced as terrifying it seems appropriate that it should be presented in a macabre tone of voice.

As in many writings on eating disorders, the narrator of *Wasted* experiences herself as hideously ugly when she binges or eats at all. Her sense of being possessed by a demonic desire for food is familiar from *Life-Size* in which Josie feels terrified of eating at all for fear that she will be overwhelmed by her true inner self—an enormously fat woman who looks like her mother. Similarly, in Evelyn Boland's poem "Anorexic" the fleshy female self is personified as a witch; in "The Bulimic Experience" the desire to binge is called a "raging beast"; and in "The Angel that Feeds Me" an angel who turns into a demon first tempts the speaker of the poem to eat and then forces her to do so. Such projections of physical desire onto other monstrous beings or monstrous inner selves are familiar from literary history. Most notably, Dr. Jekyll is

[51] I am grateful to Paul Goetsch for suggesting this reading of the text passage to me. For a general discussion of Gothic heroines see Elizabeth Mahn Nollen, *Female Imprisonment, Madness, and Escape in Selected Texts by Women Writers* (Bloomington, Indiana: Indiana UP, 1984) and Julian Fleenor, *The Female Gothic* (Montréal and London: Eden Press, 1983).

simultaneously fascinated and horrified by the dwarfish figure of Mr. Hyde, his lusty and aggressive hidden inner self, who comes to have more and more power over him and eventually kills him. Dr. Frankenstein comes to recognize that the monster, his aborted and abandoned child, will destroy him and everything he loves and force him into a freezing-cold death.

Bulimia itself and most specifically the compulsive eating that precedes a purge is experienced as monstrous by Hornbacher as well as by the speakers of poems about bulimia. The woman who binges feels the need to disassociate herself from her actions by projecting them onto something external to herself, whether it be a demon, a beast, or a distorted image of her mother.[52] In *Wasted* bulimia represents the bad or evil other, the fleshy, fat, out-of-control self. Conversely, anorexia is idealized as a Superhuman Promethean quest or as a beautiful woman, who one would like to emulate or to have at one's side.

Hornbacher states quite explicitly what bulimia means for her personally and for society in general. It represents the desirous, uncontrolled demon within her; for society at large bulimia signifies—in Hornbacher's eyes—an embarrassing lack of self-control, and if the bulimic is overweight, fat, sloth, and even poverty. As she provocatively comments: "Who worries about bulimics? They're just gross" (*W* 133). This disdain reflects Americans' Jekyll-and-Hyde discomfort with the social pressure to be thin, class prejudice associated with this pressure, and erratic eating and dieting behaviors.

I suspect then that the relative absence of extended literary accounts of bulimia has to do with more than the relative newness of the phenomenon. Rather, this lack reflects a horror authors may feel about describing experiences that society and individuals regard as shameful and monstrous.[53]

---

[52] For a discussion of monsters in literature as "liminal figures" that demarcate the border of the self, see Paul Goetsch, *Monsters in English Literature: From the Romantic Age to the First World War* (Frankfurt: Peter Lang, 2002) 15-18.

[53] Of course, the element of shame involved in admitting that one is bulimic is central to confession. Confessional logic suggests that publicly testifying about the most sensational and

Wasted is a post-modern autobiographical text that describes the evolution of an unstable identity. Just as Hornbacher can never really determine if she is just anorexic or maybe also bulimic, she never gets quite clear about who she has turned out to be. The reader receives many conflicting textual glimpses of her. She is presented as a sexy girl—good for only sex and laughs—a painfully thin, intense philosophy student, an aggressive and successful reporter, and a recovered-anorexic woman who refuses sex with her husband because she feels fat. The narrator's mercurial identity is mirrored in various tones of voice: she sometimes sounds objective and scientific and offers lots of footnotes to back up her observations, sometimes virulently angry at a culture that makes women ill, and sometimes sad. Furthermore, her instability is reflected in her abrupt shifts from an internal to an external perspective on events and her erratic, non-linear depiction of time.

Hornbacher's is a story of illness. An assumption informs the book that the more intimate details are told, the more authentic the narrator's experiences will seem and the better a case will be made against the culture that encourages anorexia and bulimia in women. Not coincidentally, Hornbacher closes the Introduction to her memoirs with a quote from James Agee in which the author summarizes his inability to express himself well with the words: "A piece of the body torn out by the roots might be more to the point" (*W* 8).

Wasted may be described as a tearing out of the body by its roots. The narrator seeks absolution by divulging the minutia of her body's sufferings. Yet rather than absolving her, Hornbacher's memoirs present a deeply troubled, fragmented, and incoherent self.

---

private details will bring about a sense of absolution and confirm the teller's authenticity. I think this sense of shame contributes to the need narrators have to "other" their bulimia; it also renders bulimic episodes both tantalizing—the attraction of the forbidden and the horrifying—and difficult to recount.

Conclusion

America Confesses its Fear of Fat and Food

This study does two things: It interrogates the culture that gives rise to eating disorders and the literary texts that interpret them; it also investigates confessionalism in contemporary American culture. In this conclusion I want to first briefly review the insights of the preceding six chapters and then move on to a more open-ended discussion of the issues that have been brought up there.

Review

The first part of this study describes what eating disorders are, why they have come to be so prevalent, and how to understand writings about them through the lens of cultural studies. The impassioned poem "Howl" testifies to the bodily and psychic abuses that forms of eating abuse entail. "Howl" also addresses two socioeconomic issues related to eating disorders in America. One, anorexia and bulimia are overly represented by Americans who are better off, whereas obesity is more the problem of America's poor. This has made thinness (and the destructive pursuit of thinness in eating disorders and chronic dieting) a powerful discriminatory class marker in America. Two, eating disorders are gender issues that result from tensions inherent to being an American woman now. I argue that the combination of rising rates of obesity in the general population coupled with a moralistic and punishing attitude towards "fat" individuals, particularly women, give eating disorders a particularly virulent edge in America. The review of literary accounts of eating disorders introduces a wide array of texts that ranges from first-person autobiographical poems and novels to third-person narratives told from the perspective of individuals who care about eating-disordered women. I justify the choice of texts to be analyzed in this study on the basis of their exemplary or literary qualities rather than their fictionality per se. The introduction also suggests that the current predominance of writings on anorexia is caused by America's condemnation of uncontrolled eating and the lack of a literary tradition about this experience.

The second chapter aims to debunk misconceptions about eating disorders. I amplify on Brumburg's analysis of anorexia and American girlhood by including Tilmann Habermas's pan-European insights into the cultural and historical roots of eating disorders. Poems are used to illustrate the three documented types of eating disorders as well as chronic dieting, with the argument that these texts reveal aspects of the eating disordered experience which medical and psychological texts cannot. These texts describe the food obsessions, body hatred, preoccupation with mirrors, loathing of the flesh, and profound sense of powerlessness many eating-disordered women have. In the discussion of the binge-eating disorder the paradox of America's becoming increasingly obese while standards of feminine attractiveness have grown thinner is addressed. The fattening of America's poor is examined as well as the issue of how women are especially made to suffer from being overweight in American society. The alteration of the focus of the feminine beauty from the face to the body and the rise of the cult of thinness is discussed to demonstrate that the meaning of anorexia has changed radically during the past century. While there are historical precedents for women expressing problems with their gender roles through food and body abuse—in Victorian times anorexia reflected the association of physical fragility with gentility and chastity in women—anorexia and other eating disorders are now often motivated by a desire to appear physically and sexually attractive. The Victorian "Goblin Market" makes an analogy between the consumption of fruit and sexual impurity. By contrast, current writings on anorexia conflate thinness with control and self-actualization.

Anorexia as we now understand it involves an obsessive fear of fat, the idealization of the thin female body, and the equation of the slim figure with success and happiness. Most women cannot achieve the standard of extreme slenderness that was initiated in the sixties with the model Twiggy. This ideal, coupled with American eating habits that encourage weight gain has led to the inception of a variety of eating disorders. The incidence of eating disorders has grown as many young women try to copy much-publicized and glamorized anorexic behavior as a way of controlling their weight. Since, however, only very few individuals can maintain self-starvation for long, many failed would-be anorectics become bulimic.

Comparing medical, psychological, and sociological explanatory models of eating disorders with one another show that anorexia, bulimia, binge eating and chronic dieting have no single cause. I argue that eating disorders can most readily be likened to hysteria at the end of the nineteenth century. Like hysteria, eating disorders are cultural malaises that are historically and culturally limited in scope. Predominantly affecting women and girls, these illnesses both reflect tensions inherent to women's secondary role in society and lead to exaggerated versions of so-called feminine behavior such as physical weakness and an obsessive interest in appearance.

The chapter regarding perspectives on literary accounts of eating disorders begins with a description of the cultural turn in literary studies. Literature is no longer treated as belonging to a separate sphere but as integrated into, responsive to, and responsible for new cultural and discursive formations. Ellmann's and Heywood's studies of starvation and literature were reviewed to show how these analyses differ from psychological explanations of eating disorders and to highlight how this study differs from their work. While offering a powerful examination of the interaction between the tropes of self-starvation, incarceration, and literary expression, Ellmann's study is ahistorical and acultural in its scope. Heywood's text makes an exaggerated case for modernity's sparse aesthetic having caused the rise of cultural anorexia. Heywood writes from a personal standpoint that stresses her painful corporeal experience. This mode of criticism reflects a trend in American public culture that I call "confessionalism," which came to a head in the intense public scrutiny of details of the Lewinsky-Clinton scandal. Texts on disordered eating examined here belong to the confessional genre; they reflect America's post-therapeutic culture in which identity is sought out in physical experience. Revealing bodily trauma or deviance comprises the center of experience and supposedly functions as a form of healing.

The second part of the study examines three extended literary accounts of eating disorders. *Life-Size* interrogates the culture that has made Josie severely anorectic. The combination of medial images, condemnation from her father and an admired youth for being "fat," her idealization of Barbie as well as her friend, the rich and thin Amanda Jane—all have contributed to her becoming severely emaciated and obsessed by thinness. Josie's anorexia imposes a penitential set of rules upon her that forces her to eat, buy, and interact with others less and less. Furthermore, *Life-Size* shows how the anorectic must constantly reinforce her fragile sense of identity in mirrors and measurements. The anorexic Josie displays dichotomous thinking about herself and her body: Either she is a thin leaping ballerina who literally flies over the heads of those who watch her perform or a fat clown who debases herself in front of a jeering audience. These exaggerated images also illustrate the romantic feelings many anorectics have about their illness: Josie perceives herself as an artist of her own "beautiful" skeletal form.

The Passion of Alice's depiction of a savvy and ironic anorectic's hospitalization also works as a "J'accuse" of American culture. The novel reviews how the adolescent Alice decided to give up desiring anything when she realized that she could never attain her mother's iconic bodily perfection. She renounces sexual, masticatory, and emotional wants. In her critical analysis of the eating disorder clinic in which she has been admitted against her will, Alice describes the economic and social dependency that makes women express unhappiness by pulling out their hair or abusing food rather than getting drunk or destroying things as men do. Her description of power structures in the clinic show that it is not conducive to health: the admitting doctor has unlimited power and coerces a patient into having sex with him; women counselors are themselves burdened by eating problems; to get out of the clinic one has to confess in some therapeutic setting to having suffered from hidden trauma.

The hybrid memoir *Wasted* offers a scathing critique of America's encouragement of young women to embrace the myth that being tall and thin and WASP-looking will make them happy. *Wasted* is also a study in narcissism. While stating explicitly that she wants to warn her woman reader from going where she went, Hornbacher stylizes herself as extraordinarily attractive to men and successful as a journalist, writer, and student during the most severe period of her anorexia. Additionally, Hornbacher appears to have emerged from her self-inflicted atrocities with a certain amount of conventional success. After all, she wrote a best-selling memoir at the age of twenty-three. In her association of fat with bulimia on the one hand and emaciation with beauty and artistry on the other hand, Hornbacher displays the polarized thinking that leads her to still idealize anorexia. This memoir erases the line that distinguishes fiction from non-fiction and presents the clearest case of how a narrator looks for, but cannot find identity and healing in the process of testifying about her illness.

Outlook

What do literary texts on eating disorders say about American society now? Reading a number of poems on eating disorders and dieting, two novels on anorexia, and a memoir about the experience of being alternately bulimic and anorexic reveals a number of issues that currently weigh uneasily on American cultural consciousness. These include an obsessive interest in physical appearance, which is specifically expressed in eating disorders, and more globally, by extremely exaggerated concerns about thinness and overweight. Moreover, many works discussed in this study interrogate American culture for encouraging women and girls to become eating-disordered. They indict a culture in which women are enculturated to equate thinness with happiness. They also bespeak America's confessional culture and the obsession with somatic experience.

I have argued that writings on eating disorders represent intensified versions of many American women's lives and preoccupations with food and weight. To a degree these texts are political protests. Hence these writings can be seen as belonging to the tradition of American novels of social protest, such as Harriet Beecher Stowe's *Uncle Tom's Cabin* (1852), Upton Sinclair's *The Jungle* (1906), and Richard Wright's *Native Son* (1940).

These texts reveal the social and economic circumstances that contribute to the creation and proliferation of eating disorders in America. "Howl" and "Conform," *The Passion of Alice*, *Life-Size*, and *Wasted* all question why their narrators became eating disordered. Each narrator makes the point that the socialization process was the major cause of her obsessive interest in being thin. Without the cultural idealization of thinness, the narrators assert, they would not have become ill.

More than half of the adult female American population is on a diet at any given time. While not all dieters become eating disordered, they experience the same problems that plague anorexic and bulimic women to a lesser degree. "Normal" women regard weight as threatening, food as harmful, and thinness and the self-control it represents as ideals. The themes expressed in the writings of eating-disordered narrators are not just interesting as accounts of the experience of one minority, but serve to document American conceptions of femininity, consumption, food, and weight. A high level of body dissociation and a tortured sense of what it is to live in one's own flesh are spoken to.

Many primary texts cited in this study demonstrate that eating disorders express class distinctions. Thinness, associated with affluence, and the arduous means to thinness is described by the narrators—all members of the well-educated, upper middle-class, white world. In America being poor often also means being fat; the far greater prevalence of obesity amongst poor population groups in America suggests that thinness is a marker of wealth in the States. That immigrant women who aspire to belong to the middle class become eating disordered soon after arriving in the States and that thin women tend to marry up in our culture suggests that being thin has far greater economic significance for women than for men.

The exclusively female narrators of literary treatments of eating disorders attest to eating disorders being a gender issue. For women and girls the importance of being slim often overrides basic considerations of health. Women are still disproportionately valued and rewarded in our society for their looks rather than their accomplishments. Body worries have in fact grown more acute during the past century and now figure prominently in American life. As dependent members of a culture that stresses physical self-presentation as a measure of personal worth, women and girls react acutely to messages about the importance of thinness. This is, for instance, reflected in the mirror theme, featured in many of the poems and all three of the longer texts discussed here. Women do not experience mirrors as sites of transformation, as Jenijoy La Belle envisions them, but as cruel witnesses or judges of their sense of self worth. Mirrors, scales, and body checks provide narrators with a means of measuring their worth.

Similarly, Joan Brumberg describes the unstable sense of identity that leads many contemporary high school girls to value themselves depending on how they think they look. High school graduates represent themselves with full-body portraits in senior yearbooks, because the body has become synonymous with selfhood. For eating-disordered women and the many American women plagued by concerns about their weight, mirrors have a threatening aspect. Like the looking-glass in the story of Snow White, mirrors have the power to decide whether a woman will—like Snow White's step-mother—accept herself or not. Mirrors determine whether a woman perceives herself as "good" or "bad," "fat" or "thin."

The stigmatization of fat and bulimia and the idealization of thinness and anorexia have a Gothic quality. The texts described here feature speakers who feel threatened by their surroundings (food), vulnerable to people around them (who would make them eat), and lost or disoriented in a nightmarish world when they go on a binge. Again and again the desire to eat or binge is depicted as a foreign entity that takes over the better thin self. Speakers liken their urge to binge to demons, beasts, or monsters. The natural need to eat is perceived as an evil outside force, and as fundamentally other. The self is fashioned as an imperiled, idealized thin creature that is constantly impinged upon by an enormous, overpowering, monstrous desire to eat.

Foods, too, appear to have personalities for eating-disordered and dieting American women; they are "good" or "evil." In all the texts cited here foods have nothing to do with nourishment but rather inspire feelings of dread or even hate. The use of military imagery in "Becoming a Woman" suggests that to be a woman in our culture requires that one be in a state of constant vigilance against the threat of invasive calories. Similarly, "Surrounded" expresses the sentiment that a woman cannot get away from the threat that food represents to her even when she tries to commune with nature. So food-obsessed is the speaker of this poem that she is reminded of Tootsie rolls by a glimpse of dog's feces while she takes a walk in the woods.

Writings about eating disorders also indict the prejudicial quality of American culture by making moralistic attitudes towards the overweight apparent. America's cult of thinness was indoctrinated into Josie, Alice, and Marya not only through women's magazines, diet books, and popular novels about slim, happy girls, but also through the message they received as girls that it was their personal responsibility to "measure up" and make themselves thin. All three narrators display disgust and reprobation to those they judge to be overweight, most particularly themselves.

Thus the American belief that with hard work one can achieve anything influenced these narrators' burgeoning eating disorders. Again, I see a collision between a popular American myth and an American reality: the reality is that the country is growing fatter. To not be getting fatter is then the exception or the oddity. On the other hand the still popular Horatio Alger story informs American society—the belief that by working hard enough, every individual may achieve his or her heart's wish and, like Ragged Dick, go from being a shoe-shine boy to a successful businessman. The female variation of this narrative is that inside every ugly, fat duckling, a beautiful slender swan is waiting to emerge. The effects of genetics and life-style are ignored in such simplistic formulae. Moreover, as Peter Stearns points out, the American faith in individualism and the benefits of hard work leads to a tendency to blame overweight or obese individuals for their apparent moral failings. This blame falls more heavily onto women than onto men.

The writings I have described here do more than interrogate American culture, they also testify to the current taste for confessional detail. This literature reflects a wider societal tendency to value the body and the testimony of bodily experience as marks of authenticity. Confessionalism describes both a trend in realistic[1] contemporary fiction and a societal pattern. By calling

[1] See Monika Fludernik's definition of realism in *Towards a 'Natural' Narratology* (London: Routledge, 1996): "*Realism* refers to a realistic portrayal of the fictional world in the sense

literary treatments of eating disorders "confessional" and treating them in a culturally critical manner, I read them in a way that reflects undercurrents in American society now. Written, as it were, from the couch, these texts document a literary sensibility and a fascination with intimate details.

In the three extended texts the eating disorder hospital unit or clinic is a setting where confession is cultivated or coerced. Patients in Seaview eagerly divulge the secret things they did with food before they were hospitalized. Similarly, the Internet sites from which many of the poems cited here were taken attest to the pervasive need to share personal details in American society. In this forum individuals can anonymously post real or embellished accounts of their experiences, and these can be read and commented on by others. These web sites grow in a pattern similar to the way participants share their experiences in group therapy, as Alice describes them: First there is silence, than a faltering testimony occurs, and then comes a rush of effusions.

The majority of the poems cited here, as well as *Life-Size* and *Wasted,* operate on the premise that telling one's secrets will effect relief if not healing. Narrators begin their tales with an admission that they are ill and their perspectives are skewed. Revealing the "worst" secrets is the narrative climax and is intended to bring about absolution. Josie describes how she once tried to eat ground-up glass before she prepares to leave the hospital in an altered if not healthy state of mind. The abundance of physical viscera in Hornbacher's memoir resembles an informational purge. Such details have a legitimate shock value: they call the reader to arms to wake up to the dangers of eating disorders. Like the poems "Howl" and "Conform" such intimate testimonies demand that society change. However, these revelations may have a compulsive quality, particularly Hornbacher's manner of relating her painful experiences.

---

that secular non-fantastic explanations can be provided for the plot and seemingly fantastic experiences are eventually explained in 'realistic' terms" (37).

I am aware that talk of compulsivity smacks of moralistic judgment making. I run the danger of sounding like many traditional, predominantly male, reviewers of literature who speak disparagingly of "confessional" writing when they want to say that texts are too full of the embarrassing details about women's lives. This, at least, is Caroline Heilbrun's charge. Narratives of pain and body obsession reveal untold aspects of many women's and hence human experience.

However, by describing purging techniques in detail and by depicting the anorexic period of their lives in glamorous and sometimes self-aggrandizing terms, writers such as Hornbacher perpetuate the values of the cult of thinness from which they have suffered. Compelling and aestheticized versions of anorexia add to our culture's wealth of romanticized visions of beautiful, dying women and may encourage young women to emulate this imagery. Finally, the demonization of fat and the othering of bulimia that occurs in texts by eating-disordered narrators may further inculcate some readers with an obsession with being thin.

The existence of so many texts about eating disorders demonstrates prima facie that these problems exist in great number and writers want to talk about them. How these writings reflect common difficulties American women have with food, weight and identity has been the farther-reaching goal of this study. Anxieties expressed by eating-disordered narrators represent heightened versions of worries most middle-class American women how much they "should" eat and weigh.

The reader will note my ambivalence about the revealing, deeply painful—and, in the case of *Wasted*, the narcissistic—quality of the texts on eating disorders I have described in this study. On the one hand it is important that attention be paid to the problems of eating-disordered women and the culture that makes them so. These texts render the experience of suffering from anorexia, bulimia, binge eating, and chronic dieting comprehensible and compelling. On the other hand I find the fetishizing of the female body that occurs in these narratives deeply disturbing. For eating-disordered narrators, identity represents the digits on the scale, the perceived image in the mirror, the shape of the thigh, and the amount of flesh that can be pinched between the forefinger and thumb. The complexity of human experience narrows down to the corporeal detail. The story of the self is told in the language of the sickened body. Although the narrators directly or indirectly accuse American culture of overvaluing women's bodies, they essentially commit the same crime. Physical appearance becomes the measure of who the narrators think they are, and what they think, feel, and may potentially do. In the reduction of women's lives to attestations of bodily obsessions, cultural scripts that equate women with somatic experience and physical weakness are perpetuated.

Narratives about binge eating, bulimia, and anorexia, like eating disorders themselves, both express and exaggerate larger trends in American culture. It is a culture, self-confirming and endlessly reinforced and reinvented, which makes many women sick. American women have of sense of being mortally threatened by food, weight and fat. Due to a sense of confusion about who they are outside of their bodily experience and appearance, women seek and express their identities in narratives that equate selfhood with their flesh.

Bibliography

American Psychiatric Association. *Diagnostic and Statistical Manual of Mental Disorders*. 4th ed. Washington, DC: American Psychiatric Association, 1994.

Anderson, Kathy. "Surrounded." *Eating Our Hearts Out: Personal Accounts of Women's Relationship to Food*. Ed. Lesléa Newman. Freedom, CA: The Crossing Press, 1993. 161.

Apostolides, Marianne. *Inner Hunger: A Young Woman's Struggle Through Anorexia and Bulimia*. New York, London: W.W. Norton & Company, 1998.

ANRED (Anorexia Nervosa and Related Eating Disorders, Inc.). 4 November 2002 <http://anred.com>.

Atlas, James. "Confessing for Voyeurs: The Age of the Literary Memoir is Now." *New York Times* 12 May 1996, 6:26.

Atwood, Margaret. *Cat's Eye*. 1988. New York: Bantam Doubleday, 1989.

________"Hair Jewellery." *Dancing Girls*. London: O.W. Toad Ltd., 1977. 101-118.

________*Life Before Man*. 1979. London: Jonathan Cape, 1980.

________ *Lady Oracle*. 1968. London: Virago, 1982.

________"Spring Song of the Frogs." *Bluebird's Egg*. London: O.W. Toad Ltd., 1983. 167-180.

________ "The Female Body," *Bones & Murder*. London: Virago, 1994. 77-84.

________ "There Was Once," *Bones and Murder*. London: Virago, 1994. 22-26.

Augustine, Saint. *Confessions*. Trans. Henry Chadwick. Oxford: Oxford UP, 1991.

Aull, Felice. "Shute, Jenefer P. Life-Size." 4 November 2002 <http://cndcavor.med.nyu.edu/lit-med/lit-med-db/webdocs/webauthors/shute145-au-.html>.

"A Very Revealing Picture: Psychology Today's 1997 Body Image Survey Findings." *Psychology Today* (January/February 1997): 34.

Axthelm, Peter M. *The Modern Confessional Novel*. New Haven: Yale UP, 1967.

Bailin, Miriam. *The Sickroom in Victorian Fiction: The Art of Being Ill*. Cambridge: Cambridge UP, 1994.

Bak, Hans and Hans Krabbendam. Introduction. *Writing Lives*. Amsterdam: VU University Press, 1998. 1-6.

Bakan, Rita C., Laird Birmingham, and Elliot Goldner. "Chronicity in Anorexia Nervosa: Pregnancy and Birth Complications as Risk Factors." *International Journal of Eating Disorders* 10.6 (1991): 631-645.

Bakhtin, Mikhail. *Problems of Dostoevsky's Poetics.* Trans. R.W. Rotsel. Ann Arbor, MI: Ardis, 1973.

________ *Rabelais and His World.* Trans. Helene Iswolsky. Cambridge: M.I.T. Press, 1968.

Bartky, Sandra Lee. "Foucault, Femininity, and the Modernization of Patriarchal Power." *Feminism & Foucault: Reflections on Resistance.* Ed. Irene Diamond and Lee Quinby. Boston: Northeastern UP, 1988. 61-86.

Bell, David E. "A Moratorium on Suspicion," *PMLA* 117.3 (May 2002): 487-490.

Bell, Rudolph M. *Holy Anorexia.* Chicago: Chicago UP, 1985.

Belsey, Catherine. "Towards Cultural History—In Theory and Practice." *New Historicism and Cultural Materialism: A Reader.* Ed. Kiernan Ryan. London: Arnold, 1996. 82-91.

Beryl, "Beginnings." 4 November 2002 <http://www.geocities.com/Hollywood/Set/1607/poem.html>.

Beumont, Pierre J. V. "The Clinical Presentation of Anorexia and Bulimia Nervosa." *Eating Disorders and Obesity: A Comprehensive Handbook.* Ed. Kelly D. Brownell and Christopher G. Fairburn. New York: The Guilford Press, 1995. 151-158.

Bidart, Frank. "Ellen West" (1977). *In the Western Night: Collected Poems 1965-90.* New York: Farrar Straus Giroux, 1990. 109-121.

Binswanger, Ludwig. "The Case of Ellen West". 1944. Trans. Werner M. Mendel and Joseph Lyons. *Existence: A New Dimension in Psychiatry and Psychology.* Ed Rolla May, Ernest Angel, and Henri F. Ellenberger. New York: Basic Books, 1958. 237-364.

_______ "Versuch einer Hysterieanalyse." *Jahrbuch für psychoanalytische und psychopathologische Forschung, I* (1909). Quoted in Habermas, *Geschichte der Magersucht*, 98.

Blair, Michelle. "The Key to Happiness—A monologue—." *Eating Our Hearts Out: Personal Accounts of Women's Relationship to Food.* Ed. Lesléa Newman. Freedom, CA: The Crossing Press, 1993. 120-122.

Bloom, Harold. *A Map of Misreading.* New York: Oxford UP, 1975.

Boehmer, Elleke. *Screens Against the Sky.* London: Bloomsbury, 1990.

Boland, Eavan. "Anorexic." *Collected Poems.* Manchester: Carcanet, 1995. 58-59.

Booth, Wayne C. *The Rhetoric of Fiction.* Chicago and London: Chicago UP, 1961.

Bordo, Susan. "Anorexia Nervosa: Psychopathology as the Crystallization of Culture." *Feminism and Foucault: Reflections of Resistance*. Ed. Irene Diamond and Lee Quinby. Boston: Northeastern UP, 1988. 87-118.

_______ *Unbearable Weight: Feminism, Western Culture and the Body*. Berkeley and Los Angeles: California UP, 1993.

Bronfen, Elisabeth. *Over Her Dead Body: Death, Femininity and the Aesthetic*. Manchester: Manchester UP, 1992.

________*The Knotted Subject: Hysteria and Its Discontents*. Princeton, NJ: Princeton UP, 1998.

Brownstein, Rachel. "Interrupted Reading: Personal Criticism in the Present Time." *Confessions of the Critics*. Ed. H. Aram Veeser. New York and London: Routledge, 1996. 29-39.

Bruch, Hilde. *The Golden Cage: The Enigma of Anorexia Nervosa*. 1978. New York: Vintage Books, 1979.

________ *Eating Disorders: Obesity, Anorexia Nervosa and the Person Within*. New York: Basic Books, 1973.

Brumberg, Joan Jacob. *The Body Project: An Intimate History of American Girls*. New York: Random House, 1997.

________ *Fasting Girls: The History of Anorexia Nervosa*. 1988. New York: Plume, 1989.

Bullitt-Jonas, Margaret: *Holy Hunger: A Memoir of Desire*. New York: Alfred Knopf, 1999.

Campbell, Neil and Alasdair Kean. *American Cultural Studies: An Introduction to American Culture*. London and New York: Routledge, 1997.

Carroll, Lewis. *Alice's Adventures in Wonderland and Through the Looking-Glass and What Alice Found There*. 1865; 1871. The Centenary Edition. Ed. Hugh Haughton. London: Penguin, 1998.

Caskey, Noelle. "Interpreting Anorexia Nervosa." *The Female Body in Western Culture: Contemporary Perspectives*. Ed. Susan Rubin Suleiman: Cambridge, MA: Harvard UP, 1986. 175-189.

Chabram-Dernesrsesian, Angie "I Throw Punches for my Race, but I Don't Want to Be a Man: Writing Us—Chica-nos (Girl, Us/ Chicanas—into the Movement Script." *American Mythologies*. Ed. Marshall Blonsky. New York, Oxford: Oxford UP, 1992. 81-103.

Chandler, Steve B. et al. "Pathogenic Eating Attitudes and Behaviors and Body Dissatisfaction Differences among Black and White College Students." *Eating Disorders: The Journal of Treatment and Prevention* 2, No. 4 (Winter 1994): 319-328.

Channon, Shelley, and Andrew Hayward. "The Effect of Short-term Fasting on Processing of Food Cues in Normal Subjects." *International Journal of Eating Disorders* 9.4 (1990): 447- 451.

Chernin, Kim. *The Obsession: Reflections on the Tyranny of Slenderness.* 1981. New York: HarperPerennial, 1994.

Cixous, Hélène. "The Laugh of Medusa." *New French Feminisms: An Anthology*. Ed. Elaine Marks and Isabelle de Courtivron. Hertfordshire: Harvester Press, 1981. 245-264.

Clinton, Hillary Rodham. *It Takes a Village: And Other Lessons Children Teach Us*. New York: Touchstone Books, 1996.

Cohen, Ed. "Constructing Gender." *The Columbia History of the American Novel*. Ed. Emory Elliot. New York: Columbia University Press, 1991. 542-557.

Cooper, Peter J. "Eating Disorders and their Relationship to Mood and Anxiety Disorders." *Eating Disorders and Obesity: A Comprehensive Handbook*. Ed. Kelly D. Brownell and Christopher G. Fairburn. New York: The Guilford Press, 1995. 159-164.

Cover. *People Weekly*. 4 December 1999.

Coward, Rosalind. "Are Women's Novels Feminist Novels?" *The New Feminist Criticism: Essays on Women, Literature, and Theory*. Ed. Elaine Showalter. 1980. New York: Random House, 1985. 225-239.

Critser, Greg. "Let Them Eat Fat: The Heavy Truths about American 'Obesity'." *Harper's Magazine* (March 2000): 41-47.

Cross, Lisa W. "Body and Self in Feminine Development: Implications for Eating Disorders and Delicate Self-Mutilation." *Bulletin of the Menninger Clinic* 57, Number 1 (Winter 1993): 46-68.

"Dating Violence Raises Risk of Abnormal Dieting." *Eating Disorders Review* 12, No 4 (July/August 2001): 8.

Davis, William N. Epilogue. *Holy Anorexia*. By Rudolph M. Bell. Chicago: Chicago UP, 1985. 180-190.

Dolan, Bridget. "Cross-Cultural Aspects of Anorexia and Bulimia: A Review," *International Journal of Eating Disorders* 10.1 (1991): 67-77.

Dostoevsky, Fyodor. *Notes From Underground*. 1864. Trans. and ed. Michael R. Katz. New York: Norton, 1989.

Drake, Nicholas, ed. *The Sixties: A Decade in Vogue*. New York: Prentice Hall, 1988.

Dubus, Andre. "The Fat Girl." *Adultery and Other Choices*. 1975. 162-172.

Dudley, Betty Rose. "Fat Kills." *Fat!So? Magazine.* 4 November 2002 <http://www.fatso.com/bigtruth.html>.

Duenwald, Mary. "A Conversation with Marion Nestle: An 'Eat More' Message for a Fattened America." *New York Times.* 19 February 2002: F6.

Duhamel, Denise. "Feather, 1948"/"Finger, 1988." *Eating Our Hearts Out: Personal Accounts of Women's Relationship to Food.* Ed. Lesléa Newman. Freedom, CA: The Crossing Press, 1993. 118-119.

Duplessis, Rachel Blau. "Reader, I Married Me: A Polygamous Memoir." *Changing Subjects: The Making of Feminist Literary Criticism.* Ed. Gayle Greene and Coppélia Kahn. London and New York: Routledge, 1993. 97-111.

Durant, Alan. "Facts and Meanings in British Cultural Studies." *Studying British Cultures.* Ed. Susan Bassnett. London: Routledge, 1997. 19-38.

Eagleton, Terry. "Introduction: What is Literature?" *Literary Theory: An Introduction.* 2nd ed. Oxford: Blackwell, 1996.1-14.

Easthope, Anthony. "But what *is* Cultural Studies?" *Studying British Cultures.* Ed. Susan Bassnett. London: Routledge, 1997. 3-18.

"eating disorder." *Eating Disorder Poetry Collection.* 4 November 2002 <http://www.geocities.com/Wellesley/ 4220/edpoetry.html>.

Edmond, Lauris. "Anorexic Girl." *Selected Poems.* Auckland: Oxford UP, 1988. 176.

Eliot, George. *Daniel Deronda.* 1876. London: Penguin Books, 1995.

Eliot, T.S. "The Love Song of J. Alfred Prufrock." 1917. *T.S. Eliot: Selected Poems.* New York: Harcourt, Brace & World, 1934. 11-16.

________ "Tradition and the Individual Talent." 1919. *Twentieth-Century Literary Criticism: A Reader.* Ed. David Lodge. London: Longman, 1972. 71-77.

Ellmann, Maud. *The Hunger Artists: Starving, Writing, and Imprisonment.* Cambridge, MA: Harvard UP, 1993.

Falk, Pasi. *The Consuming Body.* London: Sage Publications, 1994.

Fielding, Helen. *Bridget Jones's Diary.* London: Picador, 1996.

Fleenor, Julian. "Introduction: The Female Gothic." *The Female Gothic.* Montréal and London: Eden Press, 1983. 3-28.

Flemming, Anne Talor. "the new ideal: What makes a body beautiful?" *Women's Sports Fitness* (January/February 1999): 72-75.

Fludernik, Monika. *Towards a 'Natural' Narratology*. London: Routledge, 1996.

Ford, Camie, and Sunny Hale. *Deadly Diet*. Orleans, MA: Paraclete Press, 1983/1995.

Foreyt, John P. "Weight Loss Programs for Minority Populations," *Eating Disorders and Obesity: A Comprehensive Handbook*. Ed. Kelly D. Brownell and Christopher G. Fairburn. New York: The Guilford Press, 1995. 536-540.

Foucault, Michel. "Docile Bodies." *Discipline and Punish: The Birth of the Prison*. Trans. Alan Sheridan. 1979. *The Foucault Reader*. Ed. Paul Rabinow. New York: Pantheon Books, 1984. 179-187.

________ "Complete and Austere Institutions." *Discipline and Punish: The Birth of the Prison*. Trans. Alan Sheridan. 1979. *The Foucault Reader*. Ed. Paul Rabinow. New York: Pantheon Books, 1984. 214-225.

________ *The Archaeology of Knowledge*. Trans. A.M. Sheridan Smith. New York: Harper Colophon, 1972.

________ *The Birth of the Clinic: An Archaeology of Medical Perception*. Trans. A.M. Sheridan Smith. New York: Vintage Books, 1994.

________ *The History of Sexuality: Volume 1: An Introduction*. 1976. Trans. Robert Hurley. New York: Vintage Books, 1980.

Fraser Laura. *Losing It: America's Obsession with Weight and the Industry that Feeds on It*. New York: Dutton, 1997.

Freedman, Diane P. "Autobiographical Literary Criticism as the New Belletrism: *Personal Experience*." *Confessions of the Critics*. Ed. H. Aram Veeser. New York and London: Routledge, 1996. 1-16.

Freud, Esther. *Peerless Flats*. London: Penguin, 1993.

Freud, Sigmund. *An Infantile Neurosis and Other Works*. Trans. and ed. James Strachey. Vol. 17 of *The Standard Edition of the Complete Works of Sigmund Freud*. London, 1966.

"From Kate." 4 November 2002 <http://www.mindspring.com/~cwildes/kate2.htm>.

Gaia, "Me." 21 October 1998 <http://www.gurney.org.uk/eda/poetry.html>.

Gallagher, Catherine. "Marxism and the New Historicism." *New Historicism and Cultural Materialism: A Reader*. Ed. Kiernan Ryan. London: Arnold, 1996. 45-55.

Gaskell, Elizabeth. *Cranford/Cousin Phillis*. 1853. Harmondsworth: Penguin Books, 1976.

Geisler, Astrid. "Skinnygirl. 1,74 Meter, 47 Kilo." *die tageszeitung*. 27 November 2002: 6.

Geertz, Clifford. "The Impact of the Concept of Culture on the Concept of Man." *The Interpretation of Cultures: Selected Essays*. New York: Basic Books, 1973. 46-54.

Gibbs, W. Wayt, "Gaining on Fat," *Scientific American*, August 1996. 4 November 2002 <http://www.sciam.com>.

Gilchrist, Ellen. "The Gauzy Edge of Paradise." *Victory over Japan*. London and Boston: Faber and Faber, 1984. 96-110.

________"The Last Diet." *Drunk with Love*. London and Boston: Faber and Faber, 1986. 146-158.

Ginsberg, Allen. "Howl" and "Footnote to Howl." *Collected Poems*. New York: Harper & Row, 1984. 126-133.

Glück, Louise. "Dedication to Hunger." *Descending Figure*. New York: Ecco Press 1980. 107-112.

Goetsch, Paul. *Monsters in English Literature: From the Romantic Age to the First World War*. Frankfurt: Peter Lang, 2002.

Goffman, Erving. *The Presentation of Self in Everyday Life*. 1959. Harmondsworth: Penguin, 1990.

Goldbloom, David S., and Sidney H. Kennedy. "Medical Complications of Anorexia Nervosa." *Eating Disorders and Obesity: A Comprehensive Handbook*. Ed. Kelly D. Brownell and Christopher G. Fairburn. New York: The Guilford Press, 1995. 266-270.

Gordon, Mary. *Final Payments*. New York: Ballantine Books, 1978.

Gordon, Richard. *Anorexia and Bulimia: Anatomy of a Social Epidemic*. Oxford: Blackwell, 1990.

Gottlieb, Lori. *Stick Figure: A Diary of My Former Self*. 2000. New York: Berkeley Books, 2001.

Granestrand, Lasse. "*Kronprinsessan får hjälp*" (Crown Princess Receives Help). *Dagens Nyheter* 29 November 1997: A5.

Grant, Stephanie. *The Passion of Alice*. 1995. London: Hodder and Stoughton, 1996.

Greenblatt, Stephen. *Renaissance Self-Fashioning*. Chicago and London: University of Chicago Press, 1980.

"Growing Up Today." *Archives Pediatric Adolescent Medicine* 1999, 153:1184. As reviewed in "Purging: Peers and Media Influences." *Eating Disorders Review* (May/June 2000): 5.

Habermas, Tilmann. *Zur Geschichte der Magersucht: Eine medizinpsychologische Rekonstruktion*. Frankfurt: Fischer, 1994.

Hall, Liza F. *Perk: The Story of a Teenager with Bulimia*. Carlsbad, CA: Gürze, 1998.

Hanauer, Cathi. *My Sister's Bones*. London: Headline, 1996.

Hardy, Thomas. *Tess of the D'Urbervilles*. 1891. London: Penguin, 1978.

Hawthorn, Jeremy. *Cunning Passages: New Historicism, Cultural Materialism and Marxism in the Contemporary Literary Debate*. London: Arnold, 1996.

Heilbrun, Carolyn G. "Contemporary Memoirs: Or, Who Cares Who Did What to Whom?" *The American Scholar* (Summer 1999): 35-42.

Hepworth, Mike, and Bryan Turner. *Confession: Studies in Deviance and Society*. London: Routledge, 1982.

Hesse-Biber, Sharlene. *Am I Thin Enough Yet?: The Cult of Thinness and the Commercialization of Identity*. New York and Oxford: Oxford UP, 1996.

Heywood, Leslie. *Dedication to Hunger: The Anorexic Aesthetic in Modern Culture*. Berkeley: University of California Press, 1996.

Hoek, Hans W. "The Distribution of Eating Disorders." *Eating Disorders and Obesity: A Comprehensive Handbook*. Ed. Kelly D. Brownell and Christopher G. Fairburn. New York: The Guilford Press, 1995. 207-211.

Hornbacher, Marya. *Wasted: A Memoir of Anorexia and Bulimia*. New York: HarperFlamingo, 1998.

Hosenball, Mark, and Barbara Kantrowitz. "Ready for Her Close-Up." *Newsweek*, 15 March 1999: 20.

Ingrassia, Michele. "The Body of the Beholder," *Newsweek*, 24 April 1995: 49-51.

Ingris, Fred. *Cultural Studies*. Oxford UK, Cambridge USA: Blackwell, 1993.

Johnston, Anita A. *Eating in the Light of the Moon: How Women Can Let Go of Compulsive Eating through Metaphor and Storytelling*. Secaucus, NJ: Birch Lane Press, 1996.

Jong-Fast, Molly. "A World Apart." *MODE Style Beyond Size*. May 1998: 68-70.

Joyce, James. *Stephen Hero*. London: Jonathan Cape, 1944.

________ *Ulysses*. New York: Vintage Books, 1961.

Kahane, Claire. *Passions of the Voice: Hysteria, Narrative, and the Figure of the Speaking Woman, 1850 –1915*. Baltimore: John Hopkins UP, 1995.

Kakutani, Michiko. "Fear of Fat as the Bane of Modernism." *New York Times*, 12 March 1996: 15(C).

Kafka, Franz. "A Hunger Artist." 1924. *The Penal Colony: Stories and Short Pieces*. Trans. Willa and Edwin Muir. New York: Schocken Books, 1961. 243-255.

Kesey, Ken. *One Flew Over the Cuckoo's Nest.* 1962. London: Picador, 1973.

Kilbourne, Jean. "Still Killing us Softly: Advertising and the Obsession with Thinness." *Feminist Perspectives on Eating Disorders.* Ed. Patricia Fallon, Melanie A. Katzman, and Susan C. Wooley. New York and London: The Guilford Press, 1994. 395-418.

Korte, Barbara. "The 'Femme Fragile': Decline and Fall of a Literary Topos." *Anglia* 105 (1987): 366-389.

Kusz, Natalie. "A Big Fat Secret," *Allure.* July 1999: 70.

La Belle, Jenijoy. *Herself Beheld: The Literature of the Looking Glass.* Ithaca and London: Cornell UP, 1988.

Lacan, Jacques. *Écrits: A Selection.* Trans. Alan Sheridan. London: Tavistock Publications, 1977.

Lamb, Wally. *She's Come Undone.* New York: Washington Square Press, 1992.

Lasch, Christopher. "For Shame: Why Americans Should Be Wary of Self-Esteem." *New Republic* 207, 10 August 1992. Sorapure, Madeleine. "Representing Shame." *Writing Lives: American Biography and Autobiography.*

Leutwyler, Kristin. "Bulimia Nervosa, Explorations: Treating Eating Disorders:" March 2, 1998. *Scientific American,* March 1998. 4 November 2002 <http://www.sciam.com>.

Levenkron, Steven. *The Best Little Girl in the World.* 1979. Harmondsworth: Puffin, 1995.

Liu, Aimee. *Solitaire.* New York: Harper & Row, 1979.

Lyons, John. "Language and Society." *Language and Linguistics: An Introduction.* Cambridge: Cambridge UP, 1981.

Machoian, Lisa. "Risk and Resilience in Girls' Development," Harvard Graduate School of Education 2001-2002. Unpublished class syllabus.

Macleod, Sheila. *The Art of Starvation: A Story of Anorexia and Survival.* New York: Schocken Books, 1982.

Mailloux, Steven. "Rhetorical Hermeneutics as Reception Study: *Huckleberry Finn* and 'The Bad Boy Room'." *Reconceptualizing American Literary/Cultural Studies.* Ed. William E. Cain. New York and London: Garland Publishing, 1996. 35-56.

Markus, Marsha D. "Binge Eating and Obesity," *Eating Disorders and Obesity: A Comprehensive Handbook.* Ed. Kelly D. Brownell, Christopher G. Fairburn. New York: The Guilford Press, 1995. 441-444.

Marin, Rick "She's Still in Vogue." *Newsweek*, 7 December 1998: 56.

Meadow, Rosalyn and Lillie Weiss. *Good Girls Don't Eat Dessert: Changing Your Relationship to Food and Sex.* New York: Harmony Books, 1992.

Medoff, Jillian. *Hunger Point.* New York: HarperCollins, 1997.

Menell, Stephen. "On the Civilizing of Appetite." *The Body: Social Process and Cultural Theory.* Ed. Mike Featherstone, Mike Hepworth, and Bryan S. Turner. London: Sage Publications, 1991. 126-153.

Micale, Mark S. *Approaching Hysteria: Disease and its Interpretations.* Princeton, NJ: Princeton UP, 1995.

Miller, Caroline Adams. *My Name Is Caroline* 1988. Carlsbad, CA: Gürze Books, 1991.

Mitchie, Helena. *The Flesh Made Word: Female Figures and Women's Bodies.* Oxford: Oxford UP, 1987.

Monster's Ball. Dir. Marc Foster. Perf. Halle Berry, Billy Bob Thornton, Heath Ledger, Peter Boyle. Entertainment, 2002.

Morton, Andrew. *Diana: Her True Story.* London: Pocket Books, 1992.

Morton, Richard. *Phthisiologia or, A Treatise of Consumptions.* 1720. 2nd ed. Quoted in Rudolph Bell, *Holy Anorexia.*

Nassar, Mervat "Eating Disorders: Between Cultural Specificity and Globalization." *Eating Disorders Review* 9.5 (1998): 1-3.

Natriello, Gary. "The Author's Voice: Revealing the Person behind the Curtain." *Teachers College Record* 99.4 (Summer 1998): 617-621.

"A Never-Ending Battle with Anorexia." 2 July 1998 <http://www.amazon.com/exec/obidos/subst/...hornbacher-interview/002-0204924-2702259>.

Nollen, Elizabeth Mahn. *Female Imprisonment, Madness, and Escape in Selected Texts by Women Writers.* Bloomington, Indiana: Indiana UP, 1984.

Nünning, Ansgar, ed. *Unreliable Narration: Studien zur Theorie und Praxis unglaubwürdigen Erzählens in der englischsprachichen Literatur.* Trier: Wissenschaftlicher Verlag Trier, 1998.

O'Connor, Amy. "Educating Claudia," *Self.* February 1999: 28-31.

Olson, Greta, "Reconsidering Unreliability: Fallible and Untrustworthy Narrators," *Narrative* 11, No. 1 (Januar 2003): 81-97.

O'Neill, Cherry Boone. *Starving For Attention.* New York: Continuum, 1982.

"ONE MORE LAST TIME." *Eating Disorder Poetry Collection.* 4 November 2002 <http://www.geocities.com/Wellesley/4220/edpoetry.html>.

Oxford Advanced Learner's Dictionary of Current English. Ed. A.P. Hornby. 4th ed. Oxford: Oxford UP, 1989. 894.

Palazzoli, Mara Selvini. "Anorexia Nervosa: A Syndrome of the Affluent Society." *Transcontinental Psychiatric Reseach Review* 22.3 (1985): 199-204.

________ *Self-Starvation: From the Intrapsychic to the Transpersonal Approach to Anorexia Nervosa*. 1963. Trans. Arnold Pomerans. London: Human Context Books, 1974.

Palmer, Robert L. "Sexual Abuse and Eating Disorders." *Eating Disorders and Obesity: A Comprehensive Handbook*. Ed. Kelly D. Brownell and Christopher G. Fairburn. New York and London: The Guilford Press, 1995. 230-233.

Parry-Jones, Brenda, and William Parry-Jones. "History of Bulimia and Bulimia Nervosa." *Eating Disorders and Obesity: A Comprehensive Handbook*. Ed. Kelly D. Brownell, Christopher G. Fairburn. New York: The Guilford Press, 1995. 145-150.

Plath, Sylvia. *The Bell Jar*. 1963. New York: Bantam, 1971.

________ "Lady Lazarus." 1962. *The Collected Poems*. Ed. Ted Hughes. New York: Harper & Row, 1981. 244-247.

________ "Edge." 1963. *The Collected Poems*. Ed. Ted Hughes. New York: Harper & Row, 1981. 272-273.

Poe, Edgar Allan. "The Tell-Tale Heart." *The Short Fiction of Edgar Allan Poe*. Ed. Stuart Levine and Susan Levine. Indianapolis: Bobbs-Merill Company, 1976. 259-262.

________ "The Philosophy of Composition." *The Centenary Poe: Tales, Poems, Criticism, Marginalia and Eureka*. London: The Bodley Head, 1949. 499-500.

Polivy, Janet and C. Peter Herman. "Dieting and its Relation to Eating Disorders." *Eating Disorders and Obesity: A Comprehensive Handbook*. Ed. Kelly D. Brownell and Christopher G. Fairburn. New York: The Guilford Press, 1995. 83-86.

Power, Carla et al. "Monica Madness." *Newsweek*, 22 March 1999: 88-90.

Pritikin, Nathan. *Pritikin's Program for Diet and Exercise*. 1979.

Rabinor, Judith Ruskay. "Mothers, Daughters, and Eating Disorders: Honoring the Mother-Daughter Relationship." *Feminist Perspectives on Eating Disorders*. Ed. Patricia Fallon, Melanie A. Katzman, and Susan C. Wooley. New York: The Guilford Press, 1994. 272-286.

Radcliffe, Ann. *The Mysteries of Udolpho*. 1794. Oxford: Oxford UP, 1998.

Rand, Colleen S. W. and John M. Kuldau. "Restrained Eating (Weight Concerns) in the General Population and Among Students." *International Journal of Eating Disorders* 10.6 (1991): 699-707.

Ravussin, Eric. "Energy Expenditure and Body Weight." *Eating Disorders and Obesity: A Comprehensive Handbook.* Ed. Kelly D. Brownell and Christopher G. Fairburn. New York and London: The Guilford Press, 1995: 32-37.

Remnick, David. "Our Lady of Secrets." *The New Yorker*, 8 February 1999: 23-24.

Rich, Adrienne. "For Ellen West, Mental Patient and Suicide." 1971. Kim Chernin. *The Obsession.* 178-179.

Richardson, Samuel. *Clarissa.* 1747-8. Harmondsworth and New York: Penguin Books, 1985.

Robinson, Kathleen, "A How To Book For Those Who Want An Eating Disorder, May 3, 2002" *Amazon.com. Customer Reviews* Wasted. 4 November 2002. http://www.amazon.com/exec/obidos/tg/stores/detail/-/books/0060930934/customer-reviews/3/ref=cm rev_next/ 104-4996524-6277528?show=-submittime.

Rose, Debbie. "Thief in the Night." *Eating Disorder Poetry Collection.* 4 November 2002 <http://www.geocities.com/ Wellesley/4220/edpoetry.html>.

Rosen, Jonathan. *Eve's Apple.* London: Granta Books, 1997.

Rosenthal, M. L. "Poetry as Confession: *Life Studies* by Robert Lowell." *The Nation* (10 September 1959). Rpt. in M.L. Rosenthal, *Our Life in Poetry: Selected Essays and Reviews.* New York: Persea Books, 1991. 109-113.

Rosenthal, M. L., and Sally M. Gall. *The Modern Poetic Sequence.* New York and Oxford: Oxford UP, 1983.

Rossetti, Christina. "Goblin Market." Composed 27 April 1859. *The Complete Poems of CHRISTINA ROSSETTI.* 1862. Ed R.W. Cramp. Baton Rouge: Louisiana State UP, 1979. 11-26.

Rothblum, Esther. "I'll Die for the Revolution but Don't Ask Me not to Diet": Feminism and the Continuing Stigmatization of Obesity." *Feminist Perspectives on Eating Disorders.* Ed. Patricia Fallon, Melanie A. Katzman, and Susan C. Wooley. New York: The Guilford Press, 1994. 53-76.

Rumbaut, Hendle. "An Image of Myself." *Eating Our Hearts Out: Personal Accounts of Women's Relationship to Food.* Ed. Lesléa Newman. Freedom, CA: The Crossing Press, 1993. 123-126.

Salinger, J. D. *The Catcher in the Rye.* 1945, 1946. London: Penguin Books, 1994.

Said, Edward. *Orientalism.* London: Routledge, 1978.

Sarah, "The Bulimic Experience; Today Will Be The Last." 6 February 1998 <http://users.neca.com/cwildes/sarah.html>.

Schlosser, Eric. *Fast Food Nation.* New York: Houghton Mifflin, 2001.

Schnyder, Louis. "Le cas de Renata: Contribution à l'étude de l'hystérie." *Archives de psychologie* (1912). Quoted in Habermas, *Geschichte der Magersucht.* 72.

Schwarz, L. "Untitled." *Eating Disorder Poetry Collection.* 4 November 2002 <http://www.geocities.com/Wellesley/4220/ edpoetry.html>.

Seid, Roberta P. *Never Too Thin: Why Women Are at War with Their Bodies.* New York: Prentice–Hall Press, 1989.

________ "Too 'Close to the Bone': The Historical Context for Women's Obsession with Slenderness." *Feminist Perspectives on Eating Disorders.* Ed. Patricia Fallon, Melanie A. Katzman, and Susan C. Wooley. New York: The Guilford Press, 1994. 3-16.

Schneider, Karen S. "Arguing her Case." *People Magazine*, 9 November 1998: 92-95.

Shelley, "Becoming A Woman." 4 November 2002 <http://www.geocities.com./Wellsley/ 4220/edpoetry.html>.

Shelley, Mary. *Frankenstein, or, The Modern Prometheus.* 1818. London: Penguin, 1992.

Showalter, Elaine. *Hystories: Histerical Epidemics and Modern Culture.* New York: Columbia UP, 1997.

Shute, Jenefer. *Life-Size.* 1992. London: Minerva, 1995.

Sinfield, Alan. "Cultural Materialism, *Othello*, and the Politics of Plausibility." 1992. *New Historicism and Cultural Materialism: A Reader.* Ed. Kiernan Ryan. London: Arnold, 1996. 61-81.

Sobal, Jeffery. "Social Influences on Body Weight." *Eating Disorders and Obesity: A Comprehensive Handbook.* Ed. Kelly D. Brownell and Christopher G. Fairburn. New York: The Guilford Press, 1995. 73-78.

Sorapure, Madeleine. "Representing Shame." *Writing Lives: American Biography and Autobiography.* Ed. Hans Bak and Hans Krabbendam. Amsterdam: VU University Press, 1998. 106-114.

Spivak, Gayatri Chakrovorty. "Lives." *Confessions of the Critics.* Ed. H. Aram Veeser. New York and London: Routledge, 1996. 205-220.

________ "Can the Subaltern Speak?" *Marxism and the Interpretation of Culture.* 1988. *Colonial Discourse and Post-Colonial Theory: A Reader.* Ed. Patrick Williams and Laura Chrisman. New York: Harvester Wheatsheaf, 1993: 66-111.

Stearns, Peter N. *Fat History: Bodies and Beauty in the Modern West.* New York and London: New York UP, 1997.

Stein, Alan. "Eating Disorders and Childrearing." *Eating Disorders and Obesity: A Comprehensive Handbook*. Ed. Kelly D. Brownell and Christopher G. Fairburn. New York: The Guilford Press, 1995. 188-190.

Stein, Mary K. "Exploring Better Access to Care for Minority, Underserved Populations." *Eating Disorders Review* 12 No. 4 (July/August 2001): 1.

Steinhausen, Hans-Christoph. "The Course and Outcome of Anorexia Nervosa." *Eating Disorders and Obesity: A Comprehensive Handbook*. Ed. Kelly Brownell and Christopher Fairburn. New York: The Guilford Press, 1995. 234-237.

Stephenson, Heather. "Howl." *Eating Our Hearts Out: Personal Accounts of Women's Relationship to Food*. Ed. Lesléa Newman. Freedom, CA: Crossing Press, 1993. 32-33.

Stevenson, Robert Louis. *Dr. Jekyll and Mr. Hyde*. 1886. New York: Bantam Books, 1981.

Streigel-Moore, Ruth. "Statement of Ruth, PhD at the APA CoSponsored Congressional Briefing." *American Psychological Association* 2002. 4 November 2002 <http:// www.apa. org/ppo /issues/pruth.html>.

Stroiber, Michael. "Family-Genetic Perspectives on Anorexia Nervosa and Bulimia Nervosa." *Eating Disorders and Obesity: A Comprehensive Handbook*. Ed. Kelly D. Brownell and Christopher G. Fairburn. New York: The Guilford Press, 1995. 212-218.

Studer, L. "Ellen West." *WahnsinnsFrauen*. Ed. S. Duda and L. F. Pusch. Frankfurt: Suhrkamp, 1992. 226-254.

Stunkard, Albert J. and Jeffery Sobal. "Psychosocial Consequences of Obesity." *Eating Disorders and Obesity: A Comprehensive Handbook*. Ed. Kelly D. Brownell and Christopher G. Fairburn. New York: The Guilford Press, 1995. 417-421.

The Gürze 1999 Eating Disorders Resource Catalogue. Carlsbad, CA: Gürze Books, 1999: 22.

The Oxford English Dictionary. Volume III. Oxford: Clarendon Press, 1961. 293.

Tompkins, Jane P. "*Uncle Tom's Cabin* and the Politics of Literary History." *The New Feminist Criticism: Essays on Women, Literature, and Theory*. Ed. Elaine Showalter. New York: Random House, 1985. 81-104.

Trish. "Conform." *Eating Disorders Poetry Collection*. 4 November 2002 <http://www.geocities.com/Wellesley/ 4220/edpoetry.html>.

Turner, Brian. *The Body and Society: Explorations in Social Theory*. Oxford: Basil Blackwell, 1984.

Udovitch, Mim. "A Secret Society of the Starving." *New York Times Magazine*. 9 August 2002: 18 – 67.

Untitled. 13 October 1998 <http://www.geocities.com/Wellesley/4220/edpoetry.html>.

Van Leer, David. "Society and Identity." *The Columbia History of the American Novel.* Ed. Emory Elliot. New York: Columbia UP, 1991. 485-509.

Wadden, Thomas A. "Very-Low-Calorie Diets: Appraisal and Recommendations." *Eating Disorders and Obesity: A Comprehensive Handbook.* Ed. Kelly D. Brownell and Christopher G. Fairburn. New York: The Guilford Press, 1995. 484-490.

Wagner-Martin, Linda. "*Still* Telling Women's Lives." *Writing Lives: American Biography and Autobiography.* Ed. Hans Bak and Hans Krabbendam. Amsterdam: VU University Press, 1998. 283-296.

Walsh, B. Timothy. "Pharmacotherapy of Eating Disorders." *Eating Disorders and Obesity: A Comprehensive Handbook.* Ed. Kelly D. Brownell and Christopher G. Fairburn. New York: The Guilford Press, 1995. 314-315.

Washbum, Patricia J. "Losing It." *Eating Our Hearts Out: Personal Accounts of Women's Relationship to Food.* Ed. Lesléa Newman. Freedom, CA: The Crossing Press, 1993. 54-58.

Wells, Kim. "CFP: Autobiography, the Scholar, and the Essay." 4 November 2002 <http:// www.english.upenn.edu/CFP/archive/2000-04/0028.html>.

West, Cornel. "Postmodern Culture." *The Columbia History of the American Novel.* Ed. Emory Elliot. New York: Columbia UP, 1991. 515-520.

West, Cornel. "The Postmodern Crisis of Black Intellectuals." *American Mythologies.* Ed. Marshall Blonsky. New York, Oxford: Oxford UP, 1992. 689-705.

Wilde, Oscar. *The Picture of Dorian Gray.* 1891. London: Penguin, 1985.

Williams, Raymond. "Base and Superstructure in Marxist Cultural Theory." *Problems in Materialism and Culture.* 1980. *New Historicism and Cultural Materialism: A Reader.* Ed. Kiernan Ryan. London: Arnold, 1996. 22-32.

Wilson, G. Terence. "Eating Disorders and Addictive Disorders." *Eating Disorders and Obesity: A Comprehensive Handbook.* Ed. Kelly D. Brownell and Christopher G. Fairburn. New York: The Guilford Press, 1995. 165-170.

Winnicott, D.W. "Mirror-role of Mother and Family in Child Development." *Playing and Reality.* 1971. New York: Routledge, 1991. 111-118.

Woodman, Marion. *The Owl Was a Baker's Daughter: Obesity, Anorexia Nervosa and the Repressed Feminine.* Toronto: Inner City Books, 1980.

Woolf, Naomi. *The Beauty Myth: How Images of Beauty Are Used Against Women.* 1981. New York: Anchor Books, Doubleday, 1982.

Woolf, Virginia. "Professions for Women." 1931. *Virginia Woolf: Women and Writing.* Introd. Michèle Barrett. London: The Women's Press, 1979. 57-63.

Zelter, Joachim. *Briefe aus Amerika.* Stuttgart: Ithaka Verlag, 1998.

Zerbe, Kathryn J. "Whose Body Is It Anyway? Understanding and Treating Psychosomatic Aspects of Eating Disorders." *The Bulletin of the Menninger Clinic* 57.2 (1993). 1 July 1998 <http://www.olmo.com/psychnet/zerbe.html>.

________ *The Body Betrayed: A Deeper Understanding of Women, Eating Disorders, and Treatment.* 1993. Carlsbad, CA: Gürze Books, 1995.

NEUE STUDIEN ZUR ANGLISTIK UND AMERIKANISTIK

Band 1 Ingeborg Weber-Brandies: Virginia Woolfs "The Waves": Emanzipation als Möglichkeit des Bewußtseinsromans. 1974.

Band 2 Meinhard Winkgens: Das Zeitproblem in Samuel Becketts Dramen. 1975.

Band 3 Klaus Simonsen: Erzähltechnik und Weltanschauung in Samuel Butlers literarischen Werken "Erewhon Revisited" und "The Way of All Flesh". 1974.

Band 4 Renate Mann: Jane Austen: Die Rhetorik der Moral. 1975.

Band 5 Bernhard Reitz: Das Problem des historischen Romans bei George Eliot. 1975.

Band 6 Wolfgang Sänger: John Millington Synge: "The Aran Islands". Material und Mythos. 1976.

Band 7 Norbert Schmuhl: Erfahrungen des Aufbruchs: Zur Perspektivität und Aperspektivität in James Joyces "Ulysses". 1976.

Band 8 Reinhard Mischke: Launcelots allegorische Reise: Sir Thomas Malorys "Le Morte Darthur" und die englische Literatur des fünfzehnten Jahrhunderts. 1976.

Band 9 Kurt Müller: Konventionen und Tendenzen der Gesellschaftskritik im expressionistischen amerikanischen Drama der zwanziger Jahre. 1977.

Band 10 Ursula Schaefer: Höfisch-ritterliche Dichtung und sozialhistorische Realität: Literatursoziologische Studien zum Verhältnis von Adelsstruktur, Ritterideal und Dichtung bei Geoffrey Chaucer. 1977.

Band 11 Ewald Mengel: Harold Pinters Dramen im Spiegel der soziologischen Rollentheorie. 1978.

Band 12 Norbert Bolz: Eine statistische, computerunterstützte Echtheitsprüfung von "The Repentance of Robert Greene": Ein methodischer und systematischer Ansatz. 1978.

Band 13 Klaus Peter Jochum: Discrepant Awareness: Studies in English Renaissance Drama. 1979.

Band 14 Rudi Camerer: Die Schuldproblematik im Spätwerk von Charles Dickens. 1978.

Band 15 Peter Stapelberg: Sean O'Casey und das deutschsprachige Theater (1948-1974): Empirische Untersuchungen zu den Mechanismen der Rezeption eines angloirischen Dramatikers. 1979.

Band 16 Hans Ulrich Seeber: Moderne Pastoraldichtung in England: Studien zur Theorie und Praxis der pastoralen Versdichtung in England nach 1800 mit besonderer Berücksichtigung von Edward Thomas (1878-1917). 1979.

Band 17 Klaus Martens: Negation, Negativität und Utopie im Werk von Wallace Stevens. 1980.

Band 18 Angela Lorent: Funktionen der Massenszene im viktorianischen Roman. 1980.

Band 19 Rotraut Spiegel: Doris Lessing: The Problem of Alienation and the Form of the Novel. 1981.

Band 20 Edda Kerschgens: Das gespaltene Ich: 100 Jahre afroamerikanischer Autobiographie. Strukturuntersuchungen zu den Autobiographien von Frederick Douglas, Booker T. Washington und W.E.B Du Bois. 1980.

Band 21 Josef Oswald: "The Discordant, Broken, Faithless Rhythm of Our Time": Eine Analyse der späten Dramen Eugene O'Neills. 1981.

Band 22 Dietrich Strauß: Die erotische Dichtung von Robert Burns: Bedingungen, Textüberlieferung, Interpretation, Wertungen. 1981.

Band 23 Jill Bonheim: Paul Scott: Humanismus und Individualismus in seinem Werk. 1982.

Band 24 Claudia Stehle: Individualität und Romanform: Theoretische Überlegungen mit Beispielen aus dem 19. Jahrhundert. 1982.

Band 25 Helga Stelzer: Narzißmus-Problematik und Spiegel-Technik in Joseph Conrads Romanen. 1983.

Band 26 Katherine Bastian: Joyce Carol Oates's Short Stories Between Tradition and Innovation. 1983.

Band 27 Regine Rosenthal: Die Erben des Lazarillo: Identitätsfrage und Schlußlösung im pikarischen Roman. 1983.

Band 28 Beate Lahrmann-Hartung: Sean O´Casey und das epische Theater Bertolt Brechts. 1983.

Band 29 Hans-Wolfgang Schaller: William Dean Howells und seine Schule: Strukturzüge im amerikanischen Realismus und Naturalismus. 1983.

Band 30 Elmar Schenkel: Natur und Subjekt im Werk von John Cowper Powys. 1983.

Band 31 Sabine Volk: Grenzpfähle der Wirklichkeit. Approaches to the Poetry of R.S. Thomas. 1985.

Band 32 Erika Hulpke: Die Vielzahl der Übersetzungen und die Einheit des Werks: Bildmuster und Wortwiederholungen in T.S. Eliot, "Collected Poems/Gesammelte Gedichte". 1985.

Band 33 Eike Schönfeld: Der deformierte Dandy: Oscar Wilde im Zerrspiegel der Parodie. 1986.

Band 34 Kurt Greinacher: Die frühen satirischen Romane Aldous Huxleys. 1986.

Band 35 Susanne Mayer: Die Sehnsucht nach den anderen: Eine Studie zum Verhältnis von Subjekt und Gesellschaft in den Autobiographien von Lillian Hellman, Maya Angelou und Maxine Hong Kingston. 1986.

Band 36 Klaus Martens: Die antinomische Imagination: Studien zu einer amerikanischen literarischen Tradition (Charles Brockden Brown, Edgar Allan Poe, Herman Melville). 1986.

Band 37 Richard Matthews/Joachim Schmole-Rostosky (eds.): Papers on Language and Mediaeval Studies Presented to Alfred Schopf. 1988.

Band 38 Christian von Raumer: "Khaki-clad Civilians". Soziale Erfahrung in der britischen Prosaliteratur des Ersten Weltkriegs. 1987.

Band 39 Claudia Ebel: Der entwurzelte Hindu: Eine Untersuchung zum postkolonialen Kulturkonflikt in V.S. Naipauls Trinidadromanen. 1989.

Band 40 Sabine Krome: Das Vaterbild in ausgewählten Romanen William Styrons. 1989.

Band 41 Rita Stoll: Die nicht-pronominale Anrede bei Shakespeare. 1989.

Band 42 Helmut Schönhöffer: Krankheit im anglo-amerikanischen Drama der Moderne: Gesellschaftskritik im Spiegel der Machtanalyse Michel Foucaults. 1989.

Band 43 Irene Neher: The Female Hero's Quest for Identity in Novels by Modern American Women Writers: The Function of Nature Imagery, Moments of Vision, and Dreams in the Hero's Development. 1989.

Band 44 Thomas Kühn: Sir Thomas Brownes "Religio Medici" und "Pseudodoxia Epidemica": Eine ideengeschichtliche Untersuchung mit besonderer Berücksichtigung des Begriffs "reason". 1989.

Band 45 Martina Wächter: Darstellung und Deutung der Vergangenheit in den Dramen Arthur Millers. 1989.

Band 46 Jan Vester: Wirklichkeit und Text / Wirklichkeit als Text: Exemplarische Studien zum amerikanischen Naturalismus. 1989.

Band 47 Daniel Göske: Herman Melville in deutscher Sprache: Studien zur übersetzerischen Rezeption seiner bedeutendsten Erzählungen. 1990.

Band 48 Ulrich Adolphs: Die Tyrannei der Bilder - Sam Shepards Dramen. 1990.

Band 49 Vera Nünning: Die Ästhetik Virginia Woolfs: Eine Rekonstruktion ihrer philosophischen und ästhetischen Grundanschauungen auf der Basis ihrer nichtfiktionalen Schriften. 1990.

Band 50 Michael Meyer: Struktur, Funktion und Vermittlung der Wahrnehmung in Charles Tomlinsons Lyrik. 1990.

Band 51 Heinz Eikmeyer: Angst und Furcht in den Dramen Harold Pinters. 1990.

Band 52 Gerd Hurm: Fragmented Urban Images: The American City in Modern Fiction from Stephen Crane to Thomas Pynchon. 1991.

Band 53 Alexander Folta: Donald Barthelme als postmoderner Erzähler: Poetologie, Literatur und Gesellschaft. 1991.

Band 54 Reinhard Schweizer: Ideologie und Propaganda in den Marvel-Superheldencomics: Vom Kalten Krieg zur Entspannungspolitik. 1992.

Band 55 Susanne Bach: Grenzsituationen in den Dramen Peter Shaffers. 1992.

Band 56 Ulla-Carina Reitz: Dialekt bei D.H. Lawrence. 1992.

Band 57 Helga Eßmann: Übersetzungsanthologien: Eine Typologie und eine Untersuchung am Beispiel der amerikanischen Versdichtung in deutschsprachigen Anthologien, 1920-1960. 1992.

Band 58 Bärbel Czennia: Figurenrede als Übersetzungsproblem: Untersucht am Romanwerk von Charles Dickens und ausgewählten deutschen Übersetzungen. 1992.

Band 59 Bert Schwarzer: Hamlet liest "Hamlet": Produktive Rezeption eines weltliterarischen Schlüsseltextes in der Moderne. 1992.

Band 60 Birgit Bödeker: Amerikanische Zeitschriften in deutscher Sprache, 1945-1952: Ein Beitrag zur Literatur und Publizistik im Nachkriegsdeutschland. 1993.

Band 61 Beatrix Dudensing: Die Symbolik von Mündlichkeit und Schriftlichkeit in James Fenimore Coopers "Leatherstocking Tales". 1993.

Band 62 Uta Reinicke: "The Vital Soul". Naturerleben als kreative Weltbegegnung bei William Wordsworth. 1994.

Band 63 Regina Twiste: Die Evolutionsthematik in Doris Lessings "Space Fiction". 1994.

Band 64 Kyung-Ae Kim: Quest for Salvation in Saul Bellow's Novels. 1994.

Band 65 Monika Steinert: Mythos in den Gedichten Sylvia Plaths. 1995.

Band 66 Alexander Stützer: Darstellung und Deutung der Moderne bei D.H. Lawrence. 1995.

Band 67 Petra Krimphove: Mutter-Tochter-Beziehungen in der US-amerikanischen Literatur. Eine interkulturelle Untersuchung. 1995.

Band 68 Michael Maintz: Die Rosales-Romane Francisco Sionil Joses. Die Suche nach nationaler Identität in der philippinischen Literatur. 1996.

Band 69 Manfred Menzel: Klatsch, Gerücht und Wirklichkeit bei Nathaniel Hawthorne. 1996.

Band 70 Katharina Hagena: Developing Waterways: Das Meer als sprachbildendes Element im *Ulysses* von James Joyce. 1996.

Band 71 Beate Hermes: Felix Paul Greve als Übersetzer von Gide und Wilde. Eine Untersuchung zum Übersetzerstil. 1997.

Band 72 Dagmar Priebe: Kommunikation und Massenmedien in englischen und amerikanischen Utopien des 20. Jahrhunderts. Interpretationen aus systemtheoretischer Sicht. 1998.

Band 73 Isabel Kobus: Dialog in Roman und Film. Untersuchungen zu Joseph Loseys Literaturverfilmungen *The Go-Between* und *Accident*. 1998.

Band 74 Hannelore Zimmermann: Erscheinungsformen der Macht in den Romanen Margaret Atwoods. 1998.

Band 75 Gudrun Rogge-Wiest: Wahrnehmung und Perspektivik in ausgewählten Romanen Virginia Woolfs. 1999.

Band 76 Christine Ehler: Verschriftung und Verschriftlichung des Altenglischen. Eine methodisch-exemplarische Untersuchung. 1999.

Band 77 Petra Deistler: Tradition und Transformation – der fiktionale Dialog mit dem viktorianischen Zeitalter im (post)modernen historischen Roman in Großbritannien. 1999.

Band 78 Stefan Jeanjour: Der pastorale Bezugsrahmen in der Lyrik Wilfred Owens. 1999.

Band 79 Gunilla Neukirchen: Aktive Spiegelungen. Die Konstituierung des Subjekts im Werk Virginia Woolfs. 1999.

Band 80 Annette Lönnecke: Anglo-Kanadische Autobiographien der Postmoderne. Radikale Formen der Selbstporträtierung von John Glassco bis Kristjana Gunnars. 1999.

Band 81 Nicole Cujai: *And I too am not myself* – Konstruktionen weiblicher Identität in Werken der englischsprachigen Gegenwartsliteratur Südafrikas. 2001.

Band 82 Willi Erzgräber: James Joyce. Oral and Written Discourses as Mirrored in Experimental Narrative Art. 2002.

Band 83 Paul Goetsch: Monsters in English Literature: From the Romantic Age to the First World War. 2002.

Band 84 Anne-Mirjam Maczewski: *Long poems*: Englischsprachige Langgedichte, 1920-1939. Eine deskriptivistische Korpusuntersuchung. 2003.

Band 85 Paul Goetsch: The Oral and the Written in Nineteenth-Century British Fiction. 2003.

Band 86 Susanne Strobel: *Various Forms of Savagery* - Identitäts- und Alteritätskonstruktionen in Reiseberichten viktorianischer Frauen zu Süd- und Westafrika. 2003.

Band 87 Greta Olson: Reading Eating Disorders: Writings on Bulimia and Anorexia as Confessions of American Culture. 2003.

Holger Klein

J. B. Priestley's Fiction

Frankfurt/M., Berlin, Bern, Bruxelles, New York, Oxford, Wien, 2002. 807 pp.
ISBN 3-631-38869-1 · pb. € 101.20* / US-$ 89.95 / £ 61.-
US-ISBN 0-8204-5457-5

With around thirty novels, J.B. Priestley is a major twentieth-century novelist. His reputation as a dramatist, essayist and general man of letters has tended to obscure his solid and highly interesting achievement as a novelist. This monograph is the first to be wholly devoted to Priestley's novels and short stories, organised in large groups determined by theme and attitude, while not neglecting his narrative technique. The middle decades of the twentieth century, which he has helped to shape, come alive in this tracing of their fictional recreation by Priestley.

Contents: Introduction · Escape · People and work · The past and the present · Shades of gothic · Dimensions of crime · Visions and fantasies · Rebellion and commitment · Subversion and disengagement · Retrospect: lines of development

Frankfurt/M · Berlin · Bern · Bruxelles · New York · Oxford · Wien
Distribution: Verlag Peter Lang AG
Moosstr. 1, CH-2542 Pieterlen
Telefax 00 41 (0) 32 / 376 17 27

*The €-price includes German tax rate
Prices are subject to change without notice

Homepage http://www.peterlang.de